Reading Bourdieu on Society and Culture

A selection of previous *Sociological Review* Monographs

Life and Work History Anaylses[†]
ed. Shirley Dex

The Sociology of Monsters[†]
ed. John Law

Sport, Leisure and Social Relations[†]
eds John Horne, David Jary and Alan Tomlinson

Gender and Bureaucracy[*]
eds Mike Savage and Anne Witz

The Sociology of Death: theory, culture, practice[*]
ed. David Clark

The Cultures of Computing[*]
ed. Susan Leigh Star

Theorizing Museums[*]
ed. Sharon Macdonald and Gordon Fyfe

Consumption Matters[*]
eds Stephen Edgell, Kevin Hetherington and Alan Warde

Ideas of Difference[*]
eds Kevin Hetherington and Rolland Munro

The Laws of the Markets[*]
ed. Michael Callon

Actor Network Theory and After[*]
eds John Law and John Hassard

Whose Europe? The turn towards democracy[*]
eds Dennis Smith and Sue Wright

Renewing Class Analysis[*]
eds by Rosemary Crompton, Fiona Devine, Mike Savage and John Scott

[†] Available from The Sociological Review Office, Keele University, Keele, Staffs ST5 5BG.
[*] Available from Marston Book Services, PO Box 270, Abingdon, Oxen OX14 4YW.

The Sociological Review Monographs

The Sociological Review has established a tradition of publishing Monographs on issues of general sociological interest. The Monograph is an edited book length collection of research papers which is published and distributed in association with Blackwell Publishers. Recent Monographs have included *Ideas of Difference* (edited by Kevin Hetherington and Rolland Munro), *Theorizing Museums* (edited by Sharon Macdonald and Gordon Fyfe). *The Sociology of Death* (edited by David Clark) and *The Sociology of Monsters* (edited by John Law). Other Monographs have been published on consumption; caste; culture and computing; gender and bureaucracy, sport-life history analyses, journalism and many other area. We are keen to receive innovative collections of work in sociology and related disciplines with a particular emphasis on exploring empirical materials and theoretical frameworks which are currently under-developed. If you wish to discuss ideas for a Monograph then please contact the Monographs Editor, Martin Parker, at *The Sociological Review*, Keele University, Newcastle-under-Lyme, North Staffordshire, ST5 5BG. Email mnall@keele.ac.uk

Reading Bourdieu on Society and Culture

Edited by Bridget Fowler

Blackwell Publishers/The Sociological Review

Copyright © The Editorial Board of the Sociological Review 2000

First published in 2000

Blackwell Publishers
108 Cowley Road, Oxford OX4 1JF, UK

and
350 Main Street
Malden, MA 02148, USA

British Library Cataloguing in Publication Data

A CIP catalogue record for this book is available from the British Library

Library of Congress Cataloging-in-Publication Data applied for

ISBN 0 631 22186 7

Printed and bound by Whitstable Litho Ltd.

This book is printed on acid-free paper.

Contents

Introduction

Bridget Fowler

It is paradoxical that Bourdieu's social theory has come under attack for its alleged determinism and pessimism when it has always gone under the banner of a 'constructivist structuralism'.[1]. It has precisely aimed at an anti-essentialism which would reveal all the sources of domination, including the symbolic or gentle violence used by the dominants to legitimate their power. Congratulating Weber for his 'healthy materialism' in his studies of religion, Bourdieu invites the same criterion for his own studies. The term 'constructivist' may indeed possess a further sense. For it invites a parallel between the artistic constructivists of the 1910s and 20s who aimed to open wider the habitual doors of perception by 'making things strange', and Bourdieu's new scientific tools which allow us to grasp the force of the habitus, that innermost way of being-in-the-world, with its 'feel for the game'.[2] It thus permits us to throw off, by means of a new rationality, those processes within us that permit exploitation, connive at injustice or fester with the poisons of resentment. And in doing so it is linked to those sources of structural dislocation which create independently in agents both suffering and a radicalizing anomie.

Bourdieu has had three new books translated recently, *Practical Reason* (1998 (1996)), *The Weight of the World* (1999 (1993b)) and *Pascalian Meditations* (2000 (1997)) which encourage a reappraisal of the stature of his contribution. With these, we can assess the adequacy and consistency of his theory of practice. A central element of the logic of practice is agents' engagement with the objective structures of the modern world, crystallized into those patterns of relations, with their specific determining force, that we call 'fields' (economic power, politics, cultural production, etc.). Bourdieu uses the model of a scientific craft: making a 'rupture' with common sense, constructing scientific facts by means of conceptual models and confirming them through ethnographic experiments (Bourdieu, Chamboredon and Passeron, 1991: 41; 57–60). Sociology is at the crossroads of 'realism and the rational', where the real is grasped as 'the relational' (1991: 66; 158; Bourdieu and Wacquant, 1992: 232). But this is a genetic relational approach which rests generously on the analyses of philosophers, historians, art historians and literary critics rather than on sociologists alone. To test its validity, we therefore need to evaluate and apply his work, beyond any disciplinary ghettoization.

Bourdieu currently describes his work in Pascalian rather than Marxist language, acknowledging his debt to Husserl, Wittgenstein and even Heidegger (1997: 10). Yet I want in this introduction to situate his thought more deeply in the sociological tradition which has most shaped his conceptual tools and theory. It is well-known that Marx combined French socialism, Scottish political economy and German philosophy to create a new synthesis. Bourdieu in such a context cites Marx, Weber and Durkheim and, to a lesser extent, Mauss, manoeuvring Weber to think *against* Weber, or each of these thinkers to challenge the others. I shall sketch here ways in which he subsumes these sociological thinkers and has gone beyond them to produce the most powerful social theorization currently available.

In the public eye, Bourdieu is perceived as a post-Marxist. It is true that he certainly stresses the force of representations – classifications, signifiers, call them what you will – in constructing agents' principles of vision and division. Society is partly in the mind for Bourdieu, hence the enormous importance of doxic beliefs and ideology. It is also true that he has no time for the bankrupt formulae of 'dialectical' materialism. But whereas a thinker such as Derrida can insist blithely that there is nothing '*hors texte*', for Bourdieu there is an objectified or reified social reality, beyond individuals' discourse, the structure of which is detectable through empirical evidence. If Bourdieu always emphasizes the symbolic power of honour or reputation, he never denies the material force of economic capital nor underrates the historical rise of the market as the arena for its activities. One might cite numerous areas where his thought is still honourably within the Western Marxist tradition – his sharp distinction between a pre-capitalist peasant economy, like Kabylia or Béarn, and a modern bureaucratized capitalism, which invokes an underlying mode of production; his concept of modes of reproduction, with the differentiation of the twentieth century educational mode of selection from earlier patterns of inheritance and training; his concern with the progressive dispossession of workers of their collective heritage; the 'dialectic of distinction and down-classing' within work and so on.

Even his well-known analysis of a class fraction richer in cultural capital than economic capital (the liberal professions, artists etc.) is one which in important respects reinforces a Marxist theory of modernity. For you do not find in this conception of capitalism a higher valuation of cultural status over material power. On the contrary, Bourdieu emphasizes the predominance of objectified economic power. Hence, for example, the response of the French writers to the Commune in 1871, when, despite years of antagonistic rhetoric, they rallied to the support of the threatened bourgeoisie (Lidsky, 1970; Bourdieu, 1990c: 145). One could go on, noting not just the concern Bourdieu has for the economic force of the dominants, but also – against idealists – the strength of *reified* historical forms. The rose windows or the buttressed naves of the great cathedrals, for example, testify to an extraordinary educational diffusion of Scholastic ideas from medieval logicians to the building practices of stonemasons and architects (Bourdieu, Chamboredon and Passeron,

1991: 54, 191–3). Great buildings and spaces, continue to reveal the traces of the relations of intellectual and material power in which they were conceived and to shape social life (1993b: 159–63).

Here are still recognizably Marxist concepts. 'Contradiction' is a case in point. Bourdieu's prime analysis in this respect is of May 1968, after the expansion of the universities for electoral and vocational reasons. This was a crisis as Cournot defined a chance event, induced by the co-incidence of independent causal series (1988a: 174–5). Of these, Bourdieu especially stresses the discrepancy between students' expectations and their experience, the antagonistic intellectual relations between structuralists or social scientists and more traditional literary and philosophical academics, as well as the bitterness induced by promotion blockages. However carnivalesque and unsustained the university 'world-upside down', these antagonisms became the crucible for the expression of other resentments, as in those resonating between workers and employers (1988a: ch. 5).

Bourdieu never disputes Marx's theory of commodity fetishism, that theory of the magical power of the commodity, which, stripped of its basis in historical social relations of unequal power appears merely as the consequence of a contractual exchange between equivalents (Marx, 1976: 163–77). Rather, Bourdieu persuasively extends Marx's task of the demystification of ideological thought through his own writings.[3] From the analysis of commodity fetishism he proceeds to the sphere of other fetishisms, notably using Mauss's theory of magic to aid him (Mauss, 1972). He asks us to think of the cultural works that have been consecrated by means of their authors' charisma as equivalent 'fetishes' with their own mana, deriving, like sorcery, from an internal, special space (Mauss, 1972: 111–12; Bourdieu, 1993c: 35). Fetishes, then, emerge from cultural accumulation when utilized as capital. Cultural acquisition may have multiple dimensions, from the simple embodied culture, as in poems learnt by heart, to reified culture, as in the possession of books and paintings. But it is only in the emergence of certified culture, as in State certified examinations, that culture appears in its modern form as capital, operating no longer as a private, secret cult, but as 'state magic' (Bourdieu, 1996a: 118–9).

Bourdieu thus extends the concept of magical aura, used so poignantly by Benjamin on oil painting, to that sacred power emanating from the French élite, via their common graduation from the grandes écoles and universities. Not unlike the earlier followers of Calvin and Knox, a mixture of extreme asceticism and the self-assurance of a justified elect binds together the group of those graduates from the grande écoles who become, as state-certified graduates, a 'state nobility'. In turn the elect's auratic appeal undermines the working-class capacity to define their own interests. We could contrast Bourdieu very sharply with Derrida in this rigorous use of a theory of magic. Where Derrida and others have offered a neo-Surrealist account of modern phantasmagoria resting loosely on the Freudian idea of the uncanny, Bourdieu introduces a much tighter deployment of the anthropological concept of magic, borrowed from Mauss, which permits the socio-analytic understanding of the operation of magical aura within certain legitimated relationships (Mauss, 1972: 40).

The concepts of fetishism (1991: 52) and magic are developed elsewhere. Thus Bourdieu creatively takes up Austin's concept of performatives, those statements which possess their own illocutionary force, and views them as the expression of a magical linguistic power. For, as long as the correct form of language is used, the politician, minister or registrar literally makes things happen with words, just as the magician does through the use of formulae. But Bourdieu will stress the hidden structures veiled here, as in the commodity case, since the effectivity of the words rests on the social power of the dominants, vested through a rite of institution in the M.P., priest (etc). It is this which authorises them to baptise the baby and thus 'make the world' with these words (1991: 74–5; 125–6). This analysis of performatives has been profoundly challenged (Butler, 1997: 157; Lovell, below). Butler's critique, which mistakenly sees language for Bourdieu as epiphenomenal, neglects the existence for him of two types of linguistic power. For alongside the power of the dominants with their magic of institution and profits of linguistic distinction, there is the linguistic power of the representatives, mandated by the people. Their will may also be potentially (but not necessarily) usurped, through a form of *political fetishism* (Bourdieu, 1991: 205).[4]

Bourdieu's theory of practice further extends Marx's materialism to produce a less idealist model of action. The habitus is predicated on a bodily hexis, as in Pascal's 'pense-bête' or Merleau-Ponty's phenomenology of physical perception:

> The world is comprehensible, immediately endowed with meaning, because the body, which, thanks to its senses and its brain, has the capacity to be present to what is outside itself, in the world, and to be impressed and durably modified by it, has been protractedly (from the beginning) exposed to its regularities. Having acquired from this exposure a system of dispositions attuned to these regularities, it is inclined and able to anticipate them practically in behaviours which engage a *corporeal knowledge* that provides a practical comprehension of the world quite different from the intentional act of conscious decoding that is normally designated by the idea of comprehension (2000: 135).

Bourdieu has thus taken Husserl's sovereign ego and Heidegger's 'authentic being' and posited it instead as the habitus of an embodied social group whose inner experience might be illuminated with ethnographic techniques (1997: 170, 175).

Most striking perhaps is his recurrent concern with the different time perspectives possessed by divergent social groups, typified by Kabylian and Béarn peasants, the Algerian sub-proletariat and the French industrial working-class. In particular, he has argued that we need to conceptualize whether a group thinks of the future as an extension, or protension, of the present, which is immanent with the past, or rather, as in classic Enlightenment rationalism, as an anticipatory potential for divergent alternatives and thus inherently open to transformation (a calculated 'project' as opposed to a future latent in one's past and present (an *à-venire*)) (1997: 251–2). Thus the unemployed or member of the Algerian sub-proletariat, consigned to a marginal life, are unable to conceive of the future either as a project for rational aspirations or as the blossoming of their habitus. Stigmatized, they become devoid of a theodicy of existence and 'experience the free time that is left them as dead time, purposeless and meaningless' (2000: 222).

Bourdieu's conception of time offers a powerful application of ethnological analysis of cosmology, memory and time-discipline to different modes of production and class existence, parallel to the approach of an historian such as E.P. Thompson.[5] It enriches, in particular, our grasp of working-class experience and the entire historical process by which classes become made or unmade as classes (see Charlesworth in this volume). To this we should also add Bourdieu's profound structural grasp of different cultural groups' relation to the future – *their social ageing* – as in the instance of the avant-gardes vs commercial popular writers and painters (1993c: 98–101). Such a phenomenological analysis of time in these varying contexts extends the precision and subjective richness of historical materialism.

Despite his independent reformulations of Marx, Bourdieu's sociology, then, is profoundly faithful to his spirit. This applies to his suspicion of universalizing stances in philosophy and public administration, such as those of Kant (Bourdieu, 1984; 1990b) and of Habermas, to whose critique he brings an analysis reminiscent of Marx's strictures against the Hegelian interpretation of the Prussian bureaucracy as the representative of universal reason (1997: 296). Recently, he has written of the pretensions of the French 'state nobility' to stand for the interests of the dominated (1996a: 376; 1998b).

Nowhere is this more striking than in his expansion of Marx's dissection of the cultural and psychological needs of the bourgeoisie. For Marx writes acutely of the ways in which the bourgeoisie, once linked only through function, becomes culturally cohesive and ossified as a class. The *modernized* industrialists (unlike their frugal predecessors) have two impulses – the impulse to save, for consumption is a sin against their accumulation of capital, and the impulse to sensual pleasure ('At the same time there develops in the breast of the capitalist a Faustian conflict between the passion for accumulation and the desire for enjoyment' (Marx, 1976: 741)). With increased wealth, the need for saving together with the need for a legitimating imperative are both lessened. *Succeeding generations* of bourgeoisie, less prone to ascetic legitimation, progressively become more aristocratic in their style of life (741–2). Bourdieu applies this further to the haute bourgeoisie of late capitalism which recognizes itself through a certain stylization of life, one now based on a sacred relation to secular culture. The love of art, not conspicuous consumption, has become its distinctive spiritual point of honour, generating an intimate relation to canonized texts and consecrated forms. Building on this rare aesthetic disposition, the students of haute bourgeois origins come to be progressively endowed as a class with an educational legitimation, which allows them a more effective survival as a social group (Bourdieu, 1984: 72). But this requires, for its contrast, the dispossession of the dominated from the art of their time, a phenomenon peculiar to modernism and inherent in lower-class vulnerability to material necessity (1984: 44–50). The intimidation of the working-class within the art-gallery is matched by their awkward ambivalence towards the school (Bourdieu and Darbel with Schnapper, 1991; Bourdieu, 1993b: 597–608).

In the period since Marx wrote there has been a vast expansion of Department II. It is in the context of this extraordinary rationalization and concentration of capital that Bourdieu surveys the disavowed interests and covert operations of successive twentieth century avant-gardes. For these artists, rhetorically identified with anti-bourgeois radicalism and asceticism,[6] do what they can, without cynicism, to win interpreters and audiences with the highest educational or social capital (Bourdieu, 1993c: 83; 109–110). This system has forged a new, more rapid 'logic of social ageing', which has pulled a minority of 'geniuses' into becoming producers for the internationalized gallery-circuit and has left the great majority of other artists with a more precarious habitus, devoid of the commissions that trained artists were once guaranteed. Bourdieu proposed a theory of the 'permanent revolution' of the avant-garde – underpinned by a Schumpeterian cycle of creative destruction followed by consecration. Beyond the euphemistic disguises of material interests, notably through a vocabulary re-christening dealers as gallery-owners, artists have been shedding their former disdain for economic profits: 'One soon learns from conversations with [dealers] that, with a few illustrious exceptions ... painters and writers are deeply self-interested, calculating, obsessed with money and ready to do anything to succeed' (1993c: 79).

For Marx, modern painters had become divorced from dominant class patronage and, in a social world where censorship was a perpetual possibility, become compelled to create their own consumer. That is, they had to create a need, or use-value, for their work since a pre-existing one did not exist (Marx, 1973: 92–3). In the late twentieth century context, Bourdieu detects a further and unpredicted rationalization. A wider, educated public, a well-disposed set of 'authorized readers' (the critics), the disappearance of censors and a new network of international galleries which stabilized prices by conferring reputations on chosen artists: all these factors have undermined the simple rejection of market principles that once characterized bohemia.

Bourdieu's view should not be confused with the facile postmodernism that proclaims a radical collapse of the high/low divisions. At no point has Bourdieu claimed that the differentiation between the audiences of the restricted and the wide scale market is being dramatically eroded. However, we can interpret his analysis of the contemporary restricted market (1993c: 74–111; 1996) as a theory of the exhaustion of the avant-garde. Artists now still aim to subvert the persistence of consecrated art with an unfree everyday life by *revealing the mechanisms* underlying the whole art-world. But such actions are doomed to be read only as 'artistic events' (1993: 80). To explain this, Bourdieu resorts to a theory of fetishistic mystification and to the collective mandate now possessed by avant-garde curators and critics to be *celebrants of the artistic cult* (1990c: 89; 1993c: 81; 258–9).

Hence the significance of Bourdieu – in a world where spiritual values are invoked, he will risk analysis of the discreetly-concealed political economy underlying publishing or galleries; in a world where critics are assumed to be absolutely autonomous, he will show that their evaluation intimately shapes economic values in the art market. Use-value (established by favorable reviews) is converted into exchange value, but in a misrecognized form,[7] like the sorcerers' alchemical transmutation which Mauss analyses (Mauss, 1972: 74–5; Bourdieu, 1993c: 79–81).[8]

Bourdieu's method means that he should *ideally* supplement his analysis of the modern art market with a deeper account of the *subjective meanings* of the artists themselves. This has been undertaken in studies by Moulin (1967) and Myles (1999: 179–92). Myles emphasizes the emergence in Britain of a 'post-avant-garde' around the exhibition *Freeze*, including the figures of the 'artistic bovver-boy' (1999: 179) (Damien Hirst), Mark Quinn, Helen Chadwick and Gavin Turk, who flout the normal bohemian conventions and adopt conspicuously entrepreneurial virtues.[9] This latest avant-garde denies the post-Renaissance history of artistic perception which is based on the denigration of the other senses, so as to raise challenging questions about our relations to flesh, and to smell, which have been devalued in the privileging of the visual in Western culture (Myles: 188–9; see Cook, this volume). Myles's study also details the practices of other current, less entrepreneurial avant-gardes. And although he shows that some 'aristocratic ascetic' bohemian beliefs have been undermined, he still notes striking continuities. The buyers of British 1990s' artworks remain entirely either super-rich or the upper middle class (Myles: 1999: 323), just as Moulin 30 years earlier noted the absence of working-class collectors in the case of France (Moulin, 1967: 246).

While there is a place for an old-fashioned materialist exposure of economic interests behind idealizing stances, Bourdieu also stresses the difference between the 'symbolic capital' (artistic recognition) sought by the *autonomous artist* and that of the hack who just wants money.[10] At the end of *The Rules of Art*, he argues for the importance of understanding art as a practice which is dictated *neither* by capitalist principles of production nor by 'instrumental reason'. The concept of *illusio* indicates just how historically unique are these universes of religion, aesthetic production and science, even though he has undertaken the sacrilegious exposure of the determining mechanisms concealed within them. Art and literature have their specific interests and the visceral involvement, which comes when you are totally caught up in a particular project, leads to an emotional intensity where the principles fought for become a matter of life and death. Indeed, material economic interests tend now to be passed over and Bourdieu, stung by claims that he has been reductionist, concerns himself purely with 'specific' interests, both in the reputation of the works and in the specific logic of the field (1990c: 106–19; 1998a: 92–103). [11]

Finally, Bourdieu's argument revolves around a conception of a *'singular'* writer in the terms above, such as Flaubert. There are flaws here – ideally Bourdieu should include readings of other writers in the popular expanded market to demonstrate the singularity of Flaubert. Still, after the 'death of the author', this is an important new attempt to accept that the artist is *not only* a social figure, the product of a collective history, regulated by the distinctive rules of art which artistic outsiders flout to their cost, but also, as the possessor of an artistic habitus, someone who can *improvise* and – within certain limits – even *invent*. This is not to reintroduce the solitary genius, nor is it to 'return to the subject'. It is to accept that the artist epitomizes the skilled work of improvization that Bourdieu (and Becker) evoke with the image of the jazz player. Lest this be confused with aesthetic populism, Bourdieu proposes a theory of *symbolic revolution*, which is an important supplement to Marx's political revolution. The study of Flaubert is especially memorable in attributing to Flaubert an objectivist understanding of the social world: 'It is a vision that one can call sociological if it were not set apart from a scientific analysis by its form, simultaneously offering and masking it' (1996b: 31). The sociologist – far from destroying the author – offers a 'piquant sauce' to the dish provided by the latter, thus:

> Renouncing the angelic belief in a pure interest in pure form is the price we must pay for understanding the logic of those social universes, which, through the social alchemy of their historic laws of functioning, succeed in extracting from the often merciless clash of passions and selfish interests the sublimated essence of the universal. (1996b: xviii)

Subsuming and transcending Weber

The most conspicuous borrowing Bourdieu declares from Weber is his sociology of religion (Bourdieu, 1987), of which his *Religious Rejections of the World* (Gerth and Mills, 1991) has had perhaps the most influence. In this essay, Weber starkly explores the religious ethics of brotherliness and, situating these at 'the geometrical intersection of all perspectives', [12] indicates the extreme tension between these and alternative senses of reality coexistent with them. He surveys the economy in its rationalized form, and the political, erotic, aesthetic and cultural spheres. Within this fragmented world of modernity, the aesthetic and the erotic world of the couple have become particularly important as enclosing refuges from 'the cold, skeletal hands of rational orders, just as completely as from the banality of everyday routine' (Weber, 1991: 347; cf Bourdieu, 1998c: appendix). Bourdieu sees modern nation-states as organized around prolonged schooling and an extended leisure sphere, in which more and more agents are drawn into what Weber called the 'bedazzlement' of art. For both thinkers, such developments reveal underlying conflicts, for the aesthetic and intellectual spheres offer the most profound contradiction with the religious rejection of worldliness:

> The barriers of education and of aesthetic cultivation are the most intimate and the most insuperable of all status differences (Gerth and Mills, 1991: 354).

Or Bourdieu:

> But, through a kind of curse, because of the essentially diacritical, differential and distinctive nature of symbolic power, the rise of the distinguished class to Being has, as an inevitable counterpart, the slide of the complementary class into Nothingness or the lowest Being (Bourdieu, 1991: 126).

Bourdieu has frequently acknowledged his indebtedness to Weber's priest-prophet-sorcerer triplet in developing his sociological model of art. He has usefully gone beyond the more orthodox sociology of literature and art, which only addresses issues such as commodification and ideology. Bourdieu's approach will explore these questions through the genesis of a collective institution of art, made up of schools, groups, avant-gardes and critics, while his analysis follows Weber's in linking together the world of artistic production and reception (see Prior, below). Using Weber's contrast between the conservatism of the priests and the radical critique of the prophets, Bourdieu distinguishes between orthodox academicians or Right Bank theatre directors, and those artists who can be figured as *prophetic producers of new meanings* ('Words can wreak havoc' (Bourdieu);[13] 'Words can create panic,' (Joe Orton)).

Unlike other sociologists, he has a sharp grasp of the distinction between the author's and the critic's literary interests, setting in relief the more activist and participatory involvement of the traditional bard or poet, against the greater detachment of the critic/priestly engagement. Historically (and today in contemporary Kabylia) the oral poet accompanied recitations with the use of bodily actions or dances, which were immediately meaningful to the audience. This sensitivity to their audiences made the local artisan-poets (auctores) the spokespersons of the group. In contrast to 'pure poetry', they kept their style fresh by introducing small linguistic changes only, thus retaining their authority or poetic capital for intervention in bleak periods of war or diplomatic crisis.

On the other hand, critics are the scholarly readers of canonized texts (the medieval lectors). Uppermost for them is a theoretical, non-practical concern, in which all texts are equated in a distanced mode, detached from the political context and exposed to the play of intertextuality. This mode of reception is today more common, but still only to a minority. If Bourdieu frequently refers to the difficulties raised by Habermas and others, it is because they are not aware of the social and material conditions for this kind of reading and the 'communicative competence' it underpins (see Poupeau, below). Again, there are echoes here of Weber's arguments about the tension between an attachment to an intellectualist culture – or an escape to the aesthetic – and the viewpoint of brotherliness, with its imperative of 'taking a stand' (Gerth and Mills, 1991: 342; Bourdieu: 1990c: 95–106).

Bourdieu's studies (1984; 1993c) show that the aesthetic rejections of the world are themselves liable to further routinization in the interests of a dominant class, as they become sacred texts. This parallels in the artistic field Weber's account of the progressive *accommodation to power* of the originally radical and pacifist sects.

Bourdieu has not himself expanded at length on the resulting new market phenomena (summarized in 1996: 339–48), but we might mention Moulin's work, which he has frequently cited. She calculates that between 1984–88, international sales at Sotherby's increased five times, and sales of contemporary art multiplied nine times (Moulin, 1992: 56). Moulin argues that it is economic rationalization, which has led to 'refuge in the ludic artist', then to the sacralization of art, and finally (since 1914) to the triumph of the art-market. She notes the volatility of values, from the 1920s, as Baudelairean 'accursed values' become 'worldly values'. In the absence of a democratized scholarly culture, the art market became highly manipulable, with a 'continuous questioning of received values through the accelerated succession of changes' (1967: 69) (Bourdieu's 'permanent revolution'); even within the artworld, sharp conflict is endemic, including struggle over who is a charleton and who a real artist, hence '(t)he prices of living artists in sales cannot fail to be arbitrary' (1967: 407).

Finally, this research also reports the greater homogenization of the avant-garde after the Second World War, as prizes establish a normalized 'avant-garde official career': 'The recognition by the restricted milieu – national or international – of those [critics and juries] who establish the hierarchical classification of the painters and their command of very high prices constitute for the artist two modes of success, constantly reinforcing each other and each attesting to the other' (1967: 317). It is not difficult to conclude from the empirical analyses of Moulin and Bourdieu (1993c: chs. 2 and 3) that there has been a bureaucratization of the avant-garde. In what Bourdieu entitles the 'heroic' emergence of the modernist movement, in the 1850s, something was born which resembled Goethe's 'rosy dawn of the Enlightenment', quoted by Weber. By the end of the War, autonomy from the market and the prize system was impossible: the steel-hard cage had descended.

Subsuming and transcending Durkheim

Durkheim's organic analogies and his positivist pursuit of a narrow objectivism clearly have no appeal for Bourdieu, schooled as he was in the conceptions of science of Bachelard and Canguilhem. Yet Bourdieu owes to Durkheim both tell-tale phrases such as 'Everything suggests ...' and, more significantly, a focus on three major substantive issues. These are the significance of classification in social struggles; the role of education in reproduction of the most successful groups and the dynamic or transgressive potential of some forms of anomie, where agents *cannot* cut their coat according to their cloth.[14]

First, using Durkheim's notions of representations, and the classificatory struggles based on these, Bourdieu argues powerfully for the inclusion in social science of an element which Marxists often omit, viz the ordinary hierarchies and common-sense 'vision and division of the world':

> The individual or collective classification struggles aimed at transforming the categories of perception and appreciation of the social world [...] are indeed a forgotten dimension of the class struggle. But one only has to realise that the classificatory schemes which underlie agents' practical relationship to their condition and the representation they have of it are themselves the product of that condition, in order to see the limits of this autonomy (1984: 483–4).

Hence his emphasis on the crucial role of heterodoxies or symbolic revolutions which challenge such classifications or hierarchies, from the internal hierarchies of university and grandes écoles, to the hierarchies of sexuality, discipline or genre.

Bourdieu's interests have been particularly keenly focussed on the post-1960s' 'aesthetic turn' and its linked moral agnosticism. If Marx discusses the distinctive capitalist relation to production in terms of capital and labour, Bourdieu, like Durkheim, discusses modernity as consisting of a distinct *relation to consumption*, and especially the consumption of a varying range of symbolic goods (compare *Suicide*: 253–7). In Bourdieu's assessment, the aesthetic turn has to be understood in a wider context, that of the transformation of social space (1984: ch 2). This has created an extension and devaluation of qualifications, coupled with individuation. The experience of failure is no longer collectively explained but felt as a personal sickness (compare Durkheim's egoism, *Suicide* (1989: 210). It is accentuated by the school's retention, rather than exclusion, of those whom it downgrades academically. Thus, alongside the expansion of the market capacities for cheap luxuries in the sphere of adornment and the body, there is an unprecedented inner loneliness, derived not least through the refusal of the destiny of 'vulgarity', associated with the stigmatized working-class. In brief, for Bourdieu the game of culture which is at stake in relations to consumption, always has the working-class as its negative classificatory foil. In what he calls a type of class racism, the aesthetic turn heightens the recoil from the visual appearance and tastes of the contemporary working-class who are condemned to be both common and utter commonplaces (1984: 179).

Durkheim of course was preoccupied with issues of reproduction. What Bourdieu develops further is the school as the pre-eminent mechanism for the

11

selection of heirs – the 'inheritors' of dominant positions in capitalism. For this, the crucial mechanism is access to and successful use of the (class–based) dominant language, especially the *literary language* (1991: 57–61). The school is the crucial field in the struggle for the recognition of culture. It is the terrain for wars over the 'canon' of sacred authors, of course, but also over classificatory hierarchies of disciplines (eg Latin), art forms, genres etc.

Distinction's field work shows that respondents are differentiated between those with an 'aesthetic disposition' (or disinterestedness) and those with a 'naive gaze' (1984: 30–44). These groups can be related objectively to how much cultural capital (or educational qualifications) they possess. This, in turn, merely mirrors class relations: thus the dominant class (especially its dominated fraction) embodies high cultural capital – sometimes 'heavy' or 'antiquated' learning, in those with old money – whilst those with low cultural capital come predominantly from the working-class or peasantry. In brief, for Bourdieu, cultural acquisition becomes characterized by its relation to material ease and especially to the time taken to acquire it. The pleasures of the text or correct consumption become premised on others' educational and social exclusion. Thus, as Guillory comments, the underlying tendency Bourdieu detects is towards a relational *splitting* which has symbolic and ideological meaning. On the one hand there is in the legitimate aesthetic a valorization of *pure form* (the style of representation): on the other, in the popular aesthetic, a valorization of *pure content* (natural beauty or political or moral worth) (Guillory, 1993: 333–5).

Second, it was Durkheim who emphasized the significance of education for modernity, and especially the importance of education in settling competitive conflicts within overstocked educational areas. Durkheim pioneered a genetic analysis of education, particularly of the development of the modern university, with its conflicting faculties. And when, in *Homo Academicus*, Bourdieu studies his own world in a state of turbulence (1988a), he may well have drawn on Durkheim's account of medieval strikes over academic freedom between the teachers and the university chancellors (Durkheim: 1977: 83). Linking teachers' corporations to the medieval guilds, Durkheim stresses the material and intellectual interests in their autonomy that the lecturers had asserted, sometimes moving the whole university to another place in order to escape the encroachments of authoritarian chancellors (1977: 89).

Bourdieu's conception of the collective intellectual in the political postscript to *The Rules of Art* of course has some aspects which are unique to modernity – subordination of nation and patriotism to higher values, support from the universalistic rules of art and science, critique of the great economic organizations, dread of the penetration of art by money – consequently, his ethic is a 'corporatism of the universal'. Yet it has unmistakeably behind it the concern of the older corporations to defend the 'ownership by cultural producers of their instruments of production and circulation' (Bourdieu, 1996: 344). It thus echoes those uneven and fraught struggles between the corporation of the teachers and their students on the one hand and the bishops and chancellors on the other which Durkheim outlined in the twelfth to sixteenth centuries (1977: 79–93).

Third, I should briefly mention anomie: in the radical Durkheimian tradition, a source of great change. Bourdieu appears at first sight to contradict this view, for the habitus of the dominated is the orchestrator of their extraordinary capacity to scrimp, adapt, accommodate. But there are also, for Bourdieu, certain limits to the smooth operation of habitus. Most compelling is that of '*hysteresis*' (or the Don Quixote condition) where the agent, as in the condition of anomie, defines the world in terms of a set of relations which no longer apply. Hysteresis may at times create the madness with which Cervantes amuses us, but it also breeds resentment. Further, in situations of *crisis*, Bourdieu argues that more conscious calculation of interest comes into play: the collective memories and normal feel for the game prove to be no guide to action. Reflexivity kicks in, as it were, permitting the transformation rather than reproduction of existing social structures and engendering a rational utopianianism from collective intellectuals to guide this more widespread political engagement.

It is because of these ruptures that it would be wrong to see Bourdieu's logic of practice as operating solely under the doxic influence of binary or other classifications, ensuring 'pre-reflexive' action for all except theorists and cultural producers (see Bohman's criticisms along these lines: 1999: 136; Bourdieu and Wacquant, 1992: 130–1). But it is equally necessary to note the *difference* between the Bourdieusian notion of reflexivity and the recent, diluted formulations of Beck, Giddens and Lash (1994). For the latter, reflexivity inspires a communitarian undertaking founded on the social groups which are differentiated by the habitus and fields alone, leaving quietly in place all the distortions of domination (1994: 167–8).

In the contrasting case of Bourdieu, reflexivity involves a form of monitoring which would exclude the bias not just of the dominant class, but also those of the dominant gender and ethnic group (1998c).[15] It involves a repudiation of the strategies of that aristocracy of culture whose distinguished careers contribute to the domination of great families (Bourdieu, 1984: 92). And finally it implies a generosity which will eradicate the consequences of envy – or resentment – thus freeing the agent from the iron law of revolutionary routinization (Bourdieu and Wacquant, 1992: 212).

Controversies over Bourdieu

In the critical fallout from Bourdieu's efforts, we can see a certain clustering of divergent concerns. His 'realist constructivism' (see 1993b: 915) has been challenged in terms of the problem of his concept of capital; the artistic status of popular culture; the connection of his sociology with postmodernism and finally the alleged over-determinist, over-socialized character of his theory of practice.

Theory of cultural capital

Bourdieu has attempted to explain the position of the liberal professions, politicians and bureaucrats in terms of a highly controversial theory of cultural capital. This has extended Marxism by regarding the dominated fraction of the dominant class as using their educational assets in a competitive game of power. In the process, Bourdieu risks losing the specificity of economic capital and its distinctive strategies in the 'economic economy' (Calhoun, 1993: 68–9). This is not an insuperable obstacle, for Bourdieu could supplement his account of economic capital. He could elaborate on his view of the regulated body *(bodily hexis)* and *time* in connection with labour, spelling out the distinctive instrumental rationality occurring when those richest in material capital attempt to rule in their own interests.[16] Indeed, his recent analysis of the perspective of those advocating 'flexibility' and the bizarre conventions underlying their social cost-benefit analysis is an obvious case in point. Inventively applying the Durkheimian tradition, this shows how the left hand of neo-liberalism's *social costs* (crime, dislocated families etc.) is kept separate from the right hand of *economic* costs.[17]

Cultural capital is like economic capital in the sense that it is acquired through competition with others, in a zero-sum game (1996a: 373–89). Its scarcity and value mean that investments in cultural capital can easily be converted into high economic rewards. But it still lacks the precise *dependence on surplus-extraction* required for economic capital. For this reason, those 'theoretical classes' high in cultural capital may not have such a strong predisposition towards conflict, despite coming from different regions of social space from the subordinate classes (1998a: 10–11). Indeed, Bourdieu has himself noted recently that those with cultural capital are often found in autonomous universes (art, science, social work ...), within which they are committed to disinterestedness in profit-seeking terms (1998a: 75–123). Such spaces are no guarantee against 'aristocratism', of course, but it should also be remembered that conceptual models such as 'cultural capital' acquire a strong metaphorical force, which can lead to 'theory effects' of their own.

The problem of popular art

Various critics have noted the clash between Bourdieu's sympathies with working-class people and his failure to accept that there is such a thing as popular art (Shusterman, 1992: 172; Alexander, 1995: 178; Fowler, 1997; Frith, 1996: 9; 251). Bourdieu is adamant that his earlier work suffered from *illusions*, those of cultural communism (1993a: 2). But while he has justifiably connected this with an unacceptable form of populism, in which the working-class only acquire dignity if they read and write like intellectuals, his response overall to this issue is not entirely convincing.

Admittedly, defenders of rap or other forms of popular music are insufficiently aware of why Bourdieu proposes his view. Shusterman, for

example, argues that Stetsasonic encompass many of the defining characteristics of art in its consecrated modernist form, not least the self-conscious
awareness of being artistic (1992: 220). Frith argues that fans make complex
distinctions as to whether or not the music possesses value on aesthetic grounds
and that these critical rationales are elaborated in detail in the specialized music
press (1996: 66–7).[18]

In brief, these writers have applied a modified Kantian judgement about
aesthetic value to the rock music which Bourdieu would regard as irredeemably
part of the commercial field. But Bourdieu would regard this as neither here
nor there. His thesis utilizes a field or institutional theory of art in which
certain mandarin critics are 'socially mandated' to state what is and is not art.
Their judgements are the only ones that matter. The Shusterman/Frith stance
is repudiated because it neglects the fact that professionals' judgements are
themselves subject to classification according to their degree of academic
power, including their arbitrary right to exclude certain genres. This exclusion
is part and parcel of the meaning of these cultural activities for their publics
(Bourdieu, Chamboredon and Passeron, 1991: 47).

Yet we might still challenge this view. Indeed, in the British cultural space, it
is very clear that heterodox critics from the 1940s on (eg, Leavisites; Priestley,
Williams, 1984; cultural materialists) have succeeded in acquiring sufficient
symbolic power to challenge literary or artistic formalism and to consecrate
certain genres or texts of popular culture. Of course, Bourdieu constantly
reminds us of the *backstage* contempt which is characteristic of the spiritual
aristocracy, where knowledge is the stake in a game of distinction and
condescension. Illustrating this by drawing on the recuperation of bebop jazz
in France in the 50s, he pithily siezes on the intellectualist premises of such
crossovers with his thesis that 'popular art' can become consecrated but *only
when it is no longer popular*! Such a concession is telling but insufficient.
Bourdieu's thesis still over-simplifies the wider struggles over popular art. In
my view, it has underestimated the potential for reflexivity within the cultural
field and ignored the differentiated responses to popular culture, from nausea
to more subtle forms.

Feminist theorists and over-determinism

A similar debate has occurred over masculine domination. Butler has made the
strong claim that Bourdieu's theory fails to take account of performative
statements by lower-class women which provoke transformations (1990 and
1997; see, for a critique of both Bourdieu and Butler, Lovell, below).
Bourdieu's riposte is that Butler puts forward an 'idealist constructivism',
capable only of a narrow, text-based critique as the template for social change.
Gender change for Butler, he argues, is much like putting on a new set of
clothes, since she ignores the way gender is objectified and reified, both
through conditioned bodily responses and social institutions. The crux – for
Bourdieu – is that gendered structures are not vulnerable to textual criticism

precisely because only *certain agents, vested with the right to make public statements* can expect others to take their (performative) statements seriously.

This critique of Butler's voluntarism undoubtedly has some force and finds Butler's weakest spots. But in his turn, Bourdieu's theory has certain symptomatic gaps. He fails to elaborate on occasions when the performatives of the leaders chosen by the subordinate group or class clash historically with the utterances of the powerful. They do so not because they match them in legitimate linguistic or cultural capital (although this may sometimes be so). They do so because they acquire a certain weight and honour in becoming the ascetic 'spokespersons' of the oppressed group.

An affinity with postmodernism?

Bourdieu's sociology continues the main project of the Enlightenment, which is to identify the sources of *mystification* or magic persisting into modernity. As we have seen, Bourdieu notes various forms of 'fetishism'. He tells us, for example, that the mode of reception which identifies painting as 'a reality with no other end than to be contemplated, is very unequally distributed' (1997: 293). Bourdieu refers to such reception not simply as a fetish (1984: 284), but as one in which *the whole of bourgeois dignity* is invested. Thus Bourdieu's task has been to pinpoint as essentialism or *false universalizations* the experience and perspectives of the privileged. These are shown most spectacularly in the case of education or art, but also in the better-known arenas of masculine domination and heterosexuality.

Such a critical exposure of false universalism leads Bourdieu to challenge the other major theoretician of the Enlightenment project, Jürgen Habermas (see especially 1984). For Bourdieu, this project remains too close to the normative philosophical tradition with its scholastic point of view. Recognizing only external coercive domination, Habermas fails to see the forms of *symbolic* violence that have colonized the mind (1997: 80–81) and fails to grasp the material conditions for reason, including time and ease for contemplation (see 1997 chs 1 and 2; 1998a: 127–30).

Yet while critical of Habermas, Bourdieu is neither a moral relativist nor a nihilist. Various authors have *claimed* him for postmodernist (Brubaker, 1993: 230–1; Lash, 1990; Lane, 1999a). But this is a label he has never used of himself: on the contrary, he wants to avoid both the mistake of a *naive idealization* (Merton) and that of a *naive cynicism* (the strong programme in the sociology of science) (1997: 132–6).

Certainly, Bourdieu wants to adopt a type of perspectivism: this insists, for example, on describing and situating the sometimes illusory thinking of the oppressed as well as the ideological myths of the dominants (1990a: 28). We could even see his social theory as avant-garde insofar as it sees the same phenomena from several perspectives at once.[19] Such perspectivism might encourage a radical sense of contingency or nihilism in which truth becomes merely an effect of power and local discourses. But in Bourdieu, as we have

16

seen, perspectivism is woven into a realist social theory where underlying social structures, exerting a determining power, can be known scientifically. For Bourdieu (unlike postmodernists) such structures can be identified in falsifiable theoretical forms. If postmodernism takes the form of 'philosophical aestheticism' (Bourdieu and Wacquant, 1992: 155), Bourdieu wants to defend a 'critical and reflexive realism which breaks at once with epistemic absolutism and with irrationalist relativism' (1997: 133).[20]

It has been claimed recently that it is the *republican tradition* that has most strongly informed Bourdieu's political thought (Verdès-Leroux, 1998). It is true that republicanism has been an important theme within his work in the sense that he has been critical of the absence of rational pedagogy and other rational practices governing access to unequal resources within the public sphere. Moreover he deploys precisely the Machiavellian republican tactic of insisting on interests and *realpolitik* as against 'abstract moralism' (see Pinto, beneath). Republicanism is simultaneously defended as an embattled civilizational achievement but is also to be extended in new ways, which will be easier once severed from the historical form of the nation-state (1998a).

The key to Bourdieu's actions is the insistence on practicable social transformation or a 'realistic utopia', a victory which might possibly be snatched from another 'utopia fast becoming social reality' (neo-liberalism). For neo-liberalism inaugurates the atrophy of republican institutions in the sphere of welfare, law and education, once established in the name of the rights of citizens (1998b). Thus it is true that Bourdieu has identified publicly with new movements that have taken their rational kernel (and legitimacy) from the old forms of republicanism – the Etats Généraux, for example – which recalls the 1789 popular revolutionary movement for democratic representation and an antimonarchical form of executive power. However Bourdieu's politics are not limited to a narrow *national* republicanism. For he has publicly backed the emergence of a European Trade Union Federation and the European Works Council in a move decisively beyond the old French tradition, towards a 'new internationalism'. This movement is not simply to be drawn from those who suffer most: working-class, migrants, unemployed. It is also to be drawn from artists and intellectuals, whose past progressive actions permit a gamble on their solidarity in the face of the technocrats' projects for how we should live.

Conclusion

There is justifiable contention about aspects of Bourdieu's theory. Yet we should remember what has often been missed, especially in accounts of its allegedly ultra-determinist and egoistic synthesis.[21] Resources can be found for critical awareness and alternatives to economically-instrumental action in his sociology: not least his assessments of reciprocity in Kabylian gift-exchange which avoid both a profit-reductive and a romanticized account (1977; 1990). Such resources fit with his defence of the autonomous universes of science and art (see 1996b; 1998a: ch 5) and his perception of neo-liberalism as a threat to civilization (1993; 1998b). Bourdieu's rational utopianism is not a pious nod towards reflexivity. On the contrary, it represents a realist assessment of the potential for transformation given a better grasp of the many obstacles to reason. The most confusing of these are sham claims to universal openness:

> There is, appearances notwithstanding, no contradiction in fighting at the same time *against* the mystificatory hypocrisy of abstract universalism *and for* universal access to the conditions of access to the universal, the primordial objective of all genuine humanism which both universalist preaching and nihilistic (pseudo-) subversion forget (2000: 71).

Acknowledgements

I should like to thank Pierre Bourdieu who has helped the project of this book enormously. There are few writers whom one can reread and find more layers of meaning on each reading, but he is one of them. He continues to be an extraordinary influence, both in his theoretical thinking, and also in his more prominent activity, since 1995, as a public intellectual.

I am also grateful to the University of Glasgow, including the Department of Sociology, for supporting the international Conference on Bourdieu's Social Theory, from which this edited volume had its origins. This allowed an unusually intensive examination of Bourdieu's ideas, over three days.

Emmanuelle Guibé provided professional assistance with the translations, showing her flair and meticulous care over detail. John Orr in Edinburgh, together with Caroline Baggaley and Martin Parker of *Sociological Review Monographs* have all been exceptionally helpful in the process of steering this collection towards publication. I cannot go without mentioning John Fowler for his uncomplaining patience in helping me to sharpen up my ideas.

Notes

1 See Alexander (1995), Butler (1997), Bohman (1999) and others.
2 In justification of the artistic analogy, note the warnings of dangers, viz, the 'pointillism of [...] positivism' and 'impressionistic literary variations on ill-defined totalities' (Bourdieu, Chamboredon and Passeron, 1991: 66).
3 Bourdieu returns in his *Acts of Resistance* to the critical and historical understanding of contemporary economic ideologies, especially neo-liberal 'utopia', thus reminding us once more of Marx's ironic references to the 'Holy Trinity' of naturalized economic categories in his attack on the Manchester economists.
4 It is also true that Bourdieu is deeply suspicious of living 'revolutions in the order of words as though they were radical revolutions in the order of things' (1997: 10).
5 I disagree profoundly with Lane, who argues that Bourdieu's use of Proust to elucidate the time perceptions of the Kabylians is unscientific (Lane, 1999). But this is to invoke a positivist and objectivist conception of science, with which Bourdieu himself breaks (with Chamboredon and Passeron, 1991, Bourdieu, 1993b).
6 Not in the case of all avant-gardes: Gablik shows how art embraced money in New York from Warhol onwards (1984: 56–7).
7 Kabyleans encourage a sublimated view of gifts as acts of generosity because the time-gap veils the gift's obligatory and reciprocal aspect. However, Bourdieu is careful always to distinguish

between this underlying interest in reciprocity on the one hand and an interest in economic profit on the other (1977).

8 Moulin, citing information from Herbert Read, reveals that critics' 'disinterested' evaluations are also vulnerable to the pressure of gallery-owners publicity 'at a subterranean level', especially where, in 'this war of the jungle, prizes are key stakes' (Moulin, 1967: 314).

9 Moulin has also cited the change in market/critics' roles when she argues that artistic professionals may even yield in their judgements after a while to the force of market values 'In a confused dialectic, aesthetic judgement becomes the pretext for a commercial operation and a successful commercial operation takes the place of an aesthetic judgement' (1992: 79).

10 Autonomous artists or novelists do not monopolise such values, of course, but because of their entry to avant-garde fields such as 'art cinema', they do not have to attend also to other values (such as accessibility) which have been a condition of entry into the large-scale field (cf the cases of Hitchcock or Sam Mendes in Hollywood).

11 He comments: 'Mallarmé's hermeticism bespeaks his concern not to destroy the illusio ... it is understandable that we might, by another willing suspension of belief, choose to 'venerate' the authorless trickery which places the fragile fetish beyond the reach of critical lucidity' (1993c: 73).

12 The phrase is used by Bourdieu, describing not Weber, but Flaubert (Bourdieu, 1996b: 100).

13 He is here quoting Sartre (1990d: 149).

14 Wacquant has devoted his chapter to the relation between the two thinkers, so this introductory section will be brief.

15 Bourdieu's recent work has studied the continuities (and transformations) in masculine domination. He has also stressed the need to think these together, in relation to each other: 'Sexual properties are as inseparable from class properties as the yellowness of a lemon is from its acidity: a class is defined in an essential respect by the place and value it gives to the two sexes and their socially constituted dispositions ...' (1984: 107) or again, later: 'I say that masculine domination is one of the last refuges of the dominated classes[...]'(1993a: 4).

16 In 1976, Bourdieu did indeed publish with Boltanski, his analysis of the rhetoric of the dominant fraction of the dominant class, in the form of a dictionary of their discursive ideas: monetary reform, the unblocked society, the removal of the 'isms', the dependence of social evolution on élites, etc. (1976: 4–73).

17 *La Misère du Monde* and *Acts of Resistance* contribute to such an analysis.

18 A similar view is put by Grignon and Passeron (1989). They argue that the use of Bourdieu's theory has become over-routinized or formulaic, especially with regard to the concepts of 'capital, field and habitus'. In particular, popular culture encodes some recognition of the hegemonic character of dominant culture but also develops in a more autonomous manner than Bourdieu's depictions of it would suggest: a view which I share. A more nuanced view than that of Frith concerning the struggles in opening up the canon is provided by Guillory (1993). This poses admirably the significance of the canon as cultural capital but interprets the present canon wars in terms of the challenge from fractions of the dominants (eg in management schools) who no longer need such an erudite humanist culture for legitimation (1993: 46–7).

19 See such perspectivism in Picasso's various pictures of *Las Meninas* and especially in *Les Demoiselles d'Avignon*, where he represents the same face from two angles of vision simultaneously.

20 Lane has recently argued against this claim, declaring that Bourdieu depends on philosophical theorizing of the same type as postmodernists, such as Derrida: 'The inevitability of Bourdieu's failure to ground doxa [in *Outline* ...] either empirically or historically points to the conceptual weakness at the heart of the notion itself. For the state of 'originary doxa', the starting point or point-zero for Bourdieu's theories of historical change and social reproduction is inherently ahistorical ...' (1999: 99). There is no perfect science of the social world precisely because of the doxic influence of contemporary categories on us. Bourdieu surely agrees with Popper, however, that we need science as a *critical tradition* because no scientist, at present, can objectivate everything. And it is not merely Bourdieu, who, with Proustian spectacles, sees the conceptions of space and time of pre-modern societies like Kabylia as fundamentally different from those of

the modern, it is the basic historical framework of sociology and of Marxist and realist philosophy.
21 We must therefore resist strenuously Alexander's (1995) account of his reductive atomistic universe.

Bibliography

Alexander, J.C., (1995), *Fin de Siècle Social Theory: Relativism, Reduction and Reason*, London: Verso.
Beck,U., Giddens, A. and Lash, S., (1994), *Reflexive Modernisation: Politics, Tradition and Aesthetics in the Modern Social Order*, Cambridge: Polity.
Becker, H., (1982), *Art-Worlds*, Berkeley: University of California Press.
Bohman, J., (1999), 'Practical Reasons and Cultural Constraint', in Shusterman, R. (ed.), *Bourdieu: A Critical Reader*, Oxford: Blackwell.
Bourdieu, P., (1977), *Outline of a Theory of Practice*, Cambridge: Cambridge University Press.
Bourdieu, P., (1984), *Distinction*, London: Routledge.
Bourdieu, P., (1987), 'Legitimation and Structured Interests in Weber's Sociology of Religion', in Lash, S. and Whimster, S. (eds.), *Max Weber, Rationality and Modernity*, pp. 119–136, Allen and Unwin.
Bourdieu, P., (1988a), *Homo Academicus*, Cambridge: Polity.
Bourdieu, P., (1988b), *The Ontology of Martin Heidegger*, Cambridge: Polity.
Bourdieu, P., (1990a), *The Logic of Practice*, Cambridge: Polity.
Bourdieu, P., Boltanski, L., Castel, R. and Chamboredon, J.-C., (1990b), *Photography, A Middle-brow Art*, Cambridge: Polity.
Bourdieu, P., (1990c), *In Other Words*, Cambridge: Polity.
Bourdieu, P., (1991), *Language and Symbolic Power*, Cambridge: Polity.
Bourdieu, P., (1993a), *Sociology in Question*, London: Sage.
Bourdieu, P., (1993b), *La Misère du Monde*, Paris: Seuil.
Bourdieu, P., (1993c), *The Field of Cultural Production*, Cambridge: Polity.
Bourdieu, P., (1996a), *The State Nobility*, Cambridge: Polity.
Bourdieu, P., (1996b), *The Rules of Art*, Cambridge: Polity.
Bourdieu, P., (1997), *Méditations Pascaliennes*, Paris: Seuil.
Bourdieu, P., (1998a), *Practical Reason*, Cambridge: Polity.
Bourdieu, P., (1998b), *Acts of Resistance*, Cambridge: Polity.
Bourdieu, P., (1998c), *La Domination Masculine*, Paris: Seuil.
Bourdieu, P., (1999), *The Weight of the World*, Cambridge: Polity.
Bourdieu, P., (2000), *Pascalian Meditations*, Cambridge: Polity.
Bourdieu, P. and Boltanski, L., (1976), 'La Production de L'Idéologie Dominante', *Actes de la Recherche en Sciences Sociales*, Juin, 2/3, 4–73.
Bourdieu, P., Darbel, A. and Schnapper, D., (1991), *The Love of Art*, Cambridge: Polity.
Bourdieu, Chamboredon, J.-C. and Passeron, J.-C., (1991), *The Craft of Sociology*, Berlin: de Gruyter.
Bourdieu, P. and Wacquant, L., (1992), *An Invitation to Reflexive Sociology*, Cambridge: Polity.
Brubaker, R., (1993), Social theory as Habitus, in Calhoun, C., Lipuma, E. and Postone, M. (eds), *Bourdieu: Critical Perspectives*, pp. 211–234, Cambridge: Polity.
Butler, J., (1990), *Gender Trouble: Feminism and the Subversion of Identity*, London: Routledge.
Butler, J., (1997), *Excitable Speech*, London: Routledge.
Calhoun, C., (1993), Habitus, Field and Capital: The Question of Historical Specificity, in Calhoun, C., Lipuma, E. and Postone, M. (eds), pp. 61–89, *Bourdieu: Critical Perspectives*, Cambridge: Polity.
Durkheim, E., (1977), *The Evolution of Educational Thought*, London: Routledge and Kegan Paul (1938).

Durkheim, E., (1989), *Suicide*, Glencoe: Free Press, RKP.

Fowler, B., (1997), *Pierre Bourdieu and Cultural Theory*, London: Sage.

Frith, S., (1996), *Performing Rites*, Oxford: Oxford University Press.

Gablik, S., (1984), *Has Modernism Failed?*, London: Thames and Hudson.

Gerth, H.H. and Mills, C.W., (1991), *From Max Weber*, London: Routledge (New edition by B.S. Turner).

Grignon, C. and Passeron, J.-C., (1989), *Le Savant et le Populaire*, Paris: Seuil.

Guillory, J., (1993), *Cultural Capital*, Chicago: University of Chicago Press.

Habermas, J., (1984), *The Theory of Communicative Action*, Cambridge: Polity.

Lane, J., (1999), Pierre Bourdieu and the Chronotopes of 'Post-Theory', in McQuillan, M., MacDonald, G., Purves, R. and Thompson, S. (eds), *Post-Theory: New Directions in Criticism*, pp. 89–102, Edinburgh: Edinburgh University Press.

Lash, S., (1990), *The Sociology of Postmodernism*, London: Routledge.

Lidsky, P., (1970), *Les Ecrivains contre La Commune*, Paris: Maspero.

Marx, K., (1973), *Grundrisse*, Harmondsworth: Penguin.

Marx, K., (1976), *Capital*, Volume I: Harmondsworth: Penguin.

Mauss, M., (1972), *A General Theory of Magic*, London: RKP.

Moulin, R., (1967), *Le Marché de la Peinture en France*, Paris: Minuit, 2nd Edition.

Moulin, R., (1992), *L'Artiste, L'Institution et le Marché*, Paris: Flammarion.

Myles, J., (1999), *Postmodernism and Cultural Intermediaries*, PhD Thesis, Lancaster: University of Lancaster.

Pinto, L., (1998), *Pierre Bourdieu et la Théorie du Monde Sociale*, Paris: Albin Michel.

Shusterman, R., (1992), *Pragmatist Aesthetics*, Oxford: Blackwell.

Verdès-Leroux, J., (1998), *Le Savant et la Politique*, Paris: Grasset.

Williams, R., (1984), *Writing in Society*, London: Verso.

Section I: Domination

Introduction to Section I

The papers in this volume are organized into three sections: domination; rationality and politics; modern culture. The first section explores the Bourdieusian themes of gender and class domination.

Terry Lovell

It opens with Lovell's elegant comparison of Bourdieu and Butler on gender divisions. She argues that what distinguishes Bourdieu's sociology from feminist theorists of difference is his stress on the durability of the bodily disposition, yet this theory cannot allow for the self-surveillance of the body. However, poststructuralist gender theories such as Butler's lead to an equally erroneous over-flexibility of female agency. Thus if Butler's deconstructionism, like an Ovidian metamorphosis of souls, fails to take account of the embeddedness of structures in things, Bourdieu's habitus, because of its inflexible character is incapable of accounting for phenomena such as military 'passing', the pride of working-class women in their physical labour and even the phenomena of the 'lucid outsiders' such as Virginia Woolf.

Simon Charlesworth

A different view of Bourdieu's logic of practice emerges in Charlesworth's paper. Taking as his subject the nature of working-class experience in Rotherham, a region of extensive de-industrialization, Charlesworth uses Bourdieu's theoretical framework to shed light on his interviews with working-class people. Using Bourdieu's theoretical synthesis of the ideas of Marx with the phenomenology of Heidegger (Bourdieu, 1988b) and Merleau-Ponty, Charlesworth reveals the being-in-the-world and limited horizons of the poorly-paid or unemployed. He argues powerfully that their postural stance, responses and their style of expression reveal a profound uneasiness and introspective pain about their circumstances and likely future. This rupture with the conventional English empirical approaches to working-class life and unemployment and the deployment of tools from continental philosophy for addressing the subject's experience brings an immediate gain. It gives an unrivalled depth of perspective to the generic elements of class inferiority as well as the historical peculiarities of a period when identity is framed to such a degree by money and consumption. Charlesworth's argument poses difficult questions about the degree to which working-class existence is pre-reflexive and what this entails about an 'unconscious activity of self-curtailment' and 'internalized contradictions'. But is such pre-reflexivity compatible with the sense of injustice so evident from the interview quotations?

Thinking feminism with and against Bourdieu

Terry Lovell

1. Resources of/for feminism?

'... an invitation to think with Bourdieu is of necessity an invitation to think beyond Bourdieu, and against him whenever required'. Loïc J.D.Wacquant. 'Preface' In Bourdieu and Wacquant (1992): xiv.

Bourdieu's work has had surprisingly little circulation within Anglo-Saxon feminism. This is in marked contrast to the pervasive influence of Foucault and Derrida, the French philosophers against and in relationship to whom Bourdieu has positioned himself within the French intellectual field. In this paper I shall attempt to assess the value for feminist theory of Bourdieu's concepts, especially of *habitus*, and of 'cultural' and other 'capitals', whilst also addressing some of the common reservations about his work which bringing it into engagement with feminist scholarship might clarify. I shall draw not only upon what Bourdieu writes directly concerning *'la domination masculine'*[1] but also on texts such as *Distinction* (1984) and *The Logic of Practice* (1990b). I shall argue that his insistence upon the significance of social class in the formation of the individual's *habitus* is salutary in the face of those highly influential postmodernist feminisms of 'difference' which have had difficulty in keeping within the frame the difference that social class makes. Yet I shall argue that Bourdieu's sociology is in turn in danger of positioning sex/gender, sexuality, and even 'race', as secondary to that of social class.

By *habitus* Bourdieu understands ways of doing and being which social subjects acquire during their socialization. Their *habitus* is not a matter of conscious learning, or of ideological imposition, but is acquired through practice. Bourdieu's sociology rests on an account of lived 'practice', and what he terms 'the practical sense' – the ability to function effectively within a given social field, an ability which cannot necessarily be articulated as conscious knowledge: 'knowing how' rather than 'knowing that'. *Habitus* names the characteristic dispositions of the social subject. It is indicated in the bearing of the body ('hexis'), and in deeply ingrained habits of behaviour, feeling, thought.

Contemporary feminisms of difference and Bourdieu's sociology of practice share a common focus upon 'the body'. What distinguishes Bourdieu's embodied social actor is what one commentator on this paper referred to as 'the durable dispositional subject; what we might encounter in everyday life as an obstinate and tenacious loyalty to forms of life into which, for some reason, the subject has become enrolled' (Steve Hall, 1998: personal communication). The weight of emphasis of postmodernist feminism falls, rather, upon agency, fluidity, the instability of subject positionings and identities which contrasts at times very starkly with the durability of Bourdieu's dispositional subject. I have found it particularly fruitful to compare and contrast Bourdieu's approach with that of Judith Butler. Interestingly, there are common elements in their intellectual heritages, and they should have much to say to one another.

In his discussions of male domination (Bourdieu, 1990a; 1998), Bourdieu attributes its persistence in large part to gendered *habitus*, and I want to begin by confronting this account with the phenomenon of gender-passing.

2. The acquisition of a cross-gender *habitus*

> *L'habitus masculin ne se construit et ne s'accomplit qu'en relation avec l'espace réservé où se jouent,* entre hommes, *les jeux sérieux de la compétition, qu'il s'agisse des jeux de l'honneur, dont la limite est la guerre ou des jeux qui, dans les sociétés différenciées offrent à la* libido dominandi, *sous toutes ses formes, économique, politique, religieuse, artistique, scientifique, etc. des champs d'action possibles.* (The masculine habitus is only constituted or achieved in relation to a reserve space in which serious competitive games are played *between men*, games of honour of which the limit case is that of war, or games which, in differentiated societies, offer to the desire for domination, under all its forms, economic, political, artistic, scientific, etc., possible fields of action.) (Bourdieu, 1990a: 26).

> ... a sense of the game and of its stakes that implies at once an *inclination* and an *ability* to play the game, both of which are socially and historically constituted ... (Bourdieu, in Bourdieu and Wacquant, 1992: 118).

In modern/postmodern society there are few remaining 'games' ('social fields of practice') fully reserved for men, from which women are formally excluded, although many in which we are not exactly welcomed or taken seriously as players. However, women have a lengthy history of gate-crashing male enclaves, even in Bourdieu's limit case of games of honour, war. Consider the history of women passing as military men. Dutch research has uncovered some 119 cases of women cross-dressing and living as men, mostly as soldiers and sailors, in Northern Europe from the 13th to the 19th centuries (Dekker and Van de Pol, 1989). The advent of more formal regulation of military recruitment and of medical examinations saw the end of this phenomenon, with few exceptions, most notably that of revolutionary Russia (Wheelwright, 1989). The entry of women into the modern uniformed services as front-line troops has been accompanied by a high degree of resistance, often in the form of sexual harassment. Traditional male reserve spaces have often been vigorously defended against the incursions of women (Cockburn, 1991).

Until very recently, the infiltration of women into military arenas was either in non-combatant roles, or was accomplished through 'passing'. To have passed as fighting men as successfully as many of these women did suggests that what Bourdieu calls a 'feel for the game' was fairly highly developed among them: the ability to assume the bodily hexis and the *habitus* characteristic of the militia; to display the 'honour' to which their assumption of military uniform laid pretension.

However, would-be players may be ruled out of court on the grounds not of any lack of distinction, but for want of entitlement to play: to accumulate capital in a particular field. Exposure of illegitimacy, in many fields, is more likely to lead to expulsion than is incompetence. The butcher who passes for a surgeon will, on discovery of his lack of credentials, be removed from the operating theatre however skilfully he has wielded the scalpel. The *bone fide* surgeon who 'butchers' his patients (short, perhaps of killing them entirely, although there are more examples than we might care to think), has a good chance of being allowed to continue to practise his profession.

One might expect that however good the 'feel for the game' of warfare of women who passed as soldiers, exposure would have been swiftly followed by expulsion from the field. While this was indeed usually the case, it was not always so. Christian Davies, who served with the British army in the early 18th century and suffered serious injuries which led to the exposure of her sex, was granted a military pension and buried at the Pensioner's College in Chelsea. At her funeral three grand volleys were fired over her grave (Wheelwright, 1989: 169). Such women were instant popular heroines, often contributing to their own production as myth. (Warhman, 1998).

In 1914 Flora Sandes, who was at the time 38, joined a British Red Cross Unit headed for Serbia. The following year she was invited, by the regimental commander of the Serb unit to which her ambulance unit was attached, to enlist as a private soldier in the Serbian Army. She donned a man's uniform, and served for seven years with her battalion, coming under fire. Her distinction was recognized by promotion to the rank of lieutenant. She was exceptional among women soldiers in that she made no attempt to disguise her sex, her actions given official sanction by the Serbian military authorities. For the duration she lived effectively as a man among men, and was accepted as such by her comrades. She cross-dressed in donning a man's uniform but did not 'pass'. Her sex was common knowledge, and people in the towns and villages she passed through in the course of the war flocked to see her (Sandes, 1927; Wheelwright, 1989).

These instances of female infiltration of masculine games of honour lead to the first question which I wish to address to Bourdieu's sociology: how, given his account of 'the practical sense' and its acquisition, do some women manage to develop a good feel for 'games' from which they are excluded by virtue of their sex? How do some women manage to develop the masculine *habitus* demanded of 'players' in the militia, legitimate and illegitimate, 'passing' or entering under special licence like Sandes? *Ex hypothesi*, these women must have been good. How was it possible for them to acquire these skills and aptitudes, given that they would have been denied access in early life to the practices in which the masculine *habitus* is founded?

The question might be side-stepped through the consideration that, as a sociologist, Bourdieu is concerned not with the exceptional but with the logic of ordinary everyday practice: with statistical averages. But gender crossing is not uncommon, especially in societies where individuals move into communities in which their identity is not known. And as Bourdieu himself argues, war represents a limit case. That exceptions are possible even at these limits, and where the risk of exposure is very high, may indicate not just some social aberration but the tip of a large iceberg. However exceptional, it is a phenomenon that requires the attention of any theory of practice.

Bourdieu's theory, although resolutely non-essentialist and insistent that we are always dealing with 'cultural arbitraries', nevertheless makes it difficult to understand how one might ever appear, convincingly, to be what one is not, particularly where gender divides are crossed in the process. For his account of the acquisition of social identity through practice, *habitus*, emphasizes its corporeal sedimentation: in bodily hexis, speech, taste, and in the 'feel for the game' which appears to be a natural gift – markers which are almost impossible to learn or to consciously imitate, or for that matter to eradicate, because in Bourdieu's schema, they never come fully under self-surveillance and control.

This problem is inverted in the case of those feminist postmodernists, also social constructionists, who understand gender in terms of performance, or who operate with the figure of the mask; with identity as process, as becoming. Poststructuralist and postmodernist discourses celebrate flexible selves, permeable or semi-permeable boundaries, the journey traversed rather than origins or lasting determinations (Butler, 1990; 1993; Braidotti, 1994).[2]

Postmodernist theory, such as that of Butler, in its deconstruction of identity, puts the very concept of passing in question, for all identity can come to be seen as a species of passing if it is no more than its own wilful performance in the right circumstances with the right co-actors, and therefore with no ground for appeal to 'real' identities which the performances may conceal. The face behind the mask is merely another mask. The sloughing off of oppressive identities, on this view, is not to be achieved through denial and the iteration of a more authentic self but through 'queering the pitch'; destabilizing the fixities of social identity through paradoxical or ironic masquerades.

The impression is sometimes given that the removal of markers of identity and of subjective dispositions may be achieved as readily as a change of clothing or the adoption of a new mask. The flesh itself is sometimes presented as an instrument of masquerade: 'For some of us our costumes are made of fabric or material while for others they are made of skin' (Halberstam, 1994).

In postmodern ontology, all identities deceive; they depend upon misrecognition. Does what is commonly understood by the term 'passing', then, remains distinct only in that the deception is consciously intended?

Bourdieu's conceptual toolkit, like that of Butler, draws on J.L. Austin's concept of 'performativity' (Austin, 1962; Bourdieu, 1991; Butler, 1990; 1997). Performatives (utterances which enact or instantiate or bring about social statuses, as in the authorized declaration of marriage) are also always performances, but they have the force of social institutionalization behind them which *mere* performances lack. They are embedded in the social structures and norms which authorize them. For Butler, socially embedded *performatives* may be dislodged, their meanings transformed, by inspired *performances* which transgress *with authority*:

> When Rosa Parks sat in front of the bus, she had no prior right to do so guaranteed by any of the segregationist conventions of the South. And yet in laying claim to the right for which she had no *prior* authorization, she endowed a certain authority on the act, and began the insurrectionary process of overthrowing those established codes of legitimacy (Butler, 1997: 147).

Bourdieu's concept of performativity in which the authority of performatives derives from the power of social institutions on the one hand and, on the other, the *habitus* which tacitly recognizes that authority, suggests no easy freedom to adapt or change the self. For Bourdieu, although our *habitus* is acquired, our doxa (or taken-for-granted commonsense understandings of the world and ourselves), composed not of the natural and immutable but of cultural arbitraries, are as real, as difficult to shift, as any natural attribute. What Bourdieu offers that is most powerful is a way of understanding *both* the arbitrary, and therefore contestable, nature of the social, *and* its compelling presence and effectiveness. He articulates the nature of 'social reality' as precisely constructed but solid in a way in which postmodernist 'performances' often do not seem to be. The two terms qualify one another. *Social* reality is of a different kind from that of the natural world, but it is social *reality* in spite of its arbitrariness and dependence on continued reiteration in performance.

Bourdieu reads at times like a structuralist with an 'oversocialized' concept of the individual, who, like Althusser's actor, is destined to become what he/she 'always already' was: a mere *bearer* of social positions, one who comes to love and want his/her fate: *amor fati*. Equally, in spite of her emphasis on performativity as well as performance, Butler reads at times like a voluntarist whose individuals freely don and doff their masks, to make themselves over at will through virtuoso performances of the chosen self. It is no accident that her example of transgressive performance, that of Rosa Parks's assumption of a seat reserved for whites, focuses on the action of one individual rather than on a social movement.

31

Both authors have protested these readings. Butler disputes this criticism of her 1990 *Gender Troubles* in her introduction to her 1993 *Bodies That Matter*. 'Why is it', she asks, 'that what is constructed is understood as an artificial and dispensable character?' (Butler, 1993: xi). Bourdieu likewise contests the charge of oversocialization. In an interview, Wacquant poses the question:

> Does the introduction of the mediating concept of habitus really free us from the 'iron cage' of structuralism? To many of your readers, the notion seems to remain overly deterministic [...] where does the element of innovation and agency come from? (Bourdieu and Wacquant, 1992: 132).

Bourdieu answer runs to four pages. This reader remains not entirely convinced. The contrast between the two approaches is brought out very clearly in Butler's single engagement to date with Bourdieu's work. He makes social institutions, she claims, static, and because of this, 'fails to grasp the logic of iterability that governs the possibility of social transformation' (Butler, 1997: 147). Butler's own 'politics of the performative' places the possibility of agency upon the intersection of performance with performativity, as may be seen in her example of Rosa Parks. But if I read her correctly, it is performance which takes the active part here, because it is in the *performance*, ironic, playful, or otherwise subversive, that utterances may come to have *performative* power, and that, contrarily, the performative power of authorized utterances may be undermined: 'there are invocations of speech that are insurrectionary acts' (Butler, 1997: 145). Bourdieu in turn reiterates the accusation of voluntarism while noting Butler's own defence against this charge in *Bodies That Matter*. With specific reference to Butler, he writes of those characteristics which are '*profondément enracinés dans les choses (les structures) et dans les corps, ne pas nés d'un simple effet de nomination verbale et ne peuvent être abolis par un acte de magie performative*' (Those which, deeply rooted in things (structures) and in bodies, are not negated by a simple act of verbal naming and are not to be abolished by an act of performative magic.) (Bourdieu, 1998: 110).[5]

If these readings of Bourdieu as overdetermining and Butler as a voluntarist are misreadings, they are of frequent recurrence in secondary interpretations of each of these authors. Both may be readily supported by some of the formulations which each author offers, just as it is a simple matter to find quotations from Irigaray or Kristeva to support the charge of essentialism (see note 1). It is no accident that Bourdieu's and Butler's different approaches lead to these two 'misreadings'. Bourdieu's strength lies in his insistence upon the well-nigh permanent sediments and traces which constitute embodied culture, but he draws attention away from those other areas of social space where the constructedness of social reality may be tacitly acknowledged or exposed. Butler, like a number of postmodernists, particularly valorizes these, often 'less serious', spaces – of play, masquerade, carnival – *because* it is here that cultural constructions become visible as such and therefore open to challenge and to situationist-style political interventions. But, by the same token, she can only focus her own and her readers' attention with difficulty on the paradoxical immobile solidity which cultural arbitraries acquire as they are sedimented in hexis and *habitus*, custom and practice. And on the other hand, while Bourdieu's 'reflexive sociology' allows for political agency and social change, it is so successful in identifying the embeddedness of agency in institutional practice that there is no denying that it induces at times a strong sense of political paralysis.

3. Positioning and position taking

... l'effet de la domination symbolique ne s'exerce pas dans la logique pure des consciences connaissantes, mais dans l'obscurité des schèmes pratiques de l'habitus, où est inscrite, souvent inaccessible aux prises de la conscience réflexive et aux contrôles de la volonté, la relation de domination (Symbolic domination is not the outcome of the logic of conscious thought, but of the obscurity of practical schemes of *habitus*, in which relations of domination, often inaccessible to reflective consciousness and the will, are inscribed.) (Bourdieu, 1990: 11).

For Bourdieu, girl children early acquire the stigmata of femininity, boys the bearing of masculinity, due to their immersion within gendered 'practical schemes' into which they are channelled from birth as their biological sex and class position dictates. Yet it is clear that this by no means always happens, requiring as it does that female and male children *position themselves* as girls and boys, or that they are not pressed so hard against the necessities of their sex that they cannot position themselves widdershins. But for Bourdieu, *position-taking* (or 'stance') is closely related to the *positioning* of the actor in the social field: 'Both spaces, that of objective positions and that of stances, must be analysed together, treated as 'two translations of the same sentence' as Spinoza puts it' (Bourdieu, in Bourdieu and Wacquant, 1992: 105). While accounts of the pressures exerted upon girls and women by 'patriarchal ideology' lack plausibility insofar as these are construed as entirely external and constraining, those which posit a glovelike 'fit' between *habitus* and social position are in danger of binding subjectivity too tightly to the social conditions in which it is forged.

It is psychoanalytic feminism which was first responsible for insisting that girl children do not slip easily into the feminine position marked out for them by their sex. Jacqueline Rose argues that femininity is always deeply problematic, a status which is never fully and wholeheartedly embraced, always resisted (Rose, 1983). In some cultures, this resistance is tacitly recognized, and alternatives to femininity are institutionalized. The Balkan tradition of 'Albanian virgins' permitted some women to contract to live as social males in exchange for celibacy (Kindersley, 1976). Wheelwright (1989) argues that it was this tradition which eased the paths of Flora Sandes and her predecessor in the Balkans, Jenny Merkus who fought against Turkish rule in Bosnia for three years from 1873. In the absence of such opportunities fully to become social males, play and the games of the imagination usually permit the rehearsal of cross-gender identities. Certainly under some social conditions it has proved possible for young girls to refuse positioning in the feminine for long enough to acquire a masculine *habitus*. 'Amazons and military maids', like 'tomboys', have bodies that are not easy to read in terms of femininity and masculinity. Since the stigmata of gender are, according to Bourdieu, acquired so early, inscribed along the lines of sex difference, and deeply ingrained in the bodies of boys and girls, such success in passing across the lines of sex and gender becomes difficult to comprehend within the terms of his sociology.

Bourdieu ties up sex, sexuality, and gender too tightly together, and this is one reason why the charge of 'oversocialization' is taken seriously by feminists, notwithstanding his disclaimers. Butler on the other hand is altogether too successful in disaggregating them. We may perhaps accept that the perfect alignment of sex, gender and sexuality is a limit case which is rarely if ever found, but not all social circumstances permit or are conducive to the same degrees of non-alignment, or enable the effective subversion of performatives. For Bourdieu the 'scope of human freedom ... is not large' (Bourdieu and Wacquant, 1992: 199). He recognizes that 'there exist dispositions to resist' but insists on the need 'to examine under what conditions these dispositions are socially constituted, effectively triggered, and rendered politically efficient' (Bourdieu and Wacquant, 1992: 81). For Butler, on the authority of Foucault and Derrida respectively, the possibility of resistance is simply inherent in the nature of power or of language (Butler, 1997), but the conditions favourable to the exploitation of these windows of opportunity for personal and social transformation are never interrogated. They are represented by Butler as free political acts, as in the Rosa Parks example. A feminist politics must needs identify possibilities of intervention to effect social transformation, but an effective politics is one which recognizes the tightness of the constraints which bind women into the social circumstances in which they find themselves. *Habitus* may provide a powerful conceptual antidote to postmodern voluntaristic politics, insofar as it permits us to focus on the social conditions of existence of resistance, and conversely, Butler's understanding of the necessary 'leakiness' of all social power, social convention, *habitus*, heads off the Bourdieuian slippage into political pessimism.

I want to return to social class, in order to show how both Butler and Bourdieu may be brought together to provide the beginnings of an explanation of the paradox of the cross-gender *habitus* of the female soldier. My argument will be that not all women in all historical and cultural circumstances have equal opportunities to make such boundary crossings, but that certain class cultures facilitate the crossing of gender positionings provided these take place along the lines of class.

Bourdieu distinguishes between cultures which are forged through necessity and a harsh day-to-day struggle for survival, and those that can afford a more contemplative stance towards the world and the self. In the case of working-class men, a culture of necessity is generated which celebrates the physical body and the attributes of bodily strength: the form of 'cultural capital' most readily available for accumulation in these circumstances.[3] What is the necessity that generates the *habitus* of submission which Bourdieu reads in the bodies of the women of the North African Kabyle? Both men and women are constrained to use their bodies for hard physical labour, so why do working-class and peasant women not also develop the *habitus* and culture which Bourdieu identifies in working-class and peasant men?

The circumstances of the sexual division of labour and the different rhythms and movements which they impose on male and female bodies may produce the kind of strongly marked physical differences that Bourdieu found to be characteristic of the mature Kabyle sexed body. In other circumstances the differences are less marked. Sojourner Truth's speech to the Women's Rights Convention held in 1851 at Akron Ohio is famous for its refrain 'ain't I a woman?' but in it she also celebrates her physical, working body: 'I have ploughed and planted, and gathered into barns, and no man could head me – and ain't I a woman? I could work as much as any man (when I could get it) and bear the lash as well – and ain't I a woman?' (hooks 1982: 159). Hannah Cullwick, the white working-class 'maid of all work' in mid-nineteenth-century Britain wrote diaries and memoirs for her husband Arthur Munby which likewise glory in her superior physique and her great capacity for hard labour: 'I put how thick my arm was round the muscle and its 10 and a $\frac{1}{2}$ inches round thick below [the] elbow – 6 and $\frac{3}{4}$ round my wrist. My neck is $13\frac{1}{2}$, so its not as big as my arm – and Massa's muscle is but 13 and a half round' (Cullwick, 1984: 128). While the bent form of the peasant woman which speaks of back-breaking labours may also serve to symbolise the subordinate status of her sex, not all female labour produces such eloquently submissive bodily forms, for example the common practice of carrying of heavy burdens on the head.

It was working-class women, in the main, who were able to pass as fighting men, and who had the most powerful motivation for doing so – material necessity. Wheelwright (1989) adduces evidence of the ease with which European working-class women were able to pass as soldiers in the modern period. They '... found the shift from physically-demanding farm or domestic labour to the rigours of army life quite unproblematic' (19). The *habitus* of the working woman, when forged by necessity in particular work-regimes, may have given her not only the motive but also the means for passing as a (working-class) man. Bourdieu's claim that gender differentiation is less marked the higher one moves up the social hierarchy (Bourdieu, 1984: 382) must be qualified. It was among the white middle classes in the 19th century in Europe and the US that the most marked differences between the sexes were generated. The sexed bodily hexis of labouring people may at some times be less sharply differentiated. It is possible, sometimes indeed easy, to pass across the lines of gender.

At the other extreme of the social scale we have occasional examples of women passing as officers and gentlemen. The cultivated effeminacy and weakness sometimes assumed by 'gentlemen'[4] would have facilitated gender passing along class lines. Valerie Arkell-Smith, to escape a violent husband, assumed men's clothes, and in the course of her life, a number of masculine identities, including in the 1920s that of a war veteran, 'Colonel Victor Barker'. In this persona she married in style in Brighton in 1923. Again the economic motivation was evident, alongside the desire to escape the exigencies of her sex. She received a certain degree of sympathy at her trial in 1927 as a women who, as her defending counsel put it, was '... bold enough and has succeeded in earning her living as a man when she found that she could not do it as a woman' (quoted in Wheelwright, 1989: 2).

4. Gender and class in the social field

> *... la logique de l'économie des échanges symboliques et, plus précisément ... la construction sociale des relations de parenté et du mariage ... assigne aux femmes,* universellement, *leur statut social d'objets d'échange ...* (... the logic of the economy of symbolic exchange, and, more precisely, ... the social construction of kinship relations and of marriage, ... assigns to women, *universally*, their status as objects of exchange ...) (Bourdieu, 1990a: 27).

One problem with Bourdieu's work relates to the scope of his assertions concerning '*la domination masculine*'. In the 1990 article he draws heavily upon Kabyle society, which he describes as '*tout entière organisée selon la division hiérarchique entre les sexes*' (entirely organized through the hierarchical division between the sexes.) (Bourdieu, 1990a: 5, note 7, reproduced from Bourdieu, 1979: 354). He locates Kabyle society within a broader Mediterranean cultural tradition which has its origins in ancient Greece: a tradition founded on honour and shame which may be seen clearly in the writings of Homer and Hesiod. However it is not always possible to know when he is restricting his observations to the particular case of Kabyle society, when he is extending them to encompass the whole Mediterranean culture of honour/shame, including that of the modern period, and when he is offering universal generalizations. He observes that '*selon toute probabilité, la suprématie masculine est universelle*'. ('In all probability, male supremacy is universal'.)[5] (Bourdieu, 1990a: 7, note 9).

In Bourdieu's *Distinction* (Bourdieu, 1984), where the focus is on contemporary France, women still feature, in his schema of the social field, primarily as social objects, repositories of value and of capital, who circulate between men and who serve certain important functions in the capital accumulation strategies of families and kinship groups. While class penetrates right through his diagrammatic representations of the social field, like the lettering in Brighton rock, gender is largely invisible, as is 'race'. This in spite of the observations made in the body of the text which suggest the critical importance of gender in the mapping of class distinctions and relations, for

36

example: 'sexual properties are as inseparable from class properties as the yellowness of a lemon is from its acidity: a class is defined in an essential respect by the place and value it gives to the two sexes and to their socially constituted dispositions' and 'the true nature of a class or class fraction is expressed in its distribution by sex or age' (Bourdieu, 1984: 107–8). Yet while class distribution is made graphic in his diagram of 'the space of social positions' through colour-coding, so that 'the proportion of individuals from the dominant class (black) rises strongly, while the proportion from the working class (white) declines as one moves up the social hierarchy' (Bourdieu, 1984: 127), there is no similar coding which would make gender or 'race' instantly visible.

The problem arises, perhaps, because Bourdieu recognizes women's status as capital-bearing *objects* whose value accrues to the primary groups to which they belong, rather than as capital-accumulating *subjects* in social space. Insofar as women have labour market occupations, then it is possible to include them in Bourdieu's social chart, but then they would, as it were, be entered twice: in terms of their own holdings of cultural and economic capital, and in terms of the value of these holdings for their families. There is an echo here of the position taken by the British sociologist John Goldthorpe who defended the common practice of defining social class in terms which left women out of account against the criticisms of feminists (Goldthorpe, 1983; Goldthorpe and Marshall, 1992; Stanworth, 1984).

For Bourdieu, following Lévi-Strauss (1969), women are produced socially as objects who are exchanged between men, and not as subjects – objects of value ('vile and precious merchandise' Wittig) but objects nonetheless – whose strategic circulation plays a key role in the maintenance and enhancement of the symbolic capital held by men. He sees this logic as little affected by the advent of industrial capitalism.

The feminist anthropologist Sherry Ortner asked in 1974 'Is female to male as nature is to culture?' She answered her own question in the affirmative *and* the negative. Women, she argued, occupy a liminal space between nature and culture. We might mount a similar argument faced with the opposition between 'subject' and 'object'. Even if it is conceded that 'women universally have the social status of objects' it must remain questionable whether women universally and exclusively *position* themselves as objects, and indeed whether it is even possible to do so unequivocally. Here the neat correspondence between *habitus* and social field begins to come apart a little. Certainly we must follow Jacqueline Rose in recognizing that '... most women do not painlessly slip into their roles as women, if indeed they do at all' (Rose, 1983: 9).

The idea of 'producing oneself as an object' is paradoxical within a language which links identity with subjectivity and therefore with positioning as a *subject*. Nevertheless Bourdieu makes an important point when he draws attention to the fact that the maintenance of class and other social boundaries through the accumulation of symbolic capital is gendered, and that women play a very significant role in these processes. But he rarely considers women as subjects with capital-accumulating strategies of their own which may be at odds with those of their family and kin, and it is to these strategies that I shall now turn, to see the ways in which Bourdieu's inventory of 'capitals' has been used to good effect within feminist analysis.

5. Women in social space: capital investment strategies

Where would we find women as capital-holding subjects in Bourdieu's social field? Unlike the working class, which in Bourdieu's representation of the social field is clustered in regions bereft of symbolic capital, women, were they to be included in his representation, would be positioned across the entire field. Colour-coded, there would be no steady progression from pink to blue. They are not clustered together 'below', with men clustered together 'above'. The history of feminist thought since the late 1970s has been one which, of necessity, has had to recognize the ways in which hierarchies of class and 'race' are hierarchies which also separate women from each other in social space. Bourdieu is able to disregard the problem posed by this differential distribution, in his discussion of male domination, because of his under-standing of women principally as objects in that space, as repositories of capitals which are appropriated and deployed by men as assets in their jostlings for position with one another.

What I propose here, then, is an analytical focus, of the kind increasingly taken for granted within feminism, on women as subject/objects, but specified in Bourdieu's terms: that is to say, in terms of the 'capitals' possessed, the composition of that capital, its trajectory over time, and control over its deployment, to see whether these terms allow us to cast new light on femaleness, femininity and feminism. What kinds of 'investment strategies' do women follow in what circumstances? How may the existence of women as objects: as repositories of capital for someone else, be curtailing or enabling in terms of their simultaneous existence as capital-accumulating subjects? The answers to these questions must be relative to historical and cultural contexts, and to positions occupied within 'the social field'. But a few points may nevertheless be made here, drawing on the work of feminists who have used Bourdieu's analytical framework.

Skeggs identifies in Bourdieu's work three forms of cultural capital, which exists: 'in an embodied state, that is in the form of long-lasting dispositions of the mind and body; in the objectified state, in the form of cultural goods; and in the institutionalized state, resulting in such things as educational qualifications' (Skeggs, 1997: 8).

A great deal has been written about women's investments in their bodies as sexual bodies. Skeggs' study is particularly interesting in her identification of the ambivalence that the young white working class women she interviewed displayed towards any too overt investment in their bodies as (hetero)sexual bodies, because of the priority they gave to their investments in 'respectability' and the ways in which their positioning by others or themselves in terms of sexuality placed these prior investments at risk (Skeggs, 1997). This particular investment logic is historically and culturally specific, and is located by Skeggs in terms of the emergence of white middle-class femininity as the dominant femininity, in nineteenth-century Anglo-Saxon societies, in a manner which marked it in opposition to female sexuality (Gilman, 1985), especially black female sexuality.

Skeggs' third type of cultural capital is chiefly acquired through education, and Bourdieu argues that the transmission of capital over generations is increasingly mediated by formal education for the inheriting classes. Women have in the past found themselves facing obstacles to their preferred 'investment strategies' because of the value that they represent in the strategies of others for whom they constitute 'capital assets'. Women's long battle for access to educational capital is well documented within feminism. This is one instance where Bourdieu's focus on women as *repositories* of capital rather than as capital-accumulating subjects may have something to add.

Toril Moi gives a good example of the ways in which the educational investment strategies of women as subjects might be constrained by the capital value that they represented for powerful others, in her analysis of Simone de Beauvoir. Moi follows Bourdieu in recognizing the value of women at that time in France as repositories of social capital in the marriage strategies of their families, and identifies the consequences that this had in their own individual quests for the accumulation of legitimate cultural capital. She compares Beauvoir's success in gaining access to higher education with that of her schoolfriend Zaza's (Elizabeth le Coin): 'If ... Zaza's intellectual ambitions and interests were more firmly repressed than Simone's, this was almost entirely due to the different economic standing of their two families. Zaza's wealthy background allowed her – or rather her mother – to hope for a conventionally suitable marriage, whereas Simone's own impecunious circumstances forced her parents to abandon all such plans for her and her sister' (Moi, 1994: 46).

Bourdieu briefly and interestingly discusses, in the closing section of his article on male domination and in the book that followed (Bourdieu, 1990a; 1998), the gendered division of labour in the 'husbanding' ('cultural housekeeping?') undertaken by women of the symbolic, social and cultural capital of their families, and their responsibility for its transmission across generations, but from the point of view of the stake which this gives families and kin in the capital accumulated and conserved by women. In those social classes with sufficient distance from necessity to participate in the struggle for symbolic capital, there is, characteristically, a gender division of labour in family accumulation strategies. Women, Bourdieu argues, play the lead role in converting economic capital into symbolic capital for their families through the display of cultural taste:

... *elles jouent un rôle déterminant dans la dialectique de la prétention et de la distinction qui est le moteur de toute la vie culturelle.* ('... they play a determining role in the dialectic of pretension and distinction which is the motor of all cultural life'.) (1990a: 29).

Moi's concern in her study of Beauvoir is with the manner in which women's embodiment of social capital for their families may prevent them from accumulating sufficient cultural capital through educational investment to enter the lists as intellectuals in their own right without being too heavily disadvantaged. Moi was writing of France in the 1920s, and the position of women has of course changed a good deal since then. Bourdieu, in his work on male domination, recognizes this shift, but sees in the improved educational opportunities of bourgeois women, and their entry onto a labour market in which their feminine skills are increasingly in demand, as evidence merely of changes in the capital accumulation strategies of bourgeois families and kin groups (Bourdieu, 1998). Moi, however, was interested in the opportunities for, and the rights of, women to compete in their own right for intellectual 'distinction': the right of women to be intellectuals and to be taken seriously as such. She views femininity, in this context, as 'negative cultural capital' (Moi, 1991). Skeggs' study of young working class girls on a caring course takes a very different view of femininity which also draws, as does Moi, on Bourdieu's concept of cultural capital. For Skeggs, femininity is a form of cultural capital.

6. Femininity and cultural capital

Skeggs' study is primarily framed within the terms offered by Bourdieu's concept of 'capitals', yet it is significant that in analysing the investments her respondents made, she comes closer to Butler's feminism of performance/ performativity, eschewing *habitus* as an over-restrictive concept. Skeggs identifies in these young women an ambivalence towards femininity. They made 'investments' in the only forms of cultural capital available to them, and because the sanctions for refusing to make any such investment were so harsh, but, Skeggs argues, they invested in order to 'put a floor' under their economic and cultural circumstances rather than in the hope or expectation of profitable returns: 'Most of the investments into themselves are based on stopping things from becoming worse' (Skeggs, 1997: 102). The terms in which she describes these young women's relationship to femininity, as something they 'did' rather than an identity, suggests performances with some degree of consciousness rather than the enactment of the doxic. Skeggs concludes: 'Femininity is uninhabitable as a complete and coherent identity', her formulation close to that of Rose although rooted in a theory apparently untouched by psycho-analytic feminism. These women did not come to love their fate, nor even in some cases to settle for it.

These young women's investments, in the feminine identity of 'carer' and the skills which they acquired in making this particular investment in themselves, initially trained them to enter the labour market (when first interviewed they were students enrolled on a 'caring' course at a local college), but also served as preparation for traditional roles in marriage. Skeggs argues that these working-class femininities had little value as 'symbolic capital', circulating only within 'restricted markets'. However they were translatable into a currency of symbolic value that has been of historical social importance for dominated groups, and which has had widespread circulation among the aspirant working class, that of 'respectability'.

The cultural capital which working-class men have usually found themselves restricted to is, Bourdieu argues, primarily of a physical kind (the whiteness of white working-class men, as well as their sex, may be significant markers of 'distinction' but this, too, is physically embodied). In describing the cultures of the dominated, the cultures of necessity characteristic of working-class men, Bourdieu recognizes that the cultural capital, the qualities which these men honour in one another, circulates only within 'restricted markets'. Simon Charlesworth describes one such in his study of working-class life in a British northern industrial town in recession: 'the gym, the night-clubs and pubs in Rotherham are protected markets in which the competence of the people who inhabit those social fields can exist positively, in which the social properties they possess can be said to be capital and not simply a series of deficits' (Charlesworth, 1997: 154). He identifies in this restricted currency 'a stringent sense of honour, characterised by a way of walking, of moving in space, of gesticulating, of swearing, joking, "bantering", of laughing, eating, drinking and "being a lad", of being "straight as a die", a "rait lad", a "good lad"...' (Charlesworth, 1997: 156).

It is not always easy to distinguish the difference between women's 'capital accumulating strategies' and the use of women by others as bearers of capital value for their families and kin. Because of the weight of emphasis within certain schools of feminism which identify in women forms of altruism and self-abnegation, some practices in which women are active agents may risk being misunderstood, at least in part. The 'kinship work' studied by Di Leonardo which was assiduously practised by Italian-American women in Northern California referred to above is viewed from Bourdieu's perspective (Bourdieu, 1998: 105) as no more than an example of women functioning to produce and reproduce social capital, creating ties between men which serve men's interests, and indeed this may be one of the things it does. However Di Leonardo, engaging not with Bourdieu but with the Chodorow/Gilligan thesis of female other-oriented altruism (Chodorow, 1978; Gilligan, 1982), draws attention to the stake that the women themselves had in this work, which was in large part self-interested: '... the domestic domain is not only an arena in which much unpaid labor must be undertaken but also a realm in which one may attempt to gain human satisfactions – and power – not available in the labor market' (Di Leonardo, 1987: 14).

Femininities, like masculinities, may be assets on the labour market as well as the marriage-and-family market, tradeable therefore for economic if not for symbolic capital. While Skeggs refers to 'the diminishing labour market' for the skills and self-identities cultivated by her young working-class women, the demand for caring is rising rather than falling with the increase in the proportion of the population in need of care. It is the demand for masculine physicality which has diminished almost to vanishing point with the shift away from heavy industry.[6] Even the military life, increasingly mediated by sophisticated technology, places less and less premium upon those skills into which male working-class 'investments' have been largely channelled.

There is some evidence that femininity as cultural capital is beginning to have broader currency in unexpected ways. Demand for stereotypically feminine skills is generally increasing on the labour market, a reversal of the situation in which Hannah Cullwick's labouring body had transferable value on the marriage market for young upper-middle-class men for whom the labouring female body was one that was highly charged sexually (Davidoff, 1983). Bourdieu, in *Distinction*, notes that many of the newer 'petit-bourgeois' occupations demand skills that are stereotypically associated with women (108; 112; 134–5; 382). The recent dramatic closing of the gap between genders in educational achievement in Western society, and the predictable 'moral panic' over 'underachieving boys' is surely related to the manner in which the labour market is shifting. Working-class femininity may begin to have a competitive market advantage compared to the attributes of traditional working-class masculinity, and this shift may have profound effects on '*la domination masculine*'.

7. Conclusion

Space does not permit a fuller exploration of the range of themes and issues within feminism upon which Bourdieu's sociology of practice might be brought to bear, and vice-versa. Further work is in process. Bourdieu's analysis of the sexual division of labour in the maintenance and augmentation of cultural and symbolic capital has, I believe, important implications for feminist under-standings of the history of class relations. There is a far greater degree of acknowledgement of gender in relation to the maintenance of 'birth communities', especially nations and ethnicities, where some very exciting work is being undertaken (Anthias and Yuval-Davies, 1991; Gedalof, 1999; Hasan, 1994; Sangari and Vaid, 1990; Yuval-Davis, 1997). It is high time to reintegrate the concept of class, problematic though it remains, within the dominant discourses of feminist theory. Diana Coole has made an influential plea for recognition that class is 'a difference that makes a difference' (Coole, 1996) and it is perhaps significant that a number of theoretically-informed feminist studies of class have felt the power of Bourdieu's sociology (Moi, 1993; Reay, 1997; Skeggs, 1997)[7]

Feminist theory, feminist politics, are themselves 'practices' in Bourdieu's (and feminism's) terms. They demands considerable 'investments' of the self, of social, and cultural capital. Skeggs asked the white working-class young women of her study what they knew of and thought about feminism. Their answers led her to the view that the investments made in caring, familial respectability, femininity and 'glamour' 'together present a veritable resistance to acceptance of most discourses of feminism' (Skeggs, 1997: 139). Investments in feminism threaten to place in jeopardy these hard-won gains which make life more tolerable in the restricted markets in which working class women must trade. They have more to lose, after all, than their chains.

Bourdieu's 'reflexive sociology' has a certain affinity with feminist traditions of reflexivity in research, and his sociology of intellectual life may be made to resonate with long-standing concerns over 'academic feminism'. Reflexive sociology and feminist academic practice share similar anxieties and concerns. Bourdieu's characterization of the games played by '*homo academicus*' may be read as an attempt *both* to unmask the pretensions of the game itself by exposing its terms and strategies, *and* to position himself simultaneously as a serious player. His book of that title (Bourdieu, 1988) was published in 1984, and written not long after the time of his 'consecration' – his election to the chair of sociology at the Collège de France in 1981 (Bourdieu and Wacquant, 1992: 132). In accepting the highest honour of the academic intellectual field and, at the same time, exposing and deconstructing the field along with its pretensions, has Bourdieu founded a different kind of practice, in his 'reflexive sociology', which successfully eschews the 'symbolic violence' he so relentlessly exposes in the academic intellectual field?

This question is not very different from that which troubles the producers of feminism within the academy as feminist scholarship has gained a (still precarious) foothold and begun to become more accepted, and there is a mushrooming literature on feminist epistemology in which these issues are addressed (Alcoff and Potter, 1993). To what extent has it been possible to establish a new field whose practice is not based upon symbolic violence and the exclusion of women who are among the dominated by virtue of their class or 'race'? These are questions persistently raised also by feminists outside of the academy who take a sceptical stance towards 'academic feminism'. Do feminist scholars merely compete with one another for distinction in a ghettoized low-status sub-field, as Bourdieu (1990a) suggests? Do we, in so doing, establish our own forms of symbolic violence, to reproduce class and 'race' hierarchies?

Feminists tackling these questions are able to draw on a lengthy tradition of feminist utopian thinking which offers models of alternative forms of social and intellectual life. Bourdieu's model of the social, by contrast, seems to offer few such alternatives. It is at times bleakly pessimistic. In more recent writings however, alongside this dominantly pessimistic tone, there is a note which suggests the possibility of a different kind of practice, and his hopes converge in some respects with those of feminist intellectuals who have recognized not only the exclusions and marginalizations which women have suffered, but also the need to challenge the terms of the game itself and not simply to secure entry for women as legitimate players. Bourdieu is critical of 'critical theory' for its failure to recognize the conditions of its own existence. Yet, viewed in terms of the necessity of utopian thinking, the projects of feminist critical theorists may have something to offer in the task of imagining and experimenting in the construction of 'prefigurative' forms of social and intellectual life which are not exclusively agonistic, as Bourdieu's seem to be; not structured around hierarchy, male domination, cut-throat competition, symbolic violence[8] (Benhabib and Cornell, 1987; Fraser, 1997; Young, 1990). The necessity of utopianism has also been emphasized in French feminist poststructuralist thought (Grosz, 1989: Moi, 1985; Whitford, 1991). Indeed unless we think that such an alternative field is possible, there is little point in continuing to unmask the machinations of the 'social unconscious', the operations of 'symbolic violence'. Bourdieu argues for his project of 'reflexive sociology' in terms of the possibility of creating 'a continent-wide countervailing symbolic power' (Wacquant, in Bourdieu and Wacquant, 1992: 57), and he concerns himself centrally with the conditions of possibility of the production of such a development. But 'reflexive sociology, faces the same danger that stalks 'academic feminism', that of merely producing new fields for, and forms of the exercise of symbolic violence.

The project of many feminisms, like that which socialism set itself, was that of remaking our communities in greater justice *and* equality. Bourdieu's work is of great importance in the task of identifying the hidden conditions of existence of intellectual communities which have prided themselves upon their openness and objectivity. The test of both must ultimately be their success in identifying the conditions of existence and of coming into being of less oppressive forms of social and intellectual community.

Notes

1 This chapter was written before the publication of *La Domination Masculine* in October 1998 (Paris: Seuil). Most of the quotations here are from the article of the same title published in 1990. The book contains some additional material which will be referred to, but does not substantially alter the argument advanced in this chapter. Bourdieu's working paper published in 1990, generated some hostile responses from feminists (Armengaud and Ghaïss, 1993; abridged English version, *Trouble and Strife*, 31, 1995). It must be said that Bourdieu trailed his coat. Unnamed feminists are rebuked for 'offhandedly converting the social problems of a dominated group into a sociological problem ... [such that] ... one is bound to miss ... all that constitutes the actual social reality of the object, substituting for a social relation of domination a substantive entity, conceived in and for itself ...' (Bourdieu, 1990a. Trans. from Armengaud, Delphy, and Jasser, 1995). Thirty years on from the beginning of the second wave there is no single monolithic feminism, and feminist scholarship is rich and diverse. Bourdieu's decision to ignore almost all of this work is surely no unwitting exercise of the symbolic violence he knows so well how to analyse. Julia Kristeva and Luce Irigaray share a footnote in the 1990 version in which they are summarily dismissed as essentialist – a familiar charge, but one against which defences have been mounted that deserve to be taken seriously (Grosz, 1989; Whitford, 1994). Even this backhanded acknowledgement has disappeared by 1998. Bourdieu's lack of engagement with those who already occupy the well-tilled 'field' of gender studies is quite remarkable. His lack of generosity towards feminism is in marked contrast to his brief

annex to the 1998 text on the gay and lesbian movement, against which identical caveats might have been entered. Instead it is (rightly) credited with having raised questions which are among the most important in the social sciences (Bourdieu, 1998: 129–134). Likewise it is to feminism and the women's movement that the constitution of gender as an object of the sociological gaze is due. And feminism has also made a not insubstantial contribution to the development of gay and lesbian studies.

2 We should distinguish here those variants of post-colonial postmodernisms which argue that social identity, in the era of global capitalism and/or 'the postmodern condition', is acquired in passing in another sense: passing away from 'home', through a variety of successive social locations. It is a process of becoming; of a locatedness that is often provisional, temporary (Brah, 1995; Gilroy, 1993; Hall, 1990). Brah and Gilroy argue for a 'politics of location' as opposed to 'identity tourism' – in which, in spite of being endlessly re-modified through its journeying, the embodied self continues to bear the marks of the starting point and the ground covered along the way.

3 'one needs to ask oneself if the popular valorization of physical strength as a fundamental aspect of virility and of everything that produces and supports it ... is not intelligibly related to the fact that both the peasant class and the industrial working class depend on a labour power which the laws of cultural reproduction and of the labour market reduce, more than for any other class, to sheer muscle power ...' (Bourdieu, 1984: 384).

4 'Steele and Addison satirized various fashionable assumptions of bodily imperfections among the men of their time, notably the monocle and the cane, which for more than two centuries have been under fire as affectations of aristocratic helplessness ... In France about 1785 ... those who sought to lead the fashions by aping the extinguished aristocracy found nearly their whole stock in trade in the affectations of bodily imperfections and weaknesses. They peered through single-barrelled spy-glasses, leaned on canes, and could never pronounce the *r* because it 'scorched' their tender throats, which had never been hardened by unbolted flour husks or other rough food' (Utter and Needham, 1936: 182–3).

5 It is notable that in developing his argument at greater length in the 1998 book, this ambiguity remains. He adds a section which acknowledges more recent factors for change, among which he includes improved access to education and to salaried employment. He notes the postponement of the age of marriage and of childbearing, the reduction in family size, and the rise in divorce figures. But, in line with his caveat in 1990 against substituting substantive for relational analysis, he argues that these sometimes dramatic changes have done little to alter the relative positions of men and women. He returns to his analytical focus on the conservative effect of structure and habitus in reproducing relations of male domination (Bourdieu, 1998: 89–115).

6 The emergence of fictional plots of redundant working-class men turning their bodies to account as male strippers, of which the best known is the 1997 British film *The Full Monty*, may be noted in this context.

7 It is interesting that Ros Coward's *Sacred Cows*, (Coward, 1999), in which she proclaims the irrelevance of feminism to 1990s Britain, rests her case on the not-so-hidden injuries of class which, she seems to believe, have affected men more seriously than women, whom she presents, as a sex and taken in the round, as doing rather better than men. This kind of intervention is very popular with the media. It has yet to be answered effectively. To do so requires that her argument and evidence is reworked within a feminist analysis which recognizes the complex and often troubling relationship between class and gender.

8 One addition to his analysis of male domination in the 1998 publication is a brief encomium to love, in which he permits himself a rare idealism. While respecting his wish to avoid wallowing in the gloomy pleasures of disillusionment, it is difficult to resist a certain feminist cynicism here. If women are constrained to be 'the aesthetic sex': to devote so much of their energy to 'seduction' (Bourdieu, 1998: 106), then falling under the spell of this seduction is a hazard of male power, as was recognized by Leopold von Sacher-Masoch in his novel *Venus in Furs*. Bourdieu's argument that love and domination are diametrically opposed may be (cynically) read as an appeal to women to forbear to exercise such power as may fall to them in this manner. Besides, men do not

usually lay aside their male power when they love, as many, many women have discovered to their cost.

References

Alcoff, L. and Potter, (eds) (1993), *Feminist Epistemologies*, New York and London: Routledge.

Anthias, F. and Yuval-Davis, N., (1991), *Racialized Boundaries: Race, Nation, Gender, Colour and Class and the Anti-Racist Struggle*, London and NY: Routledge.

Armengaud, F. and Ghaïss, J., (1993), *'Pierre Bourdieu: Grand Temoin?'*, *Nouvelles Questions Féministes*, Vol 14: 3, 83–88. Abridged English translation, with Christine Delphy: 'Liberty, equality ... but most of all, fraternity', *Trouble and Strife*, 31, Summer 1995.

Austin, J.L., (1962), *How to Do Things with Words*, Cambridge, Mass: Harvard University Press.

Battersby, C., (1998), *The Phenomenal Woman: Feminist Metaphysics and the Patterns of Identity*, Oxford: Polity.

Benhabib, Seyla and Cornell, Drucilla, (eds) (1987), *Feminism as Critique: Essays on the Politics of Gender in Late-Capitalist Societies*, Cambridge: Polity.

Bourdieu, P., (1977), *Outline of a Theory of Practice*, Cambridge: Cambridge University Press.

Bourdieu, P., (1979), 'Symbolic power', *Critique of Anthropology*, 13/14: 77–85.

Bourdieu, P., (1984), *Distinction: A Social Critique of the Judgement of Taste*, London: Routledge and Kegan Paul.

Bourdieu, P., (1986), 'The forms of capital', in Richardson, J.G. (ed.), *Handbook of Theory and Research for the Sociology of Education*, New York: Greenwood Press.

Bourdieu, P., (1988), *Homo Academicus*, Cambridge: Polity Press.

Bourdieu, P., (1989), 'Social space and symbolic power', in *Sociological Theory 7*, no 1, 18–26.

Bourdieu, P., (1990a), 'La domination masculine', in *Actes de la recherche en sciences sociales*, 84: 2–31.

Bourdieu, P., (1990b), *The Logic of Practice*, Cambridge: Polity.

Bourdieu, P., (1991), *Language and Symbolic Power*, Cambridge, Mass: Harvard University Press.

Bourdieu, P., (1998), *La Domination Masculine*, Paris: Seuil.

Bourdieu, P. and Wacquant, Loïc, J.D., (1992), *An Invitation to Reflexive Sociology*, Cambridge: Polity.

Brah, A., (1996), *Cartographies of Diaspora: Contesting Identities*, London and NY: Routledge.

Braidotti, R., (1994), *Nomadic Subjects: Embodiment and Sexual Difference in Contemporary Feminist Theory*, New York: Columbia University Press.

Butler, J., (1990), *Gender Trouble: Feminism and the Subversion of Identity*, NY and London: Routledge.

Butler, J., (1993), *Bodies That Matter*, NY and London: Routledge.

Butler, J., (1997), *Excitable Speech: A Politics of the Performative*, New York and London: Routledge.

Charlesworth, S., (1997), *Changes in Working Class Culture in Rotherham*, Cambridge: Unpublished PhD thesis.

Charlesworth, S., (1999), *A Phenomenology of Working Class Experience*, Cambridge: Cambridge University Press.

Chodorow, N., (1978), *The Reproduction of Mothering*, Berkeley: University of California Press.

Cockburn, C., (1991), *In the Way of Women: Men's Resistance to Sex Equality in Organizations*, Basingstoke: Macmillan.

Coward, R., (1999), *Sacred Cows*, London: Harper Collins.

Coole, D., (1996), 'Is class a difference that makes a difference?', in *Radical Philosophy*, 77: May/June, 17–25.

Cullwick, H., (1984), *The Diaries of Hannah Cullwick, Victorian Maidservant*. Edited and with an introduction by Liz Stanley. London: Virago.

Davidoff, L., (1983), 'Class and gender in Victorian England', in Newton, J.L *et al.* (eds), *Sex and Class in Women's History*. London: Routledge and Kegan Paul.

Dekker, R.M. and Van de Pol, L.C., (1989), 'Republican heroines: cross-dressing women in the French revolutionary army', in *History of European Ideas*, 10: 3, 353–363.

Di Leonardo, M., (1987), 'The female world of cards and holidays: women, families and the work of kinship', in *Signs*, 12: 3, 440–453. Reprinted in Lovell, T. (ed.), *Feminist Cultural Studies*, Vol I. Edward Elgar, 1995.

Fowler, B., (1997), *Pierre Bourdieu and Cultural Theory: Critical Investigations*, London: Sage.

Fraser, N., (1997), *Justice Interruptus: Critical Reflections on the 'Postsocialist' Condition*, London and NY: Routledge.

Gedalof, I., (1999), *Against Purity: Rethinking Identity with Indian and Western Feminisms*, New York and London: Routledge.

Gilligan, C., (1982), *In a Different Voice*, Cambridge, MA: Harvard University Press.

Gilman, S.L., (1985), *Difference and Pathology: Stereotypes of Sexuality, Race and Madness*, Ithica NY and London: Cornell University Press.

Gilroy, P., (1993), *The Black Atlantic: Modernity and Double Consciousness*, London and NY: Verso.

Goldthorpe, J., (1983), 'Women and class analysis: in defence of the conventional view', in *Sociology*, 11: 2, 465–488.

Goldthorpe, J. and Marshall, G., (1992), 'The promising future of class analysis: a response to recent critiques', in *Sociology*, 26: 3, 381–400.

Grosz, E., (1989), *Sexual Subversion: Three French Feminists*, Sydney, London etc.: Allen and Unwin.

Halberstam, J., (1994), 'F2M: the making of female masculinity', in Doan, L., *The Lesbian Postmodern*, New York: Columbia University Press.

Hall, S., (1990), 'Cultural identity and diaspora', in Rutherford, J. (ed.), *Community, Culture and Difference*, London: Lawrence and Wishart.

Hasan, Z., (ed.) (1994), *Forging Identities: Gender, Communities and the State*, Delhi: Kali for Women.

Hooks, B., (1982), *Ain't I a Woman? Black Women and Feminism*, London: Pluto.

Kindersley, A., (1976), *The Mountains of Serbia: Travels Through Inland Yugoslavia*, London: John Murray.

Lévi-Strauss, C., (1969), *The Elementary Structures of Kinship*, London: Eyre and Spottiswoode.

Moi, T., (1985), *Sexual/Textual Politics: Feminist Literary Theory*, London and New York: Methuen.

Moi, T., (1991), 'Appropriating Bourdieu: feminist theory and Pierre Bourdieu's sociology of culture', *New Literary History*, 22: 1017–1049.

Moi, T., (1994), *Simone de Beauvoir: The Making of an Intellectual Woman*. Oxford: Blackwell.

Ortner, S., (1974), 'Is female to male as nature is to culture?', in Rosaldo, M.Z. and Lamphere, L., (eds), *Women, Culture and Society*, Stanford: Stanford University Press.

Reay, D., (1997), 'Feminist theory, habitus, and social class: disrupting notions of classlessness', *Women's Studies International Forum*, 20: 2, Mar/Apr.

Rose, J., (1983), 'Femininity and its discontents', *Feminist Review*, 14: 1983. Also in J. Rose, *Sexuality in the Field of Vision*, Verso 1986.

Sandes, F., (1927), *The Autobiography of a Woman Soldier: A Brief Record of Adventure with the Serbian Army*, 1916–1918. London: Witherby.

Sangari, K.K. and Vaid, S. (eds), (1990), *Recasting Women: Essays in Indian Colonial History*, Delhi: Kali for Women.

Skeggs, B., (1997), *Formations of Class and Gender*, London: Sage.

Stanworth, M., (1984), 'Women and class analysis: a reply to Goldthorpe', in *Sociology*, 18: 2, 153–171.

Utter, R.P. and Needham, G. (1936), *Pamela's Daughters*, New York: Macmillan.

Wacquant, L.J.D., (1992), 'The structure and logic of Bourdieu's sociology', in Bourdieu, P. and Wacquant, L.J.D., *An Invitation to Reflexive Sociology*, Cambridge: Polity.

Warhman, D., (1998), 'Percy's prologue: from play to gender panic in eighteenth-century England', *Past and Present*, 159: 113–160.

Wheelwright, J., (1989), *Amazons and Warrior Maids*, London: Pandora.

Whitford, M., (1991), *Luce Irigaray: Philosophy in the Feminine*, London and NY: Routledge.

Young, I.M., (1990), *Justice and the Politics of Difference*, Princeton, NJ: Princeton University Press.

Yuval-Davis, N., (1997), *Gender and Nation*, London: Sage.

Bourdieu, social suffering and working-class life

Simon Charlesworth

Over the last twenty years fundamental changes have taken place in this society that have altered the social landscape of this country and entrenched the grounds of its nationhood, making clearer the nature of Englishness as an exclusive form, forbidden for many. A series of economic policies, pursued for political as well as fiscal ends, have actively impoverished the bottom third of our society. De-industrialization and new technologies have been used to create conditions of employment that have disempowered the working-class. Certainly areas like South Yorkshire, South Wales and industrial Scotland have seen formerly proud working communities slide into confused, atomized, isolated ways of living based in low wages and state benefit amidst rising crime rates and drug and alcohol-related social problems that are clearly indices of a general change in the communities' former way of life.

A sense of what all this might mean is elucidated by looking at a locality that exemplifies the changes that have occurred. The South Yorkshire town of Rotherham was heavily hit by the economic changes of the late 1970s and 80s and its recent history manifests many of the consequences of these changes. De-industrialization and economic restructuring meant a decline in the number of available jobs and thus increases unemployment. In October 1980 the unemployment rate was estimated to be 8% in Rotherham, compared with the national rate of 5.5%. The highest levels of unemployment were recorded in January 1986, when 24,580 people were registered as unemployed, an unemployment rate of 23.5%. At that point the national unemployment rate was 13.9%. The late 1980s saw a reduction in the numbers of unemployed nationally, and by July 1990 the national figure stood at 6.4% whilst Rotherham's unemployed numbered 12,017, or 12.8%. In January of 1992 unemployment in the area had risen to 14.7% and rose again to 15.6% in January of 1993, when 14,980 people were officially registered as unemployed. Furthermore, Rotherham has one of the highest rates of long-term unemployment in the country. The link between high unemployment and a low wage economy and poverty are clear in reports like the following:

> Families in Rotherham are struggling to give their children three meals a day ... With unemployment well over the national average at 16 per cent,

and local employers offering some of the lowest rates of pay in the country, Rotherham Council's anti-poverty unit's survey paints a grim picture of debt and poor health.[1] *Rotherham Record* March, 1996.

The same report informs us that 4,000 jobs have been lost in the last five years; that this has left 20,000 people without work, and more than 55,000 people are now on income support, that is more than one in five of the borough's population. In a survey of one housing estate it was revealed that 15% of tenants said that they could not afford heating in the living room and bedroom, 13% were unable to afford a warm, waterproof coat and 21% couldn't afford new clothes. More distressing still, 9% couldn't afford 3 meals a day for their children. It cannot be surprising, then, that 80% of residents reported being afraid of not being able to continue securing the money to live and pay their bills, and two thirds reported being unable, at one time or another, to pay their gas, electric or water bills. Furthermore, between April and November 1994, 67% of people were refused lump-sum payments for basic needs from applications for community care grants through the Government's Social Fund. This number itself is an underestimate, because many people know that they will not get such a grant and, instead, apply for recoverable budgeting loans. With so little money in the pockets of local people, one would expect children to suffer, and apparently 12,100 children live in households that do not have a wage-earner, a figure that amounts to more than a fifth of the total number of children. 5,395 children were living in over-crowded conditions, that is, with more than one person to a room.

As one might expect in a town like this, the burden of debt is huge, at over £4 million, which is £23 for every adult. The replacement of the poll tax with the Council Tax has only had a minimal effect, with over 16,000 people owing Council Tax debts; which is one in every six, with an average debt of £160.71. In 1994/95 one account in four was subject to a summons, and one in eight resulted in a liability order being issued. 2,390 people were having debts recovered from their earnings, and 499 more from their benefit. In March of 1995, 112 cases were with the bailiffs. In the same period it was reported that there were 17,469 token or rechargeable key meters in use to supply electricity and recover debts, with the average debt to be recovered by Powerkey meters being £177. These are pressures on the individual that are worsening. For example, Severn Trent Water increased its charges by 35% between 1990 and 1995 and its sewerage charges by 29.1%. Similarly Yorkshire Water Services increased charges by 18.5% and sewerage by 23.4% and Rotherham Environmental Health and Consumer Advice Centre has reported that one in five of its clients need advice about debt to water companies. According to this organization its average client had five debts totalling £3,514, and the average debt per creditor was £916.

And the low wages are as important a phenomenon as the unemployment. The Yorkshire and Humberside Low Pay Unit in its work found Rotherham to be one of the lowest paid regions in the country with employers offering the lowest hourly rates for full time work in the country, notably through the Job Centres. £3.70 per hour is seen by many as a 'good' wage but it contrasts with the Low Pay Unit's minimum wage-target of £4.15, and the Council of Europe's low pay threshold, fixed at 68% of adult full time mean earnings, of £5.87 per hour. These are the conditions for a thriving black market, with wages so low that employers in the area call in unemployed men to do a day's work for an extra few pounds on top of their unemployment benefit. And the social life of these people begins to operate like the barter economy of social crises where people exchange whatever they can get their hands on and sell. The National Federation of Housing Associations, looking at the incomes of new Housing Association tenants, found that 61% of tenants had a net income of less than £100 per week and 93% had an income of less than £200, while the average income of lone parents was £38.28 below an amount believed to be necessary for a lone parent with one or two children on a low-cost budget. A further statistic that reveals the lack of money in the area is that 38% of Rotherham residents do not have a car, and among lone parents the figure is 72%. Clearly, the money that there is, is spent on essentials and there is little room for embellishment here. Furthermore, people in Rotherham also suffer worse health than in other parts of the Trent region, with mortality rates being higher in every category with the exception of breast cancer. For example, the number of households in England and Wales that contain a person with a limiting long-term illness is 24.6% and yet in Rotherham households this is 31.2%.

There can be little wonder that illnesses related to nutritional deficiencies are returning to areas where people are expected to live on such meagre incomes, little wonder that it is once again common for mothers to go without food. As one young woman described it:

> X: I've allous [always] got to se' 'no' to mi kids, an', A've [I've] got to du wiyaht [without] food an' A've [I've] got to bi 'ungry a lot, so I eat bits o'r stuff that an't [are not] good fo' yer, sweet stuff, yer know ... Ah dun't eat right an', wot's w'se [worse] is that wi't [with the] kids A'm not 'appy wot A feed them, Ah know thi dun't get enough ... an' Ah worry that it'll affect the'r 'ealth an that. Can yer imagine bein' completely on yer own? ... Yer know, well on yer own it's really ard in it an' ... that's wot bein' poor is, like. Ah just an't got enough an thi's nowt else I can giy up.

In order to consider the sense manifest in these woman's words, I would like to pause and consider what Merleau-Ponty called the 'primacy of perception'. Merleau-Ponty used this notion to call our attention to the centrality of perception to our sense of being. Simply, that perception is rooted in our practical form of life, in the forms of comportment and demeanour which embody values that are a fundamental aspect of our perception of the world of objects, of people and of culture generally. What we see in this woman's words,

51

are how the immediate situation of our economic position constitutes a horizon within which perception of life takes place. Our way of being, our comportment discloses a particular world that is manifest in perception and for the poor their situation means that the smallest aspects of existence are constituted from amidst a primal encounter with hardship and the humiliation that it generally involves. This opens working people to the world in a certain way, makes them sensitive to the world in certain ways, conditions their receptivity to certain aspects of reality. For the woman quoted above, the hardships she faces constitute a horizon within which her sense of life emerges. The immediacy that her words betray, of this primal encounter in which it seems that needs press upon her in every detail of what is closest to her in existence, from the health of her children to her own hunger, betray the continuous structuring presence of the need to withstand want that has for generations marked working life.

There is, then, a deep primacy of perception in the day-to-day experiences of working-class people: a shaping, undeniable force that destroys for them any possibility of being other than they are and which sets parameters to their ways of dealing with the world. It is a sense of the limits of their lives that one hears clanging around their speech like the tolling of a bell. It haunts everything that working people think and say and every choice they make. Their lives take place in the long shadow of freedom's light cast through the obstacle that necessity represents to them. Bourdieu suggests that the life-style of working people, the choices they are able to make about the environment in which they live, emanate from an inescapable deprivation of necessary goods, that their culture is a virtue made of necessity, a resignation to the inevitable, a sense of the limits of life which is also a forgetting of those limits as limits, a forced contentment with one's lot which, as bad faith, yet one emanating from an absence of volition, produces throughout working-class life tension-points, forms of individual and group pathology that working people are extremely mindful of in these times. Bourdieu suggests:

Taste is *amor fati*, the choice of destiny, but a forced choice, produced by conditions of existence which rule out all alternatives as mere daydreams and leave no choice but the taste for the necessary.

The taste of necessity can only be the basis of a life-style 'in itself', which is defined as such only negatively, by an absence, by the relationship of privation between itself and the other lifestyles. For some, there are elective emblems, for others stigmata which they bear in their very bodies. 'As the chosen people bore in their features the sign that they were the property of Jehovah, so the division of labour brands the manufacturing worker as the property of capital'. The brand which Marx speaks of is nothing other than life-style, through which the most deprived immediately betray themselves, even in their use of spare time; in so doing they inevitably serve as a foil to every distinction and contribute, purely negatively, to the dialectic of pretension and distinction which fuels the incessant changing of taste. (Bourdieu 1984: 178)

Merleau-Ponty suggests 'I say that I *know an idea* when there is set up in me a power of organizing around it words which make a coherent meaning' (Merleau-Ponty, 1962). For the woman who spoke of going without for her children, life has taught this woman the real meaning of necessity, that it means looking in her children's eyes as she registers the effects of conditions of privation in the natural expressivity of their bodies, seeing the disappointment in their eyes, the deprivation in their posture, the relation of 'going-without' setting into their ways. Her words are organized around a coherent centre of a deeply felt sense of the world that emerges from her life in these conditions, of saying 'no' to her children, of being 'without' heightened to a permanent state, of being under-nourished, of worrying about the effects of this state on her children and of her own loneliness amidst this stress, whilst being haunted by the desire to give up more, without having the means to give up another thing. The sense in Bourdieu's understanding of the choice of necessity that he sees as at the heart of working people's relation to the world, is manifest in the thoughts of one unemployed eighteen year old:

> X: Like, A'm from a council estate, in K, an' A've done time, rait in young offenders places an' community service an all kids doin' that shit ahr from council estates an' wi'v got nowt guin' fo us aht the'er, yer know what I mean, we've got no money, we've got no jobs, thi's just nothin' fo' us to do, we've got nowt, yer know what I mean? We'eras you look at kids, se', up M [*Middle class area which provides students for the old grammar school, now a sixth form college, which serves the wealthier areas*], or W, wi' money, o'r who's parent's 'ave got money, they've got a life an't thi? Ye' see 'em rahnd tahn 'avin' a good time wi' the'r trendy clothes an wot not, thi'v no need to gu' aht thievin'...

What is striking in this man's speech is his articulation of the absence of a 'life' in terms of an absence of income and, importantly, a difference of status and identity involved in forms of symbolic capital ('trendy clothes'). It is remarkable how far this man sees his own problems as emerging from the shared conditions of others in the area who are like himself, and how he presents their plight as emerging from an absence of the material resources that would render their lives culturally meaningful and which would allow them to ascend to the (human) status of 'having a life' – and one might add, following Charles Taylor, personhood. This man articulates clearly the extent to which having a life and being a person are dependent upon a certain basic level of income through which individuals can participate in consumption which, in these societies is one of the main ways in which individuals place themselves, experience social participation and inclusion and, through the adornment of the body with the necessary consumer signifiers, accede to a recognized form of social existence, even at this minimal level. From conditions of scarcity, with the absence of material resources, their position of exclusion comes to dominate their experience because it is the fundamental condition in relation to which their existence is constituted. That their lives issue from this inescapable deprivation of necessary goods is powerfully attested to in the connection this man makes across different domains in his deliberate but un-self-conscious repetition of 'nowt ... no ... no ... nothing ... nowt' in: 'got *nowt* guin' fo us ... *no* money ... *no* jobs, ... *nothin'* fo' us to do ... we've got *nowt* ...'

And this sense of nothingness, of abuse, of fracture, of damage is at the heart of working people's sense of life, of their being-in-the world. And this is as true for the working poor, as it is for the unemployed:

> I w'ked fifty-three hours last week fo' 'undred an' fifty quid. It's disgustin'. An' that wo on' jack-hammer. That's *'ard* labour that is, I'll tell yer, it's *fuckin' 'ard* w'k. Whoever said money in't everythin' wo' a liar. It' gets thee everythin' ... [*Pause*] ... Wi wo just unlucky, to be born wi' nowt [nothing].

These are people who have been levelled. The lack of economic power, the lack of an ability to stand above necessity with comfort and grace, is a levelling experience, and instills a profound sense of vulnerability and insecurity.

A peculiar effect of domination is that many of the most dispossessed seem unaware of the extent to which their life is circumscribed by such conditions. Conditions of dispropriation mean that people do not have access to the resources; the instruments through which their understanding might begin to constitute a concrete sense of the limits of life and, paradoxically, the more fully the limits of life enforce themselves, the more powerfully people inscribe a sense of this life as the *only* life possible. Furthermore, living a life within strict confines, or a life in which life is simply awful; there can be little incentive, (there could be no interest) in developing other forms of consciousness beyond those of the 'mindless' everyday coping skills through which it makes sense to *live* such conditions. To begin to develop forms of consciousness that make the world consciously problematic, something to be thought about; to move away from the efficiency of habits attuned to life in this world would be to invite a slide from semi-conscious frustration to absurdity and transform ordinary unhappiness into misery. Living life in the context of minimal expectations, the only strategy that makes practical sense is to maintain an ignorance of anything better, to kill one's hopes. Agee and Evans capture this beautifully:

> This arduous physical work, to which a consciousness beyond that of the simplest child would be only a useless and painful encumbrance, is undertaken without choice or the thought of chance of choice, taught forward from father to son and from mother to daughter; and its essential and few returns you have seen: the houses they live in; the clothes they wear: and have still to see, and for the present imagine, what it brings them to eat;

what it has done to their bodies, and to their consciousness; and what it makes of their leisure, the pleasures which are made available to them ... I have said this now three times. If I were capable, as I wish I were, I could say it once in such a way that it would be there in its complete awfulness. Yet knowing, too, how it is repeated upon each of them, in every day of their lives, so powerfully, so entirely, that it is simply the natural air they breathe, I wonder whether it could ever be said enough times. (Agee 1969: 289)

And this is why anyone in Rotherham who seems to have any inclination to think or care in ways other than those that are generally realized in these conditions, seems to suffer. To be a normal human being, with a degree of civility and concern for one's fellow creatures seems to lead to varying degrees of depression, suffering and misery. This must indict the conditions in which these people live out their lives. There is little wonder that the humanity of these people seems to be withering, as though human decency is a cloth that has been stretched too thin, as though it were a joke told once too often, as though liberties have been taken for too long, making such a practical morality absurd. Whatever does survive, in working people, by way of humanity survives in spite of their present conditions. Anyone who lives with working people quickly hears this philosophy of self-willed ignorance and emotional refusal, like a refrain to the naive who still hope for a better quality of life:

X: I think rahnd [round]'ere thy 'as to just try thi' best to enjoy thi'seln [yourself], gu 'aht an get pissed on weekend wi' lads, smoke a joint. I mean it's *no fuckin' good* been serious all time an' thinkin' abaht [about] it. Let's face it, if wi all sat an' thought abaht it all, rahnd 'ere, abaht us lives, we'd all top' us'selves. Tha's *not got to be* serious.

This expresses a mode of intentionality, a way of projecting being, a technique of absorbed distraction that is here being advised as a technique of coping.

It is this sense of the teaching of an attitude toward the world that is contained in the experience of a people situated in relation to certain fundamental structures, like the labour market, the education system, the state apparatus of the D.S.S. and the political system itself, that I have suggested grounds working-class existence in something that is originary for it, something that has great primacy for their subsequent experience and what they go on to become. There is a primacy to these perceptions because they define a world which must be negotiated. Something that would contradict any desire to euphemize or misconstrue one's experience. The availability of this sense of the world emerges from perceptions arising from concerned absorption in the everyday practical world in which we encounter the sedimented expression of these class experiences embodied in the comportment of others. The words of one woman illuminate the way these issues come to be involved in one's sense of life:

X: young people nahr, thi dun't look 'appy at all.

S: Du yer reckon, different from se twenny year back?

X: Oh aye, Thi' look sad, when yer look at 'em in town an that. Thi look miserable ... thi' ave a kind'a 'opelessness in the'r faces ... 'specially when thi get to the' teens, it's like thi' [they are] thinkin' to 'emselves 'we'er du a gu after school ... next?', ye' know, [*Voice rises for emphasis*] 'what is the'r fo' mi?'. Whereas when we wo' young, wi could get a job anywe'er an' not just that, wi knew wi could get a mortgage fo' a place we'er 'as ahr [our] kids nahr [now], thi' dun't know if thi'r ever gunna 'ave a 'ouse an a place. [*Pause*] Oh it affects everythin' dun' it, family and future an everythin'.

What is interesting here is the way she fixes upon the effects of such conditions on the demeanour of individuals. As though demeanour displays the primal effects of these conditions. It is as though this woman has come to be aware, through her own experience, of the fundamental existential ramifications of such social conditions because these conditions are imbued in the forms of comportment through which individuals, as part of a distinct culture, deal with, and respond to, those very structuring conditions. Furthermore, this woman is aware of the sense carried in the continuous, mindless, dispositional patterning of reactions and responses which exhibit a world experienced, felt, seen, showing up, within the light of a certain form of being, held within the confines of a highly circumscribed space of possibility. The bonds of the flesh that are common class origin and lifestyle, allow her to feel, body-to-body, the sense of this response to the world as it exists for those she knows have grown up without hope or choice. Her expression makes clear that within the phenomenal field of her immediate perception, that is, her naive, spontaneous perceptions, she feels gripped by a sense of the 'social necessity turned into nature' (Bourdieu, 1990: 69) carried in the demeanour and forms of comportment of the young people she describes. She articulates the relation between the demeanour of the young people and the relation to the future inscribed in the relation to themselves and the world that their responses, their comportment, instantiates, and this adds the sense of pathos that is so pronounced in this woman's sense of these people because, as far as she is concerned, it is as though their future is manifest in the present condition that she sees exhibited in demeanour, knowing the conditions of acquisition of those muscular patterns, postural sets and forms of gestural response and, moreover, upon a realized practical knowledge of how the world treats people possessed of those objective marks. This woman has an intuitive grasp of why what is manifest in their demeanour is so deep and so tragic, that it cuts to the heart of their existence and exhibits the lamentable condition of their soul. She perceives in the whole of the expressivity that makes the concept of person incompossible, irreducible, 'logically primitive' (Strawson, 1959: 101); in their bodies perceived as sums of dispositional patterns, muscular and postural schemes of continually-instantiated organization, the sense that they bear before the world, a sense that is not something like a style that they enact but which flows from the very grounds of their being and possesses them.

Yet from the grounds of this woman's insight, there arises a problem that is at the heart of English society. If perceiving the nature of their condition is based upon an awareness based upon shared conditions, then people who do not share the conditions will perceive their condition differently. And this is what makes these people's predicament, politically, so futile, because recognizing the pain that indicts the society, depends upon being able to perceive the 'numb imperatives' (Bourdieu, 1990: 69) made body during the long process of acculturation of position involved in growing up in places like Rotherham. In response to this woman, one can always refuse to see, with the sensibility and forms of sense that her situated life has made available for her. She recognizes that the bodies of the people she is concerned for proclaim something at the heart of their lives: a state and condition that they live with, a state that has extorted what was essentially human in them and filled their souls with a sense of their insignificance.

In response to this phenomenon one can simply be struck by the abjection of the poor, or one might simply find them ridiculous, good for a cheap laugh, or one might re-categorize the phenomenon in different ways. However, this woman's situated life has made available to her, the forms of sense, the sensitivity, that she engages the world through; and these perceptions reveal the wisdom involved in her sense of the world around her and in response, it is all too plausible to refuse to see her world under the same aspect,[2] 'in the same light', and thus to remain unable to see. She recognizes that the bodies of those around her manifest a condition that has extorted what is essential and left only insignificance.

We need to recognize that working-class people's lives are lived against this background which obtrudes, creating for them a sense of despair that is akin to an aesthetic response, in that it is part of a learned form of perceiving the significance of their environment, a form of spontaneously perceptually realized 'reading' of their world based upon an immanent sense, practically acquired, of that world. It is a state that we are used to recognizing in photographs of the past, the sense that poverty and vulnerability create, the down-and-out bleakness of black and white photo-journalism; yet too many are insensitive to the similarity in the wasted lives of those with whom they share the country. Yet many working peoples' lives negotiate this despair and the effects of the social decay of their environment. Listening to working people speak, one thus needs to appreciate the conditions from which their immediate, primary, sense of the world issues, and be sensitive to how this is inflected in their manner and way of speaking.

Living in a working-class area, therefore, it is impossible not to confront the presence of a powerful force touching all of our lives; whether it be a force that drives one to steal, be violent, use drugs, suffer mental illness or be quiet, resigned to misery, or the most usual response, going out to forget one's problems, there is something at work in our society that has affected the working-class very deeply, that has created fear, insecurity and disillusionment. Around them working people see a loss of the basic things they once relied upon, and they are acutely aware of what faces the young, that their parts of the world have indeed become 'meaner, harder and more corrupting' (Hutton, 1996: 3). These changes have had a profound effect upon the sense of life in working-class areas.

Yet, at the most fundamental level of sense-experience, what have been the consequences of the wasting of the traditional coordinates of these cultures? Thinking about the testimony that I have used here and of the experience that I have been a part of, I am drawn to Bourdieu's insights concerning the projection into the future involved in our everyday practices. Taking this Heideggerian insight seriously, then we see that when the grounds of the present are taken away, peoples' projective absorption ceases, and they are left with a debilitating experience of malaise that damages their sense of existence at the very deepest level. And this is an experience that is virtually un-capturable through the position of the scholar who retreats from the world in order to think life. As Bourdieu puts it:

> Science has a time which is not that of practice ... Scientific practice is so detemporalized that it tends to exclude even the idea of what it excludes. Because science is only possible in a relation to time which is the opposite of that of practice, it tends to ignore time and so to detemporalize practice. (Bourdieu, 1990: 81)

Moreover, from this position, there are critical aspects of phenomena that cannot be appropriately rendered. Yet, for those from the most dominated sections of social space, those condemned to a life of meaninglessness through unemployment and endless training schemes, or the never-ending cycle of poor work and the same terrible employment conditions, it is as though they are in a position akin to the one that Bourdieu describes as a:

> sudden reduction to the present, that is, to the past, the abrupt severing of the commitments and attachments to the future which, like death, casts the anticipations of interrupted practice into the absurdity of the unfinished. (Bourdieu, 1990: 82)

Many in such areas have been reduced to the same endless present which leaves them little to anticipate; rather they experience such an inability to alter the course of their lives that they come to lack the sense of themselves as having a will to affect life at all. It is as though the sense of existence that comes from involvement, the experience of initiative that comes from being able to affect one's life and satisfy one's needs or desires, becomes so eroded that individuals no longer feel any urgency to their existence. I'd like to consider the testimony that closes this chapter in relation to this insight of Bourdieu's:

Urgency, which is rightly seen as one of the essential properties of practice, is the product of playing in the game and the presence in the future that it implies. One only has to stand outside the game, as the observer does, in order to sweep away the urgency, the appeals, the threats, the steps to be taken, which make up the real, really lived-in, world. Only for someone who withdraws from the game completely, who totally breaks the spell, the *illusio*, renouncing all the stakes, that is, all the gambles on the future, can the temporal succession be seen as a pure discontinuity and the world appear in the absurdity of a future-less, and therefore senseless, present, like the Surrealists' staircase opening on to the void. The 'feel' (*sens*) for the game is the sense of the imminent future of the game, the sense of the direction (*sens*) of the history of the game that gives the game its sense. (Bourdieu, 1990: 82)

There are many who live in a condition akin to this. Their lives are absorbed in the effort involved in coping and getting by and in the stress of dealing with an unfulfilling world and they are possessed of a sense of the absurdity of this endless present which seems to be the inescapable context of life. If it is the 'history of the game that gives the game its sense', we can understand why these lives seem possessed of so little sense, because the history that the tradition that their lives instantiated has been interrupted and altered, and it has left them going through the motions of a form of life grown old. Their hearts still beat, but their sense of 'inner time', the pulse of time in their veins, the temporality they lived, has gone awry. There is little opportunity for them to exercise choices, to change their lives and they see, through the vision of their children, only more of the same. What has been destroyed for these people is the sense of the conditions of their time as something they can use, through their action in the world, to realize themselves. Instead of the future being a field that stretches beyond them, it has become a vertical face they cannot begin to conquer. Their lives try to obey the logic of working life, they try to impose, artificially, the rhythms of working culture through voluntary work and visits to the gym, but employment is in a condition of scarcity and the only thing they can do with their time is waste it. In this context, dreaming becomes pathological because it means feeling the weight of necessity more cruelly. It is a life of the absurd where hard work and self-development lead directly to a more painful experience of this condition. It makes most sense to deaden the self, one way or another. As one person explained the process:

... At first it 'its yer 'ard, when yer lose yer job, an' yer bo'ord [bored] stiff an' miserable an' yer strugglin' 'cos'r [because of] money but after a while, yer brain starts to work differently, yer don't do it deliberate, like, but if yer din't start to change yer thinkin', yer cun't [could not] live ...

This man presents the effects of changed conditions as effecting a change in the architecture of the mind, a change he sees not as an act of self-will or conscious choice but which he feels is necessary, like anaesthetic to an operation, if he is to go on living a life in which the feelings, the *sense*, of this malaise are not so acute as to completely nullify his capacity to cope. It displays the embodied situation of consciousness, the extent to which our conscious life is located in and thus affected by a more primordial, pre-objective phenomenal realm of the lived body entwined in a world that encroaches, affecting me, moving me, leading me to feel at the heart of me, what is given to me in perception of the world. That is, in perceptions given to the lived-body, which are infused, not merely, with the sense of the world, but of myself and my position. This man's words illuminate the process whereby individuals struggle to deal with impoverished existences by never developing into certain possibilities, learn to refuse the soul's endless pressing into its possibilities. It is like an unconscious activity of self-curtailment; of accommodation to the necessary carried out through the practical mediation of being throughout one's daily life. Yet this process is based on conditions of deep alienation from the sources of recognition, presence and value that can animate the flesh with the gleaming sense of people of objectively assured value; those possibilities for life given whose condition is a valuing public context that most, in these societies, find in the realm of work and the companionship and position it ensures. This man's condition excludes him from the possibility of human connection and respect, and what he describes is a process of alienation from his own self-actualization; the presence of otherness at the heart of subjectivity; an invisible dispossession of the ordinary initiative of existence; a state brought about by his changed relationship to the source of the ability to alleviate necessity, the source of life for working people that the wage represents. The words of Rainer Maria Rilke seem strikingly appropriate:

> ... we are alone with the alien thing that has entered into our self; because everything intimate and accustomed is for an instant taken away; because we stand in the middle of a transition where we cannot remain standing. (Rilke, 1993: 64)

What was most intimate for these people, the customs of the culture that was theirs, have been washed away, and this man's voice hails from amidst a transition that has left many behind and many unable to stand with any security. However, this transition is historical and economic, and it involves a transition for a whole category of individuals, all required to remain standing through the transition. And their problem is that the 'space to stand', so to speak, is contracting. It has left many growing to despise their human capacities because they have been dispossessed of the conditions in which they might experience their humanity positively, in which they might fulfil their potentiality. Hence, they cannot understand their capacities non-negatively and come to hate what they see as the faculties responsible for their inability to 'be happy'. As one unemployed man said of his time at college, 'Ah regret it nahr.

All it seems t' 'ave done is med mi mo'ore aware a ahr bad life is 'cos Ah'm still in same position as when Ah went.' Another man expressed it even more poignantly: 'Ye'v got to bi brain dead to live in Rother'am'. This is a state to be aspired to because so many people are now experiencing their desires and human capacities as things that only bring them suffering. The more they develop, the more accustomed they become to the pleasures that an income allows, the more, potentially, they will suffer, because their culture is a culture of necessity, of 'going without':

> We're allous [always] 'avin' to calculate what wi' need, yer know, if wi buy one thing, then wi' 'ave to gu wiy'aht sum'at [without something] else, an' then it's w'kin' up that time again at w'k [work]: somehow, gettin' that money back an' startin age'an [again].

The more they become, the worse they will feel; the more their sensitivity connects them to others, the more they will experience the suffering around them, a suffering all the more poignant and severe for its being a shared condition, their suffering, a suffering they live with, that obtrudes issuing from the background of their culture, manifest in the lives of those among whom they live. This is something that marks working people very deeply, it characterizes their lives, and in so doing becomes part of their characteristics and hence character.

This is what makes them recognizable, from above, as figures in a landscape; it gives them their 'realism' and 'cynicism'. Many of the pathologies of their culture stem from this, but here I want to concentrate on why a philosophy of self-fulfilment can make little sense for these people, and why the force of their perception forces them to characterize their lives as 'doing nothing'. The pain involved in living in conditions in which one's life lacks an embedding in a public world of reference and self-respect was well expressed by one man who was unusual in talking about himself as 'depressed', a remark he was asked to confirm in what followed:

S: Du yer feel depressed, then?
B: ... Ye, I feel guilty fo' not w'kin' [working]. An' Ah [I] started to feel depressed early on [S: Ahr early?] er ... abaht [about] a month, when tha's bi'n [you've been] through lookin', an' dole an that, ... [S: Can yer describe yer feelin's?] fuckin' boored, a sort'a bein' totally bored ... thi's now't 'ere is the? ... [*Pause*] ... Ahr lass comes 'ome an Ah feel terrible [*voice rises*] 'cos shi's bin to w'k an' shi'll se', 'what 'ave yer done today?' An' Ah 'ave t' se', 'well nowt'. An' w'se [worse], Ah just dun't seem to 'ave 'will anymo'ore to du 'owt [anything], stuff that Ah used t' du, and yet Ah feel restless, right pent-up, in mi'self but I can't settle to du owt [anything] ... [*voice trails off*] ... [*Pause*] ... an' him that dun't [does not] work, dun't 'ave no money, either! [*laughs*]

Questions about the nature of happiness in working-class people's lives are worth considering because what this man is articulating emerges from a way of life that he knows has always been heavily circumscribed, such that what satisfactions there were, the happiness that might be expected, was of a particular form, and yet even that has gone. This man described to me how he had lost interest in fishing and his garden, two things that, in the context of the world, of work he had enjoyed; but now, the loss of will he describes has taken these pleasures away from him. What has gone is the overall, habitual context that gave his life its sense and meaning; and the pain and despair are just other ways, barely conscious ways, of his realizing that his cultural 'lot' in life, his fishing, gardening and boozing, were not really life-sustaining. But in the absence of the resources for the reproduction of life, there is little but the restless contemplation of a condition ever more subtle in its effects, as life leaks away into the sterile grounds of a dying way of life. In this light, it seems that Bourdieu's formulation of the question is insightful:

> I think this question of happiness is very important. The doxic attitude does not mean happiness; it means bodily submission, unconscious submission, which may indicate a lot of internalized tension, a lot of bodily suffering ... I have discovered a lot of suffering which had been hidden by this smooth working of habitus. It helps people to adjust, but it causes internalized contradictions ... One may be very well adapted to this state of affairs, and the pain comes from the fact that one internalizes silent suffering, which may find bodily expression ... (Bourdieu and Eagleton, 1992: 121)

This internalized tension and silent, barely expressed, suffering, is evident in much of the testimony which reveals individuals struggling to alter their expectations and to accommodate to a realm of much frustration and little humanity. What is manifest is the tension involved in trying to change one's embodied sense of the world, to re-learn how to *be*, but to learn how to be *less* than one formerly was; to give up the pleasures that one had become habituated to; to foreshorten one's taste for existence, to give up the immediacy of the chase of life; to live, as it were, in the shadow-world of unsatisfied need. This 'smooth working of habitus', which accommodates people to changes in their social conditions whilst minimizing their awareness of suffering, is captured by Walter Brierley, writing about a similar time of despair for working people:

> That agony-day once a month, he dreaded it, more for Jane's sake than his own; it almost killed her every time. And he was so helpless, had to see her suffer and couldn't say anything comforting. And this was a pointless, hopeless existence. He suffered one way, she another. He opened his eyes, turning to look at her. She was lying on her back heavy in sleep ... about her nostrils was a pallor like death. Lines beneath her eyes and on the forehead cut into the soft, smooth flesh; it must be upon these that folks

based the assertion that the past three years had aged her. Unless, of course, they had seen that she, like him, had lost the spiritual vigour they once had. He turned back to the world of fire again, struggling against an impatience tinged with hate and anger. But there was no fire in the emotion, it was merely a faint emphasis of the general attitude of mind which had come to be part of him. Always now something pressed him down, holding him below a level which he ought to be on, which his being was rightly fitted for. If he could forget this, if he could tune himself wholly to this lower level, his existence might be smoother, he might move freely again. But he could not, he knew he could not, and therefore the attitude of mind must continue, the impatience, the anger, the hate, the concrete unhappiness. (Brierley, 1983: 3)

What were once called 'the appetites' have become things of shame because they bring, in the absence of the means of their satisfaction, only a bitter frustration and a deep cynicism. And these matters involve forms of sense that require us to move beyond the model of the conscious-subject linguistically constituting experience, they involve the totality of being that language and sense emerge from. They are existential, to do with these people's being-in-the-world; to do with the heart of their being human. 'What is there?', 'What can I hope for?' and when these are answered: 'Is this because of what I am?', 'Is this misfortune mine?' These are questions that delineate the deepest confusion. As one person confided to me: 'I'm scared. I spend most of my life being afraid and I try and say to myself that I'm alright but I never feel it.' These are ontological questions; they are matters deeper and more important than the usual questions that are asked about working-class life. For it is a world in which issues of income and education are only the most basic indices of life in a class-divided society, which indicate little of the sense arising from what they indicate. Moreover, we must realize the fundamental sense the world has, even the world of objects that we perceive with least ambiguity, because of the ways that world comes to be meaningful through the forms of shared comportment by which we come to inhabit the world as a place immanent with a sense we cannot ignore.

Reading Bourdieu, it seems to me there is a deep commitment to understanding the lives of working-class people which is too often obscured, as this collection of essays exemplifies, in the academic reception of his work. I hope this piece says enough about why I believe Bourdieu's insights to be of importance in understanding the lives of those condemned to live out lives of struggle beyond the confines of legitimate, consecrated, culture.

Notes

1 No author's name was given with this short piece.
2 I am using the notion of 'aspect perception' here.

Bibliography

Agee, J. and Evans, W., (1969), *Let Us Now Praise Famous Men*, London: Panther.

Bourdieu, P., (1984), *Distinction*, London: Routledge.

Bourdieu, P., (1990), *The Logic of Practice*, Cambridge: Polity Press.

Bourdieu, P. and Eagleton, T., (1992), 'Doxa and Common Life'. *New Left Review*, 191: 111–121.

Brierley, W., (1983), *Means-Test Man*, Nottingham: Spokesman.

Hutton, W., (1996), *The State We're In*, London: Vintage.

Merleau-Ponty, M., (1962), *Phenomenology of Perception*, London: Routledge.

Merleau-Ponty, M., (1964), *The Primacy of Perception*, Evanston: Northwestern University Press.

Rilke, R.M., (1993), *Letters to a Young Poet*, New York: W.W. Norton & Company, Inc.

Strawson, P.F., (1959), *Individuals*, London: Methuen.

Taylor, C., (1985), *Philosophy and the Human Sciences*, Cambridge: Cambridge University Press.

Taylor, C., (1989), *Sources of the Self*, Cambridge: Cambridge University Press.

Section II: Rationality and politics in Bourdieu's social theory

Introduction to Section II

Franck Poupeau

Bourdieu shares with writers like Foucault a critique of universalistic claims to represent humanity as frequently merely masks of domination (eg. Bourdieu, 1984: 485–500). Poupeau nevertheless considers Bourdieu's concern in the 1990s for universalizability, in the context of a confrontation with the other seminal thinker of our period, Habermas. This essay takes up issues which have been neglected in Habermas's defense of rationality. Poupeau follows Bourdieu in claiming that forms of symbolic violence, such as the greater influence of those using a dominant dialect, could still be concealed within Habermas's communicative action. Bourdieu, by contrast, advocates a *Realpolitik* of the universal, in which the interest in the universal found in science are applied to a realist politics. Against Habermas's scholastic bias towards a merely normative model for democracy, Poupeau persuasively proposes Bourdieu's alternate model, with its focus on a socioanalytic theory of the prerequisites for communicative rationality of a certain level of material ease and leisure.

Louis Pinto

Raising questions once explored by Antonio Gramsci and Walter Benjamin, Pinto explains the Bourdieusian project of political commitment based on sociological reflexivity. This envisages a movement of intellectuals working at the intersection of the scientific and political fields (see Pinto, 1998). The ideal would be to combine their specific expertise in the analysis of social reality with receptivity to the requirement of rationality, as well as to the 'immanent creation (non-relativist) of values'. Avoiding both Althusserian revolutionary romanticism, which was devoid of empirical foundations, and the new philosophers' courting of scepticism and irrationalism, this aims to give a public voice to those who are normally silenced by the discourse of technocrats and to enable them to acquire the instruments of decoding the media and their own social world (cf Bourdieu, 1993, 1998 (*On Television and Journalism*)).

Loïc Wacquant

Wacquant's essay develops further the case above for seeing Durkheim as one of the main pedestals of Bourdieu's sociological thought. It succeeds in sustaining a claim that Bourdieu has in fact taken from Durkheim an approach founded on cognitive confrontation with common-sense and a rupture with scholarly myths. Wacquant locates Bourdieu in a heritage from Durkheim which is far more complex than the problematic of 'organic unity' at the keystone of the American structural-functionalist temple. Identifying him instead with the Durkheim who was the historian of social transformation, he shows how Bourdieu has created a new and innovative synthesis. The Appendix, on *Distinction*, adds a fresh and detailed presentation of the parallels between them.

Reasons for domination, Bourdieu versus Habermas

Franck Poupeau

The question of universality – universality in question

One theme takes on a growing significance in the reflection of Pierre Bourdieu: that of universality. Not that he recants from his critique of universalization used as a strategy of legitimation ... nor that he ceases to assert that interest in the universal is the principal factor in promoting the universal; but he increasingly places the accent on *the conditions for realizing universality*, whether it be at an historical level – with the study of strategies of monopolization of the universal in 'Spirits of the State' (1998: 58–60) – or whether it be at the level of the constitution of social fields (political, scientific ...), the agents of which may have an interest in the advancement of the universal (1998: 90–1, 137).

If we count as reason not solely the fundamental principles governing thought, but also the rules which make for collective understanding within a given social group, we have to acknowledge that Bourdieu never goes so far as to grant the *a priori* universality of reason: he differentiates himself from a typically philosophical approach to universalism by demanding a *Realpolitik of reason*, which would permit *'thinking universally', without presupposing universal reason*. It is within this perspective that we can make complete sense of his increasingly frequent allusions to Habermas.

In brief, the latter tries to rethink human action by elaborating a theory of society founded on reason (or even by elaborating a theory of knowledge constructed like a theory of society (Habermas, 1987)). But while he (Habermas) pre-supposes the universality of reason and the existence of universalizable interests in order to lay the foundations for both rational consensus and a potential for social existence, Bourdieu takes the uniqueness of social interaction as his starting-point in order to study the conditions for the emergence of the universal and rationality.

It would, however, be an error to adopt an opposition of the type: Habermas the Philosopher versus Bourdieu the Sociologist. Without neglecting the fact that their respective approaches go in opposite directions, the question is rather whether they can meet – without ceasing also to confront one another – over a certain number of theoretical stakes. Indeed, points of convergence are not lacking ... philosophy and the social sciences seem today to be succumbing to the modern imperative of 'scientific' specialization: no philosopher worthy of the name who is not an expert on a period or on a 'great issue'; no serious sociologist who does not have a specific research area. In answer to the eminent specialists in metaphysics one will now find the technicians of social investigation, in answer to those who disdain experience, those who would never consider rising beyond it ... Yet the works of Jürgen Habermas and Pierre Bourdieu are distinguished by the diversity of subjects that they tackle and by their theoretical ambition: the former wants to identify the conditions for true communication, that is, an intersubjectivity permitting the establishment of universal rules and a theory of society; the latter elaborates a reflexive anthropology by taking up once again the project of turning sociology into a rigorous, independent science, capable of making sense of the social world without allowing any concessions to common sense. Granted, it is difficult to dissociate sociology and philosophy within each of these projects. Furthermore, both agree that sociology offers a fresh treatment of what Habermas sees as 'the fundamental issues of philosophy': that is, reason (Habermas, 1984: 1).

But the point common to both Bourdieu and Habermas is not merely the scope of each theoretical enterprise; above all, it rests on the critical perspective that runs through their work: critical in the Kantian sense, knowledge delimiting itself internally, but also critical in a much more political sense, because it is a question of the critique of domination and an analysis of its major types in today's society.

It is perhaps when it is necessary to think about domination that the inextricably philosophical and sociological projects of Bourdieu and Habermas merge, for this is the point at which theoretical ambition for a critical project is confronted by social reality, by a violent domination, whose mechanisms and reasons require explanation. Will the presupposition that reason be universal serve as the necessary, and sufficient, basis for undertaking successfully such a critique?

Domination and legitimacy

In elaborating on their respective theories, both Bourdieu and Habermas aim to transcend a certain number of traditions of thought or intellectual cleavages, such as the opposition between the relations of power brought to light by Marx (the fact of domination) and the relations of meaning studied by Weber (the justification for domination: its rationale). They both possess the (iconoclastic) ambition to combine, in a single theory, an analysis of the nature of domination and the mechanisms by which it is made acceptable, but while they both agree on these perspectives, this does not imply that they are in accord on the ordering of the relationship between power and meaning. Comparison of their respective approaches can only help to clarify any analysis of the grounds of domination.

The specificity of the Bourdieusian theory of domination is the fact that it is not presented like a classical philosophical theory: there is no enquiry about the essence of power, no attempt to 'ground politics' ... Pierre Bourdieu starts from objects which escape traditional philosophical attention: peasants from the Béarn and Kabylia regions, museum-visiting, photography, or even the French educational system. In demonstrating, for example, that the latter is an example of social selection and segregation which benefits the higher social classes in that, despite its apparent neutrality, it contributes to the reproduction of relations of domination, Bourdieu shows how the school legitimates the dominant social order by naturalizing social differences through the ideology of 'natural gifts' or through the allocation of scholastic qualifications.

Like Weber, Bourdieu underlines the connection between domination and legitimation: if all forms of domination must be rationally justified to be accepted as legitimate, then one must also explain the mode of rationalization which gives the power of reason to those who have the greatest power. The production of legitimate relations of domination cannot be reduced to the external constraints of physical relations of obedience, nor to the generalized lie of a purely ideological persuasion: it can be explained by the differences in position in the social hierarchy. Thus the recognition of an order can only be understood if the power of imposition is linked not just to an 'illocutionary force' (to accomplish an action by saying something) but to its conditions of effectivity within society, and in so doing, referring to the dispositions to take such an order for what it is, and to the structure of the field where these dispositions are produced. The dominant groups derive their authority from the loyalty of the dominated, in the name of their alleged 'gifts', which would be as nothing without the recognition from which they benefit and which they keep up through the exercise of their authority. Bourdieu calls 'symbolic violence' this power to produce acceptance for a domination misrecognized as such, by imposing meanings which serve to obscure the truth about social relations.

Consequently, if the dominated acquiesce in the principle of their domination, it is because, like those who dominate, they accept the social order which is established and legitimated by these 'gifts'. The ideological function realized here through culture – or, more exactly, the social uses of culture – appears in this analysis as the symbolic aspect of domination: symbolic violence is that form of violence which only acts on social agents with their complicity. But how does this complicity allow us to explain the production of a consensus about the maintenance of social order, and, furthermore, loyalty to the dominant values?

According to Bourdieu, recognition can only occur due to a 'misrecognition founded on an unconscious adjustment of subjective structures to objective structures'. The doxic adherence to the world created by this correspondence is anchored in the very depths of the body, where the schemata of action, perception and appreciation, that is to say the schemata of the habitus, are internalized. These structured structures, adjusted to the objective conditions

71

of which they are the product, are also structuring structures allowing one to constitute the world as though it were self-evident, a world all the more readily accepted given that these structures operate at a pre-reflexive level of motor behaviour:

> Symbolic violence is achieved by means of an act of recognition and misrecognition, which is situated beyond the control of the conscious mind and the will, in the misty regions of the schemata of the habitus (Bourdieu and Wacquant, 1992: 168).

Domination is thus inscribed in the most everyday practices: the theory of domination proposed by Bourdieu takes the form of a theory of practice, centred around the concept of habitus, explaining the process of recognition and misrecognition through which domination is legitimated.

Thus within the order of cultural practices, Bourdieu demonstrates that the dominant culture, by making itself recognized as universal, legitimates the interests of the dominant group, thus forcing other cultures to describe themselves negatively in relation to it.[1] From being a socio-historical *fact*, domination also becomes a *category* of political analysis; the division between those who dominate and the dominated functions like an explanatory schema in the different domains studied by Bourdieu (intellectual field, artistic field ...).

By contrast, for Habermas, domination seems to remain within the order of the factual: theoretical activity should be translated into historical reality, as Marx recommended. If domination really is an illegitimate exercise of power by a fraction of the population, which masks particular interests under the general interest, the critical project is then linked to an emancipatory interest, and to an action *on* society: it is its normative impact which orientates its relation to the real. But it is insufficient to interpret any exercise of power by linking it solely to the power-relations inherent in wage-labour: it is also necessary to observe the 'anonymous constraint of indirect command', since the system does not survive simply through the exploitation of workers. Analysing work in its social context should not allow one to neglect the dimension of interaction: as Weber showed, domination is:

> the probability that a command with a given specific content will be obeyed by a given group of persons (Roth and Wittich, 1978, I: 53).

Domination is not merely power *over* a given group, it is also a relationship of meaning *between* individuals in which recognition of legitimacy ensures the persistence of power. If the Weberian characterization of modernity as a process of rationalization (marked by the calculation of the future and the disenchantment of the world) brings new weapons to the task of critique, social theory must then resort to categories of analysis other than mere instrumental rationality, which fails to take into account interaction outside work.

Indeed, the problem for Habermas is to link rationalization and domination without ending up with a critique of reason as the Frankfurt School would have done. The only solution, then, is to show that rationalization is not simply the development of instrumental rationality: going beyond the notion of rational action oriented to an end (strategic), it is necessary to distinguish *a model of communicative action*, represented as 'interaction mediated by symbols'. In relation to the ideal of communication, revealed in action (meaningful relations), relations of power appear as if distorted: the supposition of an intersubjective world exempt from domination (the ideal speech situation) allows critical thought to attain its normative role in terms of action *on* society by establishing criteria of evaluation. From the distinction 'work/interaction', Habermas has moved to a distinction between the model of strategic action and that of communicative action, *a new political category from which domination is excluded and considered solely as the historical face of a distorted social order*.

At the end of the day, Habermas elaborates a theory of society where power relations are replaced by relations of meaning, where the fact of domination is effectively effaced by the normativity of analytical categories. In order to be brought to fruition, the critique of the grounds for domination must presuppose that reason escapes from domination – and it is communicative action which, after the 'linguistic turn' taken by the German thinker, serves as the criterion. Indeed, the rules of interaction have a claim to validity which can only be honoured through discussion: the necessity to arrive at a rational consensus leads to the practical hypothesis of an ideal speech situation (Habermas, 1995: 110), due to which agreement can be realized (Habermas, 1984, I: 286–8; 307–9).

Although somewhat schematic, this characterization of the relations established by Bourdieu and Habermas between the fact of domination and the categories employed to grasp it, permit us in any case to show that, despite their specific differences, an analysis of the grounds for domination leads to an analysis of human action: practice for Bourdieu, action for Habermas. In this way, it will perhaps be possible to ask whether in order to 'preserve reason' (and its universality), it is necessary to think about it outside the relations of domination.

Strategic action and communicative action

In his analysis of the rationality of human action,[2] Habermas deploys the distinction between 'cognitive-instrumental' rationality, designating the application of a descriptive knowledge (1984, I: 2–3) and communicative rationality, which designates the 'non-violent force of argument which permits the agents to reach agreement and thus gives rise to consensus' (1984, I: 10).

Three models of action (which may be reduced to two) are thus constructed and explored systematically *in The Theory of Communicative Action*:

- instrumental action and strategic action, which relate to the same type of action, namely 'success-oriented actions' (1984, I: 285–6), actions adapted respectively to things and to persons: for the former, adequacy of means (technical rules of action) with a view to success and, for the latter, a considered choice of behaviour (rules of rational choice) to influence the behaviour of others.
- communicative action, which refers to plans of action 'which are co-ordinated not through egocentric calculations of success but through acts of reaching understanding (1984, I: 285–6), that is, the rational pursuit of objectives which have been collectively set on the basis of a discussion oriented towards an agreement.

It is, above all, the distinction between communicative action (CA) and strategic action (SA) which illuminates the nature of social activity, instrumental activity being no more than a (technical) variation of SA.

CA relates to a consensus between agents who do not seek their own, or specifically individual, success, because they desire, above all, to harmonize their plans of action on the basis of common definitions of situations. The problem with this account is that it fails to eliminate all idea of success: it thus has a problem in distinguishing between CA and SA, to the extent that it is difficult to conceive of this consensus other than as a collective end chosen by all for everyone. It is therefore necessary to see if SA is only differentiated from CA through the *collective* character of the success which is pursued – in which case there is no great interest in distinguishing them (CA and SA) – or if SA can be differentiated from the type of actions rendered rational by their final objective, accounting for success-oriented action, that is, their orientation to success.

It is, then, the notion of understanding envisaged in CA which permits one to distinguish it from SA, oriented to an end. This notion designates 'a pre-theoretical knowledge of competent speakers who can themselves distinguish situations in which they are causally exerting an influence *upon* others from those in which they are coming to an understanding with them' (1984, I: 286). It is a 'process of reaching agreement' (1984, I: 287), and one which can in no way be imposed, even strategically, by agents pursuing their own success. Habermas recognizes the possibility of objective constraints, but 'of a visible type', operating through external intervention or by the employment of violent means, and which thus do not 'count subjectively'.

In the end, the distinction can be seen at the level of intentions, thus it is necessary to clarify whether:

(i) it is a purely conceptual distinction, intended to separate, from a purely theoretical point of view, two analytical descriptions of the same action. Habermas *rejects* this solution (1984, I: 286): it does not throw any real light on social interaction because the action (orientation towards a goal) is identical in both cases. The only difference would be at the level of intention, of which nothing can be known from the outside: 'only you know whether you are good or cruel, loyal or bigoted', said Montaigne, explaining the limitations of any attempt to judge the behaviour of another;

(ii) or, alternatively, this distinction cannot be reduced to the subjective and psychological styles of experiencing action, but must account for the real logic of action. Yet that means '*reculer pour mieux sauter*': nothing permits a clear distinction between the two attitudes, that oriented towards success and that oriented towards understanding. How can we avoid ending up looking for indiscernable individual motivations? Habermas at this point has recourse to the need to pass from a theory of knowledge to a theory of communication:

meanings attain their validity not with respect to the intentional structures of the subject but through relations between subjects (Habermas, 1995: 56).

It is necessary, then, to concern oneself with the very conditions for inter-subjective understanding. Utilizing Austen, from whom he takes the distinction between illocutionary statements ('to act *in* saying something') and perlocutionary statements ('to bring about something *through* acting in saying something) (1984, I: 289), Habermas affirms that the efficacy of language is inherent in language itself, and thus that the purpose of communication is understanding: ('Reaching understanding is the inherent telos of human speech' (1984, I: 287). SA would seem to be attached only to perlocutions, external to the meaning of what is said, while the internal force of illocutionary statements would seem to guarantee that communicative actions (CA) arrive at an agreement:

Communicative action [...] is distinguished from strategic action by the fact that all participants pursue illocutionary aims without reservation in order to arrive at an agreement that will provide the basis for a consensual coordination of individually pursued plans of action (1984, I: 295–6).

If inter-subjective agreement is, as Habermas affirms in his 'Analysis of the Concept of Communicative Action' (in *Logic of the Social Sciences*), a pre-theoretical knowledge shared by agents, which engages them in interaction (1988: 165), it is, equally, opposed to the individual goals of strategic action in which the agent is cut off from any links with others, withdrawing into the closed sphere of his egoistic interests. The consensus made possible through language permits co-ordination of action, and involves three claims to validity: the truth of the utterance; the appropriateness of the action (taking into account the norms in operation) and the sincerity of the speaker's intentions (1988: 186).[3] The fact that an agreement can be founded on the basis of a lie, for example, escapes this logic and enters into the category that it is possible to call 'distorted communication': agreement in this case is understood in a limited sense only, in which the engagement in a course of action is separated from inter-subjective understanding. The obvious and somewhat facile objection would consist in saying that one can achieve one's ends through persuasive language and that anyone can impose agreement on others through non-rational motives; yet it takes on its full meaning if one considers that there is a dimension concerning *the exercise of power through language* (symbolic power), which Habermas excludes from his analysis. The notion of inter-subjective understanding thus appears insufficient for a clear distinction between different types of social action. Or, more precisely, the analysis deploys these distinctions, but only at the price of a problematic classification of actions, based on the postulate that:

> validity claims are *internally* connected with reasons or grounds (1984, I: 301), and thus that whereas validity claims are internally connected with grounds and give the illocutionary act a rationally motivating force, power claims have to be covered by a potential for sanction to be a binding force (1984, I: 304).

What, then, is the validity of this distinction between SA and CA, which dissociates the reasons for domination from the reasons of discourse? Pierre Bourdieu totally rejects this distinction (Bourdieu and Wacquant, 1992: 139): absent in the case of pre-capitalist societies (where, lacking the foundations of the economic market to maintain it, domination operates more through language),[4] it would not even be enough for understanding more differentiated societies – for is not speech here the main vector of power? But his critique draws on his theory of practice:

> a philosophy of action designated at times as *dispositional* which notes the potentialities inscribed in the body of agents and in the structure of the situations where they act, or, more precisely, in the relations between them (Bourdieu, 1998: vii).

The concept of habitus (allied to that of field) can then be found at the heart of the problem: it even permits one to go beyond the opposition between communicative and strategic action.

First of all, the idea of 'strategy', as it is employed by Habermas, is striking in terms of the restricted field of action that it is supposed to cover: it designates the action of rational subjects only, striving to obtain an explicitly-formulated objective as the goal of their action. To study it, it would be sufficient to isolate the rules which underpin success. This calculative rationality would be able to generate models in which others are taken into account in the perspective of the objective, but any agreement between individuals would remain inexplicable. Habermas never enquires whether agreement is (or is not) the condition for action, and whether he can use a model of strategic action to account for it. The anthropological parameters as to the nature of the agent are restricted to such an extent – conscious, rational, calculative – that he reduces them almost to the condition of *homo economicus*.

Consequently, Bourdieu need feel in no way concerned about the Habermassian characterization of strategic or instrumental action. In an interview, 'From Rules to Strategies' (Bourdieu, 1994a: 59–75), he explains the confusion which may arise when one speaks of rules: one never knows whether it is a question of juridical rules, of a collection of objective regularities or of a model. For this reason, the use of the concept 'strategy' is designed to avoid the theoreticist use of the term 'rule' (which takes one back to structuralist thinkers whose *objectivism* leads them to put forward, as the real principles of action the theory which they themselves have constructed to explain them) but without falling either into the opposite *subjectivism* (reduction of practice to individuals freely deciding their actions): one finds in the Habermassian use of the concept of rule a similar 'scholastic bias'. The Bourdieusian concept of strategy should not be understood as a choice, subjective and rational, but as a feel for the game: a practical sense, emanating from a system of dispositions, the habitus. This concept indeed brings back the agent at the point at which structuralism only presupposes an unconscious system of rules, yet without falling into an equally theoretical fiction of *homo economicus*. Thus Bourdieu shows in *The Logic of Practice* that matrimonial strategies are not the result of obedience to rules but of the agents' feel for the game, in the light of the 'game' available (given the hand they have been dealt).

Inter-subjective understanding between individuals can thus be clarified in a new way, thanks to the habitus: as participation in the same game, commitment to the stakes in the game, in the light of the hands which people have at their disposal, putting into play their feel for the game, which in turn is the product of a habitus, the basis for the elaboration of strategies. The idea of habitus allows one to account for the practical elaboration of strategies without having recourse to some specific strategic calculation: the latter intervenes only when the logic of the habitus is denied. Habitus explains the participation in the social game, the contribution made by the agents, their illusio.

This image of the game allows one to recognize that there may be statistically-observable regularities (but not rules), insofar as they are produced on the one hand by the sum of individual actions subjected to the same constraints inherent in the structure of the game and, on the other, by the incorporation – unequally distributed – of the feel for the game:

> The objective homogenisation of a group or class habitus which results from the objective homogeneity of conditions of existence is what creates the possibility for practices to be *matched objectively, in the absence of any strategic calculation* and outside all reference to norms, and mutually *adjusted outside any direct interaction and, a fortiori, outside any explicit coordination* (1990: 102).

In contrast, within the framework of Habermas's SA, agents are only considered as speakers and as listeners, each referring to a common aspect of the world, and putting forward validity-claims in relation to those of others which are susceptible to dispute or acceptance: inter-subjective understanding contents itself with co-ordinating action, since it allows the mutual recognition of validity-claims made on a mutual basis by agents. Sociology is thus reduced to the analysis of social discourses and denies itself the opportunity of accounting for observable empirical regularities.

It could be objected that Habermas opens up new perspectives for sociology by introducing the concept of 'life-world' to explain the very possibility of communicative action (1988: 126–7): it is an implicit, non-thematized knowledge which forms the back-drop of common understanding. The life-world is not solely the context of CA but is the constitutive process of inter-subjective understanding: a sort of pre-communication which is not the subject of an explicit knowledge, a knowledge which is not yet articulated conceptually.

Habermas elaborates the concept of 'life-world' with reference to Husserl (in the *Crisis*), to the later Wittgenstein and to Searle (1988: 116–127). But this non-conceptualized knowledge remains within the framework of the classical view of the agent: that of a conscious agent. In no case is it explained how the life-world becomes the object of a pre-theoretical, pre-reflexive knowledge, involving a 'take' on a world which escapes consciousness. The relocation of the relationship with the world towards the body, which was undertaken by Merleau-Ponty, following Husserl, is not taken up by Habermas, who remains the prisoner of intellectualist positions incapable of accounting for the 'ontological complicity' between the agent and the world' brought to light by Bourdieu. The fact of an involvement in the game, the *illusio* created through contact with a field, is ignored by Habermas. He privileges the model of subjects who are not simply conscious but who possess total mastery of their speech acts and the situations in which they find themselves: for him it is impossible to analyse anything operating outside and beyond discourse, which the concept of habitus would take account of.

Furthermore, the logic of habitus permits an account of the distinction between SA and CA in Habermas's sense. It is sufficient to refer to the general type of action that they both eliminate: the fact that it is possible to have *an action objectively orientated towards an end without being consciously orientated towards that end*. Starting from this latter model of action, it is possible to distinguish different cases:

- the model is kept exactly as it is: it is the relation between the habitus and the field which explains the *illusio*, the interest in the game on the part of those who take themselves seriously as players. This model works for most social action. Pierre Bourdieu brought it to light in his ethnological works and then applied it afterwards to differentiated societies in *Distinction*.
- the model can be specified as SA when the agents are masters of the reasons for their actions, or when a calculative rationality is deliberately

resorted to in a determinate field, that of the modern economic field, for example.

- the CA has a place but only if it is understood on the basis of a *practical* mastery of the situation, of a practical sense taken as the sense of a communicative situation. Inter-subjective understanding is not automatically rational. It is, first of all, a practical acceptance of the stakes and thus of common values, which the rationalist concept of 'lifeworld' forged by Habermas cannot explain, since this concept omits the relational dimension of action (the link between habitus-field). It is then no longer necessary to state the maladaptations which are distortions in relation to normal communication – the ideal speech situation – but rather to grant that the transparency of inter-subjective understanding is only one case, resulting from 'ideal' conditions in the everyday sense. Far from being the norm, CA is a very particular case, although this does not exclude it from playing the part of a normative ideal.

Consequently, *inter-subjective understanding can no longer be understood as an agreement with a rational foundation, based on common convictions and independent of external pressures*: it is, on the contrary, the *illusio* which explains the common basis of relationships, the practical recognition of common stakes, consensus. Hence there can be conflict, or rational discussion, in the particular case in which the relations of competition in a given field are euphemistically glossed over (theoretical work, for example).

The non-rational foundations of consensus

It is at the level of the very conception of language that it is necessary to grasp the consequences of the divergence between Habermas and Bourdieu; it is no longer possible to reduce language either to a medium of transmission of information (SA) or to the source of social integration (CA) without evacuating the problem of symbolic violence and the conditions of its efficacy. There should be, according to Habermas, a 'force rationally motivating agreements leading to sympathetic understanding': in no circumstance does he perceive language as an instrument of domination, a vector of symbolic violence in its very effects. His theory of domination stops at the gates of language and philosophical foundations.

If it is true that an agreement can be initiated by means other than rational argument, a critique of the Habermassian conception of language may take either of two directions:

1. Neglect of the fact that *language derives its authority from external sources* (Bourdieu and Wacquant, 1992: 147).

The performative character of words requires a good deal more than the acceptance of their validity: that is, a *social belief*. The analysis of the 'performative magic of all rites of institution' (Bourdieu, 1991: 117–126) allows one to shed light on the fact that, in the same manner, the belief in ritual which exists before the ritual itself is the condition for its efficacy, the belief in the authority of the subjects who speak, which exists before their speech-acts, is the condition for the efficacy of their acts: 'the magic of words merely releases the 'springs' – the dispositions – which are wound up beforehand' (1991: 126). The 'illocutionary force' of words is not in the words themselves: to be performative, they must meet certain conditions of efficacy, that is to say, the dispositions constituted socially for the conditions of their performative action to be recognized and accepted. To name a boat, it is not enough for someone to say 'I name this boat the ...' but it is necessary that the one who names it is authorized to proffer the performative utterance which constitutes the institution of naming, and that this authority be recognized by the people present (or absent) who have any dealings with the boat, which, in the event, generally flows from the official investiture of the person who is authorized to name a boat: we are thus brought back to habitus, to the system of socially-constituted dispositions predisposing one to accept an authority vested as such, and therefore to the 'delegated power of the institution' (Bourdieu and Wacquant, 1992: 147).

Consequently, the performative efficacy of words depends in part on the status of those who utter them: communication is not just transmission of information, it is an exchange between people who are socially situated. Linguistic competence is not alone sufficient; it is necessary to have a 'situated competence' (Bourdieu and Wacquant, 1992: 146). The communicative action model founding inter-subjectivity merely on language is shown to be invalid in the example of the delegated power of the spokespersons who give meaning to what they say not simply through what they say but because they say it (in their capacity as spokespersons) and because those to whom they say it recognize them as possessing the authority to say it, or rather, recognize, through them, the institution which gives them the right to say it. They can act on the real through words (the performative aspect) because they act on those representations of the real which their situated authority permits them to impose. Communication is then not exempt from relations of power, which are born from differences of status between speakers and listeners: but it is necessary to understand that the relations of power are also relations of symbolic force, which means that the relationships of power between speakers and the groups to which they belong take on a euphemised form in linguistic relations (Bourdieu and Wacquant, 1992: 143).

Thus a strictly linguistic analysis omits one crucial element of the act of communication: communicative meanings go beyond the strict bounds of words and grammar. The recognition of validity-claims should not be limited to analysing the conditions of truth but should also be concerned with determining the value of truth, which is much more than a relation between words and things (truth-adequacy) or a relation between abstract speakers (truth-consensus): but a relation between real speakers, endowed with both a body and a social status. Failing to grasp that linguistic practice is a practice like others, that language itself is a 'bodily technique',[5] bringing into play a linguistic habitus linked to the class habitus of the speaker, a strict analysis of language neglects a major part of the production of meaning, which results from the concrete interaction of the speakers. It is then easy to understand that communicative action, if it were to hold as a partial model, can never account for the real conditions of agreement between speakers, because these conditions are not born from language: as we have seen,[6] there is no need for an explicit formulation of a consensus.

More precisely, the act of communication can lead to agreements and consensus, but not because of an illocutionary force or purely rational motives: a strict linguistic analysis neglects the symbolic violence which slides into every 'speech act', of which the formative element lies rather in the perlocution and its conditions (doing by the fact of saying) than in the illocutionary force (doing through saying); in order to do through saying, it is necessary first to posit the concrete act of speaking, within the given situation. Belief precedes the communicative act, persuasion extends beyond explicit reasons and brings us back also to the belief in the authority of those who speak,[7] who hence possess the power to say *what is*, to act on reality by the symbolic act of representing reality:

> Symbolic power, the power to constitute the given by stating it, to act upon the world through acting upon the representation of the world, does not reside within 'symbolic systems' in the form of an 'illocutionary force'. It is defined in, and by, a definite relationship that creates belief in the legitimacy of the words and of the person who utters them, and it operates only inasmuch as those who are subjected to it recognize those who wield it (Bourdieu and Wacquant, 1992: 148).

Thus what Habermas evades, along with the concrete aspects of communication, is the social dimension of language, which is indeed curious when it is a question of building a theory of society on linguistic acts and communicative acts. Why does he come to neglect the fact that 'every linguistic exchange contains the *potentiality* of an act of power' (Bourdieu and Wacquant, 1992: 145), in other words, to fall into the illusion that the linguistic sphere is autonomous, resulting from this neglect of the social conditions for its efficacy? Here the second level of critique is appropriate:

2. If *the power of words is not of a purely rational order*, the explanation of their recognition returns us to the 'institutionalized circle of *collective misrecognition which is the foundation of the belief in the value of a given discourse*':

The conditions for the efficacy of the performative acts of words only allows them to persuade, or to be recognized, as a result of the symbolic violence which they exert. For example, the reason for which a text is recognized as philosophical, authoritative, is often very far from being rational: Bourdieu has shown in relation to Heidegger and Althusser how a text can have claims made for it in terms of its philosophical character, in stressing its high level of rhetorical address and theoretical content. There is an imposition of form tailor-made for each field, or each linguistic market, for which the message is destined, a formal encoding which consists in respecting the forms defined by this market and incites one to produce effects in accordance with those legitimately produced and accepted by that market.

The misrecognition by Habermas of the symbolic violence of language appears clearly from the very remarks he made on Heidegger and in which he neglects the highly-elaborate style through which a text becomes recognized as philosophical. Bourdieu, in contrast, asks how 'such a great thinker' (Heidegger) was able, in his Rectorial Address of 1933, to 'stoop to such an obviously elementary mode of thought, which any lucid analysis can discern in the unstylized pathos which is that of a German University yearning for self-assertion' (1991: 152, trans. mod.). This elevated level, this sense of distinction, inherent in traditional philosophical discourse, heralds Heidegger's usual discourse as authorized, vested with the authority to exert its 'magisterial theoretical propositions' (1991: 142–153; 1988b).

In making such specific considerations, Habermas thus neglects the very conditions for his own reflections on language. As Pierre Bourdieu says furthermore:

> The symbolic violence that any ideological discourse implies, in so far as it is based on a misrecognition which calls for re-misrecognition, is only operative inasmuch as it is able to make its addressees treat it the way it demands to be treated, namely, with all due respect, observing the proper formalities required by its formal properties (1991: 153).

Digressing between philosophy and social sciences: how to undertake philosophy today?

Habermas thus only treats language as an object of analysis, forgetting its practical dimension, and the often non-rational aspects which are the corollary of its everyday usage. It is then possible, in applying Bourdieu's analyses, to see that this purely theoretical vision of language, this scholastic vision, is nothing but the 'product of the scholarly apperception and situation' (Bourdieu and Wacquant, 1992: 141) which gave birth to it. Habermas's writings, with their claims to universality, are thus dependent on the specificity of the point of view of the university professor Habermas, little *au fait* with the realities of power, of language, and with the powers of language: those writings take us back to the speech of someone accustomed to being listened to as an eminent professor, for whom certainty about the universal truth of what he says is reinforced by the recognition due to him as 'Professor Habermas', not seeing at all that it derives from the fact that he is a professor whose speech, in his professorial capacity, is recognized as worthy of being heard.

It is not solely a reflexion on the social conditions of his theoretical production which is thus at issue: it is also the relationship of philosophy to the social sciences. Habermas's discourse on sociology is a meta-discourse, little concerned with the very exercise of these sciences; the opposite approach is, namely, that of Bourdieu, who starts from concrete studies and elaborates concepts and theories deriving from that exercise. What characterizes Habermas's theory is an incapacity to get closer to the facts: could communicative action apply to anything other than the private conversation of professors of philosophy, who believe in the rational power of words and have signed a 'pact of symbolic non-aggression'? Which perhaps explains a certain attraction towards Habermas amongst French philosophers, more inclined to discuss the foundations of society and the moral order than to reflect on existing social problems, more inclined to rediscover the privileged pitch of the thinker above the scrum – above the empirical and the factual – than to analyse their own time. They have not even the desire to be untimely, like the preceding generation: to stand against one's time, then, was still being of one's time. Acceptance of the thought of Habermas is indicative of a retreat to the timelessness of *philosophia perennis*, towards the theoretical prerogatives of the professional thinkers who form the philosophical institution.

Actually, what is at stake in Bourdieu's critique of Habermas is a relationship to philosophy which questions the very existence of philosophy today or, more exactly, current 'philosophical investigations': not because philosophy ought to prostrate itself in front of sociology, but because the competition which the social sciences exert on its own terrain compel it to re-define its objectives, its methods, its 'manners', in the sense of manners of doing and of being, and force it to take into account these new conditions, without simply accounting for these 'from a distance' (or rather, from on high), at the level of 'principles' ... Habermas represents perhaps the last attempt to undertake philosophy 'as before': a will to encompass specific knowledge within a universal rationality which would still be the domain reserved for philosophers. Bourdieu is perhaps the first 'modern philosopher': not one who stands for the dissolution of rationality, but someone who stands for reflections on the conditions for its emergence within the specific social universes in which it is at work; someone who suggests a new relationship, disengaged from any 'scholastic bias', between theory and practice, speculative reason and concrete phenomena. A new relationship, also, between philosophy and the social sciences, where empirical research enriches theory without being reduced to its simple application, where scientific methods are incorporated within thought other than as 'rules' ... The problem is that these differences in attitude seem to have repercussions on the subjects, theories and conceptions of each thinker. If Plato, or Descartes, to take only such pillars of the philosophical institution, had been content with examining 'from afar' the rules of geometry or of physics, their works would not have obtained the conceptual heights that are still admired today by both philosophers and non-philosophers ...

It is certainly possible to object that the situation of the social sciences is not the same as that of the other sciences, that it is a question of further taking society as the 'foundation-stone' of this new knowledge, unlike physics, which rests on more assured foundations. Perhaps the quest for a 'point which might be fixed and certain', as Descartes said, is the first step towards science ... provided that science be practised. It is necessary to recognize here that the attraction of Habermas's thought resides more in reflections on the normative character of sociological discourse than in any concrete analysis of society.

A politics of rationality

To return once again to the critique undertaken by Bourdieu, it is possible to say that it questions again that Habermassian attempt to use the concept of illocution as the key for a new theory of reason and society (1988: xiv). But, beyond Habermas, the critique of the illusion of the purely rational force of discourse touches on nothing less than the status of reason: if the foundations of consensus are not rightfully considered rational, it seems difficult to think about rationality outside the relations of power (symbolic or otherwise) which underpin the social world. Can a study of rationality afford to bypass reflections on the social conditions for implementing this rationality? Can a theory of society afford to avoid the objectification of its own context of objectification?

As against the universal pragmatics of Habermas, Bourdieu opposes a praxeology (Bourdieu and Wacquant, 1992: 139) which insists on the symbolic violence inherent in the use of language: it is necessary to complement the quest for the conditions for truth with an assessment of the value of truth and the meanings inherent in concrete situations, beyond the linguistic sphere. Relations of meaning, Bourdieu shows, do not constitute a separate domain: they are crosscut by relations of power, which they reinforce even while masking them. To try to separate them, even in a normative form, can only accentuate the misrecognition of their social function.

It is not the project *per se* of a critical theory of society that is at issue: it is rather the attempt to found it by resorting to purely normative concepts such as that of rational consensus or the ideal speech-situation. If the 'linguistic turn' made by Habermas has the merit of showing that critique cannot afford to do without a return to the values which he uses as criteria, it is by no means certain that the price to be paid is worth it: to ignore the real conditions of the utilization of language amounts to evacuating the symbolic dimension of domination – and of having recourse again to the unjustified presupposition of a universal rationality.

Because he cannot admit the 'absolutism' of the new rationalism incarnated in Habermas, Pierre Bourdieu reminds us that rationality has a history (Bourdieu and Wacquant, 1992: 189). This 'historicist rationalism' takes an opposite position on a number of issues from the German philosopher:

1. To the ethical and universalist Kantianism which inspires the morality of communicative action, Bourdieu prefers the critical and methodological aspects, which he develops in instigating a debate about the social conditions for the possibility of discourse, notably, critical discourse (1994a: 32–33). It is in a way a 'critique of scholastic reason' which is the thread running through his theory of the knowledge of the social world.

2. Two different conceptions of reason are thus at issue in the comparison between Habermas and Bourdieu: for the latter, reason has a history, for it is not 'inscribed within the structures of the human mind nor in language. It is found rather in certain types of historical conditions', in certain 'social structures of dialogue and non-violent communication' (Bourdieu and Wacquant, 1992: 189). It is no longer possible to do without the relationship 'habitus-field', which introduces a double historicity: that of socially constituted mental structures and that of the social structures which shape them. Consequently, the schemata of perception, appreciation and action of the habitus invalidate the presupposition of an ahistorical universal rationality. The latter must thus be re-contextualized, brought back into relation with the social structures which determine the conditions for its emergence. Then a new domain of research is on offer: the study of the constitutive principles of human rationality, highlighting the schemata of the 'historical transcendental' (Bourdieu and Wacquant, 1992: 189), which is indeed the habitus. Instead of transcendentalizing the social, like Habermas, it is better to socialize the transcendental, that is, to show the historicity of the mental structures conditioning the perception of the world. As Bourdieu writes in *Practical Reason*:

the history of reason is the peculiar history of the conditions of the genesis of these particular social universes which, having *skholè* as a prerequisite and scholastic distance from necessity (and from economic necessity in particular) and urgency as a foundation, offer conditions propitious to the development of a form of social exchange, of competition, even of struggle, which are indispensable for the development of certain anthropological potentialities (1998: 138).

3. A new domain of action also opens up where theory and practice are linked together: a *Realpolitik* of Reason. Without having to presuppose some 'transhistorical universals of communication' (Bourdieu and Wacquant, 1992: 188) as Habermas does, it is possible to recognize the existence of 'forms of social organization of communication, that are liable to foster the production of the universal' (Bourdieu and Wacquant, 1992: 188; 1998: 234).

Only a realistic politics of scientific reason can contribute to the transformation of structures of communication, by helping to change both the modes of functioning of those universes where science is produced and the dispositions of the agents who compete in these universes, and thus the

institution that contributes most to fashioning them, the university ...
(Bourdieu and Wacquant, 1992: 188)

Scientific reason realizes itself when it becomes inscribed not in the ethical
rules of a practical reason or in the technical rules of a scientific
methodology, but in the apparently anarchical social mechanisms of
competition between strategies armed with instruments of action and of
thought, capable of regulating their own uses, and in the durable
dispositions that the functioning of this field produces and presupposes.
[...] It is the scientific field which makes scientific reason possible through its
very functioning (Bourdieu and Wacquant, 1992: 189; cf also 1998: 234–5)

Realpolitik of reason and realization of the universal are here joined
together: the universality of rationality is not presupposed but constitutes the
goal to be attained, rationally and institutionally. The favouring of the
institutional conditions for a universal interest goes alongside the elevation of
the conditions in which to practice scientific rationality. It is a collective matter,
as Bourdieu explains in *Raisons Pratiques*: it consists in obtaining 'the
sublimated essence of the universal' (1994b: 80) via the operational rules in the
different social fields, these 'peculiar social microcosms, in which agents
struggle, in the name of the universal, for the legitimate monopoly over the
universal' (1998: 139).

It is in this relation between reason and its institutional conditions that the
Realpolitik of reason takes on its meaning: a realist politics in the degree to
which it allows for a critique of the strategies of legitimation by the universal,
and the means to combat them thanks to 'tests of universality' (1998: 144) in
each field; but also a realist politics which can seek support from certain
anthropological laws, such as the fact that there are benefits from submitting
oneself to the universal (1998: 142). And if, against Habermas, it is necessary to
recall that claims to universality might possibly mask domination, one can
always hope that the presupposition of an 'ideal speech situation' will be
allowed to play a regulative role in the structures of communication,
institutional bases for rational thought: the question is to know whether the
ruses of reason, laid bare by struggles in which agents have an interest in the
universal, will be allowed one day to promote the universal through the
collective search for a rational consensus – without for all that handing over to
domination arguments for legitimating itself.

Notes

1 In this article *Sur le Pouvoir Symbolique*, Bourdieu writes: the dominant culture contributes to
the real integration of the dominant class by ensuring immediate communication between its
members and by distinguishing them from the members of other classes; to the fictitious
integration of society as a whole, thus to the demobilization (and false consciousness) of the

dominated classes; to the legitimation of the order created through the erection of distinctions (hierarchical) and the legitimation of these distinctions. This ideological effect is what the dominant culture produces when it veils its pattern of division by means of its function of communication: the culture which unites (medium of communication) is also the culture which separates (instrument of distinction) and which legitimates distinctions by constraining all other cultures (designated as subcultures) to define themselves through their distance from the dominant culture'.

2 Action defined by Habermas as the 'mastery' of situations' (1984, II: 141).

3 In *Sociologie et Théorie du Language* (1995), Habermas refers solely to truth and adequacy in relation to communication, and sincerity in relation to action, a distinction which does not really change the basic assumptions of the problem, at least to the degree to which it is the logic of interaction which is envisaged.

4 Bourdieu and Wacquant (1992), section on types of domination.

5 The expression used by Mauss is taken over by Bourdieu in Bourdieu and Wacquant, 1992: 149.

6 The function of communication masks that of distinction, as suggested in note 1 above.

7 There is no clearer example than that of naming: to endow persons with a name is to grant them a social essence, to summon them to be what they have to be, to indicate to them that they must conform to their name. This 'performative magic' underpins the rites of institutions.

Bibliography

Bourdieu, P., (1978), *Distinction*, RKP.

Bourdieu, P., (1980b), *Le Sens Pratique*, Paris: Minuit: OMIT?

Bourdieu, P., (1982), *Ce Que Parler Veut Dire: Les Economies des echanges Linguistiques*, Paris: Librairie Arthème Fayard.

Bourdieu, P., (1988b), *The Political Ontology of Martin Heidegger*, Cambridge: Polity.

Bourdieu, P., (1990), *The Logic of Practice*, Cambridge: Polity.

Bourdieu, P., (1991), *Language and Symbolic Power*, Cambridge: Polity.

Bourdieu, P., (1994a), *In Other Words*, Cambridge: Polity.

Bourdieu, P., (1994b), *Raisons Pratiques*, Paris: Seuil.

Bourdieu, P., (1998), *Practical Reason*, Cambridge: Polity.

Bourdieu, P. and Wacquant, L., (1992), *Invitation to a Reflexive Sociology*, Cambridge: Polity.

Habermas, J., (1984), *The Theory of Communicative Action*, Vols I and II, Cambridge: Polity.

Habermas, J., (1987), *Knowledge and Human Interests*, Cambridge: Polity.

Habermas, J., (1988), *The Logic of the Social Sciences*, Cambridge: Polity.

Habermas, J., (1995), *Sociologie et Théorie du Langage*, Paris: P.U.F.

Roth, G. and Wittich, C., (eds) (1978), *Max Weber: Economy and Society*, California: University of California Press.

A militant sociology: the political commitment of Pierre Bourdieu

Louis Pinto

As a renowned sociologist who has put his scientific capital at the service of ethical and political principles, Pierre Bourdieu finds himself exposed to all those criticisms which, varying with the occasion, are directed at the intellectuals who presume to teach a lesson, the expert who are not quite as rigorous as they would like us to believe, the committed individuals who take extremist paths, and even at the individuals who find themselves stigmatized by a boundless appetite for power.[1] In short, the transgression of the limits bestowed on the scientist, the contradictions inherent in such an approach: these are the lacunae or the defects of the intellectuals under attack. Let us pass over the details of these (often malevolent) criticisms, over a bad faith which dispenses with any explicit criteria for what should be, in this domain, a 'proper' intellectual attitude, and over the 'sociology' of a pathological or policing character which is relied on to supply 'explanations'. The fundamental issues raised by Bourdieu's public commitment are those of the nature of the positions taken at different points in a social and scientific trajectory, and of their coherence: what is the nature of these declarations, initiatives, petitions and reflections on contemporary events and to what extent are they compatible with each other on the one hand, and with the prerequisites of scientific work on the other hand.[2]

It might appear natural, in addressing these issues, to seek to distinguish the basic ordering principles from which these positions are supposed to be deduced. But, however justified it might be, this procedure presents some major obstacles against which, precisely, Bourdieu's work has always warned: indeed, it presupposes an intellectualist theory of practice, where practice is made virtually the exclusive application of those ideas or rules constructed or chosen by the theorist; furthermore, it contains a strand of essentialism, which makes it impossible to ask to what degree the positions taken derive from a specific context and from the meaning associated with that context; finally, it more or less takes for granted a political sphere which is in fact arbitrarily mapped out. To escape these limitations, it would be necessary, logically, to construct methodically the sociologists' trajectory whilst also relating it to the transformations which have affected the different fields, notably the intellectual and political fields, etc. Which is another way of saying that it would require a meticulous study which would rely on quite a considerable range of materials.[3]

Without going so far as to risk such an undertaking, it is proposed here to elucidate another essential point which, without replacing the preceding issue, would at least have the merit of clarifying the relations between intellectual work and political action. It is a question of asking what understanding of the intellectual and of knowledge is implied in the distinctive manner in which Bourdieu (and possibly, others) undertakes political action. There is no need to pose the relations between scientific space and political space in terms of a deductive model explaining one in terms of the other (according to the need of the moment: politicize science and scientizing politics): it is enough to manage to draw out a 'family resemblance' between the two spaces, which are reciprocally expressed, without ever reducing one to the other, because they exhibit quite distinct time structures and logical patterns. It is, indeed, on the basis of a *set of dispositions* that this kinship emerges. Of course, one might say, this empirically-tested proposition may apply to any intellectual. It should be added that Bourdieu's merits lie in taking full responsibility for his public action by drawing the practical conclusion from his scientific work, that is to say, by extending this scientific work into a commitment which offers a relatively coherent programme of action, without giving up the demands of sociological reflexivity.

Commitment and intellectual traditions

To understand this commitment, it is not sufficient to consider the objectives or the strategies which flow from it, but it is first of all necessary to mention the idea of militant action which springs from it, a kind of militant action which one might call 'specific', to paraphrase the expression 'specific intellectual' favoured by Michel Foucault. In effect, intellectuals who campaign do not have any intention outside self-metamorphosis and they will have to renounce a number of attractive temptations, starting with that of populism, so as to offer what they alone can contribute, in principle better than others, as a result of their work: knowledge used to serve emancipatory aims. A corollary of this is that intellectuals must recognize the knowledge and know-how of other 'militants', whom they should presume capable of doing what they do well, without such a presumption at all implying the need to give up the prerogative of critical analysis. Science and militancy are linked together here in a dialogue which imposes neither complacency nor unanimity. The domains of action are inevitably multiple and bear specific characteristics, varying degrees of urgency, generality, publicity, etc. Off-the-cuff, vague general declarations may be of interest to those who find themselves content with short-lived ideological agitation, far from the noble provinces of theory, but they may prove disastrous for sociologists, that is, for those whose intellectual credibility is tied to the requirements of scientific argument and who possess a double responsibility, at once towards the science of which they are practitioners and towards the social and political consequences of their analyses.

This model of specific militancy is also that of collective intellectuals: it introduces a critique of these contemporary intellectual models which fail to set out convincingly the relationship between the registers of thought and action. Having to innovate, breaking away from blind activism – the habit of those who persist in thinking with whatever comes to hand, usually of little use for a rational understanding of reality – finding another way proves to be difficult and initially to go unnoticed. One of the constant features of intellectuals, indeed, both within the intellectual, as much as in the political, order, has for a long time been a form of blackmail which rests on a dramatization of all alternatives, erected as a real entry-barrier into the intellectual field. It is a question of either ... or: either one is a 'revolutionary' or one is a 'reformist' (or a 'revisionist'); either one is a 'democrat' or one is a 'totalitarian'; either one is a 'European' or one is a 'nationalist'; either one is a 'radical' or one is a 'realist', etc. ... As for the journalists who cover 'intellectuals', they tend to reproduce the categories of the political field, like those of their number who have no hesitation in labelling Bourdieu as 'extreme Left', without noticing that, on many issues, there has been a shift of the centre of gravity of public debate to the Right, labelling as 'extreme' ideas which, some years earlier, would have been simply part of the collective inheritance of the Left. Thus intellectual debate, the essence of which, we are told, is to be liberal, open and complex, is eventually reduced to a series of simplistic options, over which one is hard-pushed to see how one could hesitate for an instant, except for a culpable 'ideological' stubborness. Now the truly independent mind consists in keeping one's cool, in never giving in to blackmail, in making for one's own the maxim of Karl Kraus 'between two evils, I refuse to choose the lesser'.

Another characteristic of the intransigeance of intellectuals is the dissociation between those position-takings defined as explicitly political and the truly intellectual work of knowledge. Curiously, as Jacques Bouveresse has underlined in the case of postmodern philosophers, one is given the impression that the most exacerbated and impatient forms of progressivism can go hand in hand with the prejudices of a philosophical *aristocratism* devoid of complexity (1984: 20).[4] A single thinker may, in the same move, come to hold a perspectivist relativism echoing with a Nietszchean resonance, and to praise 'rebellion', not to speak of those who would go so far as to celebrate the 'just' struggles of workers and students.

With the passage of time, radical intellectuals, disappointed by the masses, have changed their trajectory but not necessarily their tone, as on one point at least, they have not changed much at all – judging from the propensity to label and to stigmatize, usually based on nothing but the current intellectual doxa. The curse of being 'a reformist from the petty-bourgeoisie' has given way to that of being a 'Marxist'. Cursed be the latecomers, cursed be the absent-minded or the naive ones who get caught out; it is easy enough for anyone, no matter who, to learn the current rules. When everything alters, it is enough to keep on holding to the major principles of one's position-takings to suffer from 'trend- lag', a lag in which one is condemned never to be where one ought be at the right time.

Thus are legends made. Pierre Bourdieu, would have found himself 'radicalized', discovering belatedly a commitment that he had neglected in his earlier period as a scientist. People who argue in this way, obsessed only with choices viewed at face-value – which are the easiest to identify (I am *for* the 'just struggle' of 'people' X, I am against the Gulag), reveal themselves to be insensitive to the analytical principles which ought to be, in theory, essential for intellectuals. It should be essential to raise questions about the ongoing blinkered views that Bourdieu's works have had to put up with, in particular on the part of French readers. The progressivism of the first works, nevertheless fairly obvious, began by being, if not unnoticed, at least under-estimated by those amongst intellectuals who are the most 'radical'. The least one could say is that Bourdieu did not start to become politically active in 1995. It is easy to demonstrate that the whole of his work, from the beginning, has had political implications. But much as the critical bearings of *The Inheritors* have been stressed, they have also been seriously minimized, and as if cut off, dissociated from their theoretical implications by the dominant progressive discourse which was organized at that time around more grandiose stakes. In 1965, when Althusser's *For Marx* was first published, there was already so much time devoted to reading *Capital* – as indeed later, to studying 'ideological state apparatuses' – that there was hardly any left to put the labour into the empirical analysis of educational inequalities, and even less time to decode the emerging theoretical approach which put front-stage, amongst other things, a notion as basically humanist as a 'relationship with culture', essential in order to understand a number of scholarly readings of philosophy but of very minor significance in connection with subject-less structures and other fundamental considerations.

The provocative slogan launched, admittedly belatedly, by Althusser: 'at last, the crisis of Marxism', could also have been Bourdieu's if he had not had a spontaneous repugnance for these sterile, ill-defined controversies on the 'isms'. Because what is at issue in such a crisis is not something which might concern a facile repertoire of concepts such as 'historical materialism', 'instances', 'dialectic', and other vague and supposedly 'theoretical' issues from which was generated, without too great a cost, the integration of a number of 'progressive' intellectuals. It is very much less, or very much more than that: it is the crisis of an intellectual habitus combining extreme pretensions to political radicalism with a phenomenal conceptual laxity. From this point of view, the climax seems to have been ushered in by an ultra-left oscillating between extremes, 'proletarian' anti-intellectualism and avant-garde esoterism, Mao and Bataille (or Sade, not to speak of Mallarmé). A similar hysterical mood was able to affect the different slogans, issues and authors thrown into the limelight by the conjuncture. In talking of the 'Revolution', in preference to more obscure, intermediate tasks, these 'intellectuals' had no need to explore a reality undoubtedly too vulgar and too poverty-stricken for them since they already possessed in advance all the answers they needed through the simple, peremptory repetition of some pre-established beliefs, proof against any refutation. Revolutionary fantasizing is, in such a case, one of the consequences of the professional over-estimation of the power of words and ideas: what would you expect from a Nietszchean converted, in less than a few months, to ultra-populism? As for all this insubstantial radicalism – which may have been, for some, accompanied by genuine enthusiasm and actual suffering, but which, for others, remained more or less a game – Marx, with the eradication of his 'former philosophical consciousness', had already made key points, still relevant today.

Instead of raising the poorly-formulated question of when did Bourdieu change his attitude towards politics, it would be more worthwhile to ask whether it was not rather the transformations within the intellectual field that made it possible for him to take an original position, until then improbable or untenable, defined by the possibility of an open dialogue between science and current affairs. This choice of an active and critical knowledge, simultaneously demanding and modest, was, if not fully acknowledged, at least publicly expressed, by 1986, in an article in *Actes de la Recherche en Sciences Sociales* entitled, precisely, 'Science and Current Affairs'. Throughout the articles collected in this issue, Bourdieu foresaw a common intention which might stand as the profession of faith of a scientific militancy:

> No-one can dispel (...) the hope that these limited contributions, subject to revision and often at odds with current understanding, might serve as an antidote to the scepticism, verging on irrationalism, which has been set in train by the failure of the great prophecies. (Bourdieu, 1986: 3).

Indeed in 1986, people were prepared – doubtless more than earlier – to accept the idea of the exhaustion of older intellectual models. The intellectual prophets seemed no longer able to supply resources sufficient to oppose a conjuncture that had become altogether less euphoric, nor to resist those agents[5] camped on the frontiers of the media and intellectual fields (the 'new philosophers'), of the intellectual and administrative fields. In France, the first experience of socialism under the Fifth Republic (1981–6) ended in disillusionment with managerial realism; in Eastern Europe, the Soviet model was entering its final crisis, testified to by the rise of the Polish movement, Solidarnósc (and to which were dedicated two articles of the issue). In order to escape from the pessimistic and cynical alternative, it was necessary to invent an intellectual stance which would combine attention to social reality with the understanding of essential values.

Bourdieu's growing importance in the public debate can be linked to the flocking around this consistent and improvized stance of a growing number of teachers, researchers, students, and also militants and journalists, both readers and non-readers of his works, who could identify with this language, having been forced by circumstances to repudiate mere rhetoric, while at the same time seeking to give the values in which they already believed an anchorage indispensible for a progressive action.

Commitment as symbolic subversion

Intellectuals as conceived by Bourdieu refuse 'pharisaism', both in its former radical variants (Marxism, 'desire' ...) as in its current conservative variants (democracy, ethics ...). One might call them 'revolutionary' if one wanted to foreground their global, critical vision of a social order unveiling the relations of domination between social groups. But they could just as easily be called 'reformist', as is shown in the analyses and propositions of ARESER,[6] in view of the great importance they give to the specificity of the social universes under debate, those for which social science is particularly aiming to account. In effect, sociological theory as conceived by Bourdieu should hold together two complementary aspects of social reality. The first concerns the reproduction of structures or, if one prefers, the reproduction of the distributional modes of the different types of capital between various social positions situated within a hierarchised social space, itself both the stake in, and the terrain for, a competition between groups. Far from the comfortable mythology of a mechanistic and immutable reproduction which, after all, contented the radical intellectuals of former times, relations of domination between groups introduce specific models, degrees and types which require analysis and explanation. Consequently, the interest of the comparative method, in particular, which allows the methodical understanding of a diversity of cases. The second aspect concerns the regional logic of spaces, and even sub-spaces, that contribute to the reproduction of social structures. One of the principle criteria of analysis is the degree of autonomy which these spaces possess relative to external forces, political and economic forces in particular. If the stakes and means of struggle are, each time, specific to these spaces respectively, the struggles between agents have a wider impact than those which seem to affect them more obviously: it is sufficient to think of the case of the School, a place where different groups of professionals compete over defining different modes of internal assessment and certification which, in fact, are never totally reduceable to the immanent demands of the scholarly institution since they inevitably concern, also, the values and external interests of different social groups. The distribution of goods and opportunities does not take place in an automatic manner but, to a large extent, occurs through the mediation of spheres in which the value of the different resources for social reproduction which the agents have appropriated is played out. The State and the School constitute central illustrations of this logic: they contribute, as institutions, to the reproduction of social structures while being at the same time sites of cleavage and confrontation.[7]

One might well believe that Bourdieu's sociology, which persists in speaking of an opposition between the dominants and the dominated, would irritate a number of 'theoreticians' who believe that they have discovered a social world cleared, at last, of the weighty issues of former times, and available for stakes far more intelligent. One should not be too surprised to observe that, on examination, most political-intellectual debates in the post-Marxist era of the 1980s and 90s, concern the opposition between a materialist vision of a history presumed to be attached to the economy, or to production, and a new brand of spiritualism which claims to demonstrate the necessity of supplying brand-new concepts to formulate a brand-new history. Now, the infatuation with the new flatters the sense of intellectual originality more than it fits the demands of research. At the time when the sociologist, patiently, studies worlds as complex as the School, cultural production, the field of power, etc., the impatient grow in numbers such that they manage to give the allure of evidence to a vision of modernity (or postmodernity) intended to transcend both Marxism, condemned by history, and old-fashioned conservatism. Amongst them, in particular, are a few essayists whose access to the intellectual field has gone hand in hand with the power to impose spontaneous categories for the perception of the real beyond their own sphere, essentially a function of the elimination of the old intellectual models. They have found crucial supporters firstly amidst those journalists who occupy in the field of the press a homologous position to theirs, and who, for this reason, are predisposed to interpret current events in terms of the rebuttals which the latter offer to 'dogmas' and 'ideologies', which is to say, in fact, also to those legitimate intellectuals who chose to rig themselves out in these inadequate thoughts. The intellectual doxa results, partially, from the social and cultural affinities linking journalists with intellectual pretensions to philosopher-journalists, both sets of whom have benefited from the support of modernizing agents within the political field, themselves preoccupied with breaking with the traditions of the Left and with celebrating individualism and the market. Paradoxically, instead of favouring a real transcendence, the spectre of merely going beyond archaic terms ('Marxism', 'social radicalism', with its strongly Third Republican flavour), removes the possibility of being open to those which, perhaps, might really possess the merit of being categorized as new. And, it results from this that being at all costs up with the flavour of the month engenders a form of senseless discourse, which owes nothing to traditional forms of classical thought. To finish off these 'old stories' of the dominants and dominateds, which they think they have already done the rounds of and which they reduce to the exotic and moralistic question of 'the excluded', the writers of editorials in the quality press have hardly had anything to offer but for variations always replayed on new orthodoxies such as the 'return of the subject', 'the coming of the individual', the emergence of new 'challenges', not to mention the 'revenge' of philosophy ('political' if possible) on sociology, which has been irreparably damaged by its 'scientistic' straying.

The scientific opposition between objectivism and subjectivism, which is the object of numerous elaborations in Bourdieu's work,[8] is now rephrased in more directly political terms by the tension between analyses in terms of objective structures and analyses in terms of beliefs. This tension alone permits one to escape, on the distinctively political terrain, from the alternative between activist voluntarism and a determinism more or less given up to fatalism. A social order, such as that which the neo-liberal utopia wishes to bring about, imposes itself on the consciousness and on the unconscious of agents without any purposeful action from the dominants being required: sociological lucidity consists in seizing back everything which has been acquired from the dominateds through the sole force of things, by this 'structural violence' which is at the heart, for example, of the situation of unemployment, with the terror and pressure which it itself creates. So that the 'techniques of rational subordination', which have been initiated by the new types of management, owe part of their efficacy to operating conditions producing these 'precariarized habituses'.[9] The action of the dominants may only be resisted successfully insofar as these conditions reach the explicit level of discourse, and would then be linked to the most ordinary experience of work and employment.

The mode of sociological understanding, far from remaining only at the objectivist level in relation to distribution (of goods, titles, ...) and mechanisms of reproduction, takes for its object the work of representing social reality against which an objective knowledge must be seized. Because the order of things resides first in both mind and body, political action, like any conscious action concerned with the transformation of reality, is, par excellence, inscribed within the 'subjective' world of representations and beliefs: it is not a matter of simply designating a vision which can be rejected, but of accounting for what is in fact its explicit force, its unquestioned rationale. Thus one of the strategic questions in the struggle against the neo-liberal doxa is that of belief: through which mechanisms has the vision of the 'rational' individual and his exclusively-economic motivations come to be shared so widely, even by those who bear the cost? Led, by the very nature of their work, to exert a counter-symbolic violence, sociologists deconstruct through analysis what militants undo or disturb through action. In this way their meeting and co-operation are possible, indeed desirable.

Neither confusion of roles, nor division of labour, are adequate to characterize meaningfully the relations between intellectuals and militants. For their part, sociologists should not think of using the projects of militants as applications or illustrations for their discourse about the social world: rather, they might discover there one of the ways in which sociological discourse is being tested, so to speak, and put to the proof. We might call this way that of 'militant experimentation': theoretical analysis is both extended and enriched by all the information prompted by the different forms of public action, amongst which it is necessary to include the sociological discourse itself. Whether they wish it or not, sociologists are confronted with approbation, hostility and censure (this is what makes it different from a purely academic proposition, which leaves things and minds in their original state): their hypotheses must to a certain degree be sensitive – positively or negatively – to the reception of their research once published.

When Bourdieu published his small book on television (1998b), he contributed, before everything else, to demystify the workings of public debate, through the contents of the book itself as much as through the very sharp response of the agents it concerned. Indeed, to take as its object those journalists endowed with the highest social power, the stars of television, tends, in itself, to be perceived as a transgression of the norms of public discourse. Because of the audience it attracts, or at least because of the beliefs circulating about its supposed effects, television is becoming an increasingly central stake in this field and perhaps even in other spaces. Since journalists are news professionals at the service of the public, one would appear to be attacking their acknowledged status, if not their honour, when one interrogates their professional hierarchies, their modes of thought and their interests, etc., a quite normal task for anyone who undertakes the study of a professional group (doctors, who are not the only ones who care, teachers, who are not the only ones who teach). The 'attack' is all the more inadmissable when these stars are treated simply as a relatively delimited and restricted sub-group in which are concentrated some of the diffuse effects at work in the field of the press as a whole. And what to say about this slander of the 'profession', which sociological discourse tends to dispossess of its chief prerogative, namely the capacity to reject any critique except that which it has formulated on its own approved terms? The famous 'professional code of ethics' would appear to have the function of reducing collective vigilance to the simple compliance with a set of inoffensive, general rules designed for the individual consciences of journalists: it seems to be too cheaply virtuous a route by which to by-pass an authentic collective auto-reflection. Now, precisely, all Bourdieu's efforts have consisted in avoiding false trials and false debates through the tangible demonstration of the mediations through which external constraints are translated, for example, into a specifically journalistic logic, in the anodyne form of a series of tricks of the trade guiding the choice and the treatment of subjects. Granted, the analysis which he suggested rested on multiple research, presented itself not as a finished body of work, but rather as an annotated sketch of studies to undertake and hypotheses to refine. And, for such a programme, the support of all agents concerned would have been, definitely, welcome.

The effective reactions were predictable, almost too propitious for easy bets. The journalists who were in a position to express themselves on this matter were the very same who conformed to the dominant values of orthodoxy, and had nothing to fear in the way of a sanction from their undertaking: either they denied everything *en bloc*, most indignantly, or they wrote ironically about the banality of a discourse which revealed things so well-known already, at least by them. In any case, they were careful not to formulate any positive suggestions to contribute to the growth of knowledge and the reinforcement of lucidity. The only lessons of the book, for them, were those to be drawn about the boundless ambitions of its author. Thus, despite their own intentions, they brought about a confirmation of sociological hypotheses, in particular on the question of the social importance of the stakes associated with television. Incontestably, television turns out to be a central element in any circuit of communication, above all when such a circuit is submitted to a commercial logic, and this is the reason why the passion expressed by some acquired an intensity to which Bourdieu's position-taking on a good number of other subjects would not have given rise. To demonstrate the 'journalists' power' threatens the interests of all those who, directly or indirectly, draw from journalism a set of profits, either material or symbolic.

Well then, why a book on television? If it has not convinced the holders of journalistic authority – and for good reasons – the book has had a success which leaves one to posit the existence of another public, at the heart of which the place of grass-roots journalists was doubtless not negligeable: to give this public the instruments of decoding, however provisionally, the work of journalists and the production of news was one of its intended functions. In this respect alone the analysis in question had exemplary value. On the one hand, it made it possible to show that the sociologist provides real means for understanding everyday reality, familiar to the professionals as much as to the profane, by escaping the horizon of conventional discourses, which are never absent in such a terrain, such as the memoirs of famous journalists, the views of 'mediologists', semiological studies, technological prophecies, whilst also escaping all the purely militant denunciations which keep to the level of abstract explanations, precisely where it should rather be a question of connecting together a set of structural constraints with the everyday experience of agents. On the other hand, it revealed, in practice, the principles of a sociological vision irreducible to the dominant discourse of politicians, political scientists or experts, and partially transposable to other spheres of the social world.

The book, *The Weight of the World* (1999), constructed around a series of interviews, was an effort to invent an original formula able to go beyond a series of divisions, often reinforced by the academic tradition, between science and politics, the abstract concept and the singular lived experience.

Far from marking a deviation from the programme of scientific work, it responded to the concern to communicate a sociological stance, as effectively and rigorously as possible, so as to put it to work within domains habitually proliferating with the discourse of every possible professional (journalists, economists, psychologists), to reveal how the apparently most personal experiences are in fact dependent on the actions of very general mechanisms, which themselves possess nothing fateful about them, being the result of a history the course of which might be reversed or altered. The strictly political intention of the book was to testify that sociology can be faithful to its scientific objectives, whilst continuing to speak of things which matter to people in their public as much as in their private concerns; better: in letting them express themselves, in letting them be heard by others who will be able to experience a feeling of closeness to them. In breaking the solitude of those who bear the cumulative effects of social suffering and symbolic violence, this new discourse showed a progressive use of a knowledge which carries the potential for mobilization. This dimension of the work has indeed been clearly noticed by non-sociologists, and, amongst them, by certain professionals of the theatre who have promised to stage some of the interviews.

The Weight of the World, which seeks to give a voice to those who are not usually heard or who are hardly heard (due especially to the operation of certain semi-technical categories like 'exclusion', etc.) is a very natural continuation of all those efforts – as much scientific as political – to bring to light the requirements of domination. In a social world marked by the specific form of legitimacy which the State Nobility has come to impose, the dominated are consigned to an apparently well-reasoned dispossession, which relates to their 'intelligence': lacking 'competence' and 'overall vision', they are condemned to be subjected, uneasy and dissatisfied, to the effects of an order of things which conforms however to the judgement of those *experts* who decide *expertly*. This philosophy of history intended for reasoning dominants (recognized twenty years ago in a study on the commonplaces of technocratic discourse produced at the Institut d'Etudes politiques, at the Ecole Nationale d'Administration, within the committees of the Plan, etc.) (Bourdieu and Boltanski, 1976: 2–3) has proliferated in spaces where one would have least expected it, such as that of social democracy of which one of the recent turn-arounds, sometimes imputed to the 'government culture', has been marked by the division between the fecklessness of the masses and the lucid and courageous resistance of the rulers to what appeared to them as 'populist temptations': certain media prophets, sociologists or philosophers, have gone as far as advancing a theory of the necessary rupture between the 'Left' and the restricted proletarians (in any case condemned to extinction by history).

Now one of the stakes of the social movement of December, 1995, was precisely the fate of the ideological consensus established around measures of rationalization ('savings') concerning the Social Security and certain pension rights: outside the government of Alain Juppé and his parliamentary majority, many trade-unionists, (notably CFDT), journalists, intellectuals, and others, have also supported the necessity of 'reform', and under-estimated the discontent that they would provoke and the capacities for mobilization. And while the government, assured of the support of a newly-elected President and numerous MPs, seemed to possess in its hands every means of imposing the measures announced, railway-workers, postmen, civil servants, went on strike in a context which did not seem at all favourable. Of course, the latter could count on the traditional support of the extreme Left, but they risked being highly isolated, faced with a front graced by famous names coming, in part, from 'the Left'.

This situation was very propitious for the mobilization of dissident intellectuals against the political/intellectual doxa incarnated in the 'reform'. It was thus hardly surprising that it should be Pierre Bourdieu who became the main figure of the intellectual resistance to this doxa. What was new was less the content of the position-takings, which could be deduced from numerous earlier texts, but the meeting between the intellectual and scientific capital that he embodied, and the 'social movement'. The 'act of resistance' of critical sociology gained visibility in the public sphere, bestowing intellectual weapons on the struggle against neo-liberalism. Some remarkable aspects of the social movement are worth recalling. First, the consensus worked out by the 'state nobility', with the support of the high-profile intellectuals, was challenged in the name of alternative values. Next, the 'base', which had been given its notice by the upper bureaucratic echelons, reminded everyone of its existence, and this outside the pacts and politico-trade union rituals, amidst a mixture of confusion and rejection. Ultimately, confronted with the 'reformism' of the dominants and the cult of the market, the preservation of the idea of public service was not just defended on the basis of a protective rationale of work or wages, but was further presented as the guarantee of universal values of dignity and solidarity: according to Bourdieu, what was at stake was 'civilization' itself.

A key stage in the work of collective mobilization of dissident intellectuals was the creation of the group 'Reasons for Acting (Raisons d'Agir)', which, despite its modest means, inaugurated all sorts of public initiative congruent with the ideal of a scientific militancy. Thus the series 'Liber-Raisons d'Agir' made available, for a very affordable price, books reflecting on the subjects of current affairs, (television, higher education, the petitions of intellectuals and the 1995 'social movement', the spread of neo-liberal ideas, the Sokal hoax). An original design, which sought to go beyond the two alternatives of a 'neutral' science and a militant, but scientifically-vulnerable, literature.

Is it possible, setting off from the position-takings linked to a particular historical occasion, to develop from it something like a political programme? Yes and no. No, if one understands by that a direct intervention into the political field. Yes, if it characterizes simply the reasoned definition of concrete objectives on which intellectuals can make a specific contribution: on culture, on all types of inequality, on questions concerning the representations of reality (the media, the social uses of science), on the social foundations of authority (political, academic) and even on the economy; they have things to say thanks to the tools of knowledge and analysis or, very simply, from their 'will to treat scientifically, coolly, burning questions' (Bourdieu, 1986: 2) The programme, which implies the possibility of escaping both horns of the dilemma – omniscience and ignorance – perhaps consists only in the encouragement to see things differently, in going only so far as is allowed by the state of current knowledge in relation to certain issues held to be strategic. A counter-utopia, breaking with the neo-liberal utopia, has the power to truly reveal the state of things existing by the act of going beyond it. Thus, supporting a policy like the Tobin tax, as did the ATTAC movement[10] is not conceived as a dogma but as one of the ways of coming out of the torpor in the face of 'globalization', of recalling the preeminence of the state as the expression of the collective will in relation to private powers, and of inviting the setting-up of mechanisms of international and organized resistance. Something like the European social state might be envisaged as part of the same logic, which would introduce a truly universalistic European dimension to the citizens' collectivity, endowed with civil, political and social rights.

A militant rationality

Sociology possesses a view of the social world that one can categorize as realist: it is a question of describing, explaining and understanding what people do, decisively not by taking refuge through abstaining, as in the 'axiom of neutrality', but by taking as one's guiding principle that the intellectual and ethical stakes are always immanent within the real and ought not to be imposed from the outside by a detached thinker. The sociological critique of scholarly reason shows that there is no detached view and that the most abstract of thinkers are haunted by problems the origins of which tend to elude them: it leads to the cultivation of a certain mistrust for all the temptations of deductivism which consist of reconstructing the real in terms of a number of pure axioms. For example, those philosophers who talk about questions of 'equity', while all the time trying hard to detach themselves from the ideological discourses of ordinary agents, would do well to ask themselves what such a question owes to the demands for rational justifications of the 'choices' which those in the political and administrative fields are compelled to make by operational constraints (especially budgetary). They could ponder on the fact that these choices are not to be evaluated solely in terms of the criteria of values of pure reason, but rather in terms of their effects on social groups, who are not neatly docketed into users of the School, users of the Social Security, users of civil rights, etc. Instead of concerning themselves with the ideal problems of the criteria of distribution and redistribution, they would benefit from asking themselves about the effective functioning of a mode of domination which embraces many other aspects than just goods, services and opportunities. One guesses that it is not a matter of the sociologist resigning himself to keep silent about the essential questions of legitimation which he might be incapable of treating fully: what is at issue is the relevance of the act of questioning itself and the possibility of an alternative subsequent to that scholastic vision of action that has been incorporated into 'pure' theories of all type, economic, ethical and political,[11] etc.

As against an entire positivist tradition which argued for the heterogeneity of objective knowledge and norms,[12] social science allows the proposition of an immanent creation (non-relativist) of values. Norms are not as external to the intellectual work as is believed, in the sense that this work implies, simply by its own existence, something like an ethic or a politics: it is necessary to be able to clear away the uncontested evidence of doxa, of everything which creates the power of the dominants, in order to seize the true gains of knowledge. Sociologists can only but feel how socially incongruous, if not scandalous, their activity is in contrast with the academic depiction of it: they identify beliefs, interests, cleavages, when one would expect them to name only the positive, if not the harmonious, course, or the ineluctable nature of things. But not every position is equivalent in this respect: some are more favourable than others to knowledge, to autonomy, to the universal, as Kant showed in his analysis of the 'conflict between the Faculties', of which Bourdieu offered certain developments. While sociological relativism consists in simply holding that values are socially conditioned and that such conditioning is irreducible, it is also true that the demands of rationality are inscribed at the very heart of an understood and accepted historical process.

The somewhat paradoxical concept of a *Realpolitik* of Reason (Bourdieu and Wacquant, 1992: 174), the consequences of which seem far from having been drawn out as much as they might deserve, implies a deliberate refusal to place the debate about reason on the terrain of moral and political philosophy, the refusal of a scholastic rationalism with its intellectual – and also ethical and political – presuppositions. If intellectuals want to be honest and straightforward with themselves, they must stop being naive: instead of contenting themselves with establishing crucial distinctions between the acceptable and the unacceptable or the intolerable, and setting off on a quest for cast-iron foundations, tacitly leaving actual humanity to get itself into a mess with a social reality which it is difficult to master, they would do better to understand the concrete ethical stakes that the social world never stops raising. The first duty of the ethical is the need to be in accord with its proclaimed objectives, and in this respect, this means pushing as far as possible empirical information, that is, renouncing an *a priori* decision as to the division between noble questions of principle and subordinate questions of 'facts'. For example, some individuals clash daily over issues about knowing whether, in such and such an area, authority must be claimed by those with certified knowledge, talent, or experience: these are, in one sense, ultimate questions, but are posed in an unrecognizeable form because they appear dressed in disguises which are quite unknown to the scholarly readers of Plato, Kant and Hegel, who would in turn have a great deal of trouble locating these questions in very basic squabbles about classifications, the opinions of hierarchical superiors, and rewards (everything which, incidentally, university teachers know very well when they come to inform themselves as to the criteria for promotion, merit, seniority, etc.). It is enough to consider the current reclassifications of workers' skills – roughly, 'know-how' as opposed to 'qualifications' – to grasp to what extent apparently technical controversies reflect struggles over classification, which is one of the major forms in which the struggles over class manifest themselves. As to the principle of these struggles, there are no logical or ontological criteria with which to define reality, but it is solely a question of the capitals possessed by agents and utilized to impose the definition of reality that most fit the characteristics of these capitals. In the event, the down-grading of acquired knowledge, and in general of 'experience' (authorized by the state of the power relations between groups), is often an instrument for undoing the protections seized by the dominated in history. All the while, in another context, the act of questioning 'skills' might appear 'progressive'. According to each individual case, sometimes formal qualifications or sometimes experience are variably conducive to collective emancipation.

In other words, this realist politics of reason is one way of acknowledging how reason is enacted in different specific arenas, and rarely in the grandiose form of a decisive struggle between heroic protagonists: in the concrete situation, it is necessary to think in terms of degrees, with variable amounts of ambiguity, paradoxical classifications, unexpected turns, etc. And if, nevertheless, a pattern appears to emerge, it is undoubtedly because sociology provides us with weapons: it allows the laws immanent in different fields, the forms of capital accumulation and the mechanisms of domination to be defined, and by this, sociology contributes to a better understanding of interests to and of the universal.

In the most autonomous fields, the major criterion of rationality is provided by precisely the demand for autonomy: that which follows more deeply from the immanent forces of the field, rather than from external powers, is rational, and it is this that deserves to be preserved and developed. If the struggle against neo-liberalism is so central for the politics of reason, this is not solely because this challenges a set of ethical and anthropological conceptions, it is also because the market threatens to flatten out the functioning of these autonomous spaces insomuch as they contain resources for rationality and thus for emancipation. Saying this, and providing a few good reasons, should not be confused with adherence to an archaic doctrine of the extreme Left: it is rather to discern, between distinct spheres, some analogies, or parallelisms, capable of suggesting simultaneously hypotheses and lines of action.

Should it be necessary to say that the role of the intellectuals is in symbolic subversion, when so many examples of it have already been given in the past? This role, which would today require some readjustment in the name of a less naive and better-informed vision, made easier by the development of the social sciences, ought not to be confused with an obsession for general and radical interrogation, but consists in showing the role of the historical arbitrary, contingent necessity, in social order, and in the forms of authority which contribute to perpetuating and to justifying it. Such is the contribution, perhaps the most specific, that intellectuals can make at the moment when militants, engaged in the urgency of struggles and often dispossessed of that scholarly capital which guarantees the required confidence, are sometimes inclined – making a necessity into a virtue – to take refuge in a combination of borrowed doctrines and popular common sense, and are therefore poorly-prepared to confront the weapons of the legitimate holders of politico-economic knowledge. To resist the evidence of the doxa and the educated fatalism which it encourages, it is a great strength to be able to count on an informed and rational sociological criticism of the social foundations of that authority which one intends to fight. A struggle which occurs on two 'fronts' at once: on the front of temporal power, where it is a question of a population of experts and weighty economists; on the front of spiritual power, where one has to deal with these essayists who work to elaborate and spread the 'philosophy' of a world henceforth dedicated to the couplet 'democracy' and the market, a world where the voice of the 'individual' makes itself at last recognized.

Scientific militancy is absolutely indissociable from intellectual reflexivity: it is not a question of imposing on one's contemporaries (by virtue of a 'sociological imperialism') arbitrary and contingent choices, those of an individual or a group, but of communicating that which, by profession as well as by vocation, the intellectual militant is the only one able to do. It is a matter of taking intellectuals more seriously than they usually do themselves, taking them at their word. Or again: of allowing them to take on, effectively, the collective and public consequences of that universality which is claimed by science.

(Translated by Bridget Fowler and Emmanuelle Guibé)

Notes

1 To give an idea of the extraordinary lengths to which certain journalists will go, I could mention a weekly which, in 1998, had as its front-page banner headline: 'The most powerful intellectual in France' – which, behind this apparent expression of aggressive ignorance, pays an unwitting homage to the power of ideas.

2 I take the liberty to refer to my book, *Pierre Bourdieu and the Theory of the Social World* (1999): 175.

3 I should but refer here to the article by Gérard Mauger (1995) and also to the work in preparation by Nicholas Caron.

4 On an exemplary instance, the aristocratism of G. Deleuze, see Pinto, (1995).

5 The term 'agent' has been used here, in conformity both with the French word 'agent' and the usual convention for translating the texts of Pierre Bourdieu. It possesses the same sense as the sociological concept 'actor' and should not be thought of as having any connotation of passivity (Trans.).

6 See ARESER (*Association de réflexion sur les enseignements supérieures et la recherche*) (1997).

7 And who would dare to argue that, society having undergone such transformation, our instruments of comprehension would have become obsolete? So as not miss the target it would be better to take it out on the dogmatic versions of Marxism, as on the question of social class, for example, Bourdieu's sociology has introduced some very important innovations, which ask to be understood independently rather than assimilated to memories of a distant dialectical materialism.

8 See, amongst others, Bourdieu (1990).

9 On this point, see P. Bourdieu (1998a).

10 This is a movement aimed at the taxation of capital circulating between different countries, inaugurated by Tobin, the Nobel Prizewinner in Economics.

11 Bourdieu, linking together writers as different as Rawls and Habermas, criticises the propensity to 'reduce political questions, already fairly remote from reality, to problems of "rational ethics"' but not without also evoking the respect which is elicited in the 'homo scholasticus which lies dormant within (him)' by such theoretical constructions (1998c). Besides, is it not disturbing to become aware of the break between the lofty heights of theory and their swithering on the position to be taken within the public sphere?

12 On this question, see H. Putnam (1984: 145).

Bibliography

A.R.E.S.E.R. (1997), *Some Diagnoses and Urgent Remedies for a University in Peril*, Paris: Liber–Raisons d'Agir.

Althusser, L., (1969), *For Marx*, Harmondsworth: Allen Lane.

Bourdieu, P., (1979), *The Inheritors*, Chicago: Chicago University Press.

Bourdieu, P., (1990), *The Logic of Practice*, Cambridge: Polity.

Bourdieu, P., (1998a), *Acts of Resistance: Against the New Myths of Our Time*, Cambridge: Polity.

Bourdieu, P., (1998b), *On Television and Journalism*, London: Pluto.

Bourdieu, P., (1998c), *Méditations Pascaliennes*, Paris: Seuil.

Bourdieu, P., (1999), *The Weight of the World*, Cambridge: Polity.

Bourdieu, P. and Wacquant, L., (1992), *Invitation to a Reflexive Sociology*, Cambridge: Polity.

Bourdieu, P. and Boltanski, L., (1976), The Production of the Dominant Ideology, *Actes de la Recherche en Sciences Sociales*, Juin, nos. 2–3: pp. 4–73.

Bourdieu, P., (1986), 'Science and Current Affairs', *Actes de la Recherche en Sciences Sociales*, 61: 2–3.

Bouveresse, J., (1984), *Rationalité et Cynicisme*, Paris: Minuit.

Mauger, G., (1995), 'Sociological Commitment', *Critique*, August–Sept., 579–580.

Pinto, L., (1995), *The Nephews of Zarathustra*, Paris: Seuil.

Pinto, L., (1999), *Pierre Bourdieu and the Social World*, Paris: Albin Michel.

Putnam, H., (1984), *Reason, Truth and History*, Cambridge: Cambridge University Press.

Durkheim and Bourdieu: the common plinth and its cracks

Loïc Wacquant

For lack of being able to offer here a systematic comparison between Bourdieu's sociology and the thought of Durkheim, which would require an historical-analytic monograph capable of reconstituting the double chain, social and intellectual, of the ramifying causations that link them to each other and to their respective milieus, I would like, by way of selective soundings, to bring out four of the pillars that support their common base: namely, the fierce attachment to rationalism, the refusal of pure theory and the stubborn defense of the undividedness of social science, the relation to the historical dimension and to the discipline of history, and lastly the recourse to ethnology as a privileged device for 'indirect experimentation'.

I am quite conscious of the fact that such an exercise can all too easily take a scholastic turn and fall into two equally reductive deviations, the one consisting in mechanically *deducing* Bourdieu from Durkheim so as to reduce him to the rank of an avatar, the other in *projecting back* the theses dear to Bourdieu into Durkheim's work so as to attest to their intellectual nobility. Its aim is to bring out some of the distinctive features of that French School of sociology which endures and enriched itself at the cost of sometimes unexpected metamorphoses.

Far from seeking to reduce Bourdieu's sociology to a mere variation of the Durkheimian score,[1] I would like to suggest that, while he leans firmly on them, Bourdieu imprints each of its pillar-principles with a particular twist which allows them, ultimately, to support a scientific edifice endowed with an original architecture, at once closely akin to and sharply different from that of the Durkheimian mother-house. This is another way of saying that Pierre Bourdieu is an inheritor who – contrary to Marcel Mauss for example – could and did, in the manner of an intellectual judoka, use the weight of the scientific capital accumulated by Durkheim the better to project himself beyond his august predecessor.

Passio sciendi, or the rationalist faith in action

Bourdieu shares with Durkheim first of all a rationalist philosophy of knowledge as the methical application of reason and empirical observation to the social realm, an application that demands, on the one hand, perpetual mistrust towards ordinary thought and towards the illusions which it continuously generates, and, on the other hand, an endless effort of analytic (de/re)construction which alone is capable of extracting from the teeming tangle of the real the 'internal causes and hidden impersonal forces which move individuals and collectivities'.[2] One could go so far as to say that our two authors harbour the same *scientific passion*, in the sense of an irrepressible love for and faith in science, its social value and mission, which they express the more vigorously the more strongly they are contested.

One recalls that Durkheim's avowed goal, from the inception of his work, was 'to extend to human behavior the scientific rationalism' that had proven itself in the exploration of the natural world. 'What has been called our positivism', he hammers away in the long reply to his critics that opens the second edition of *The Rules of Sociological Method*, 'is but a consequence of this rationalism'.[3] Likewise, Bourdieu forcefully asserts the unity of the scientific method and the membership of sociology in the great family of the sciences:

> Like every science, sociology accepts the principle of determinism, understood as a form of the principle of sufficient reason. Science, which must *rendre raison*, supply explanations for what is, postulates thereby that nothing is without a *raison d'être*. The sociologist adds *social*: without a specifically social *raison d'être*.[4]

The 'absolute conviction' which he attributes to Flaubert in his task as writer, Bourdieu himself possesses in the task of the sociologist. Contrary to a number of his contemporaries who have packed up and gone over to the 'postmodern' camp and revel in the abandonment (indeed, the derision) of reason, and whose international vogue has recently given new life to that typically French specialty, the export of designer-label concepts, Bourdieu has remained faithful to the 'party of science, which is now more than ever that of the *Aufklärung*, of demystification'.[5]

Durkheim and Bourdieu hold this rationalist faith, besides the national predilection for 'distinct ideas' inherited from Descartes, from their mentors in philosophy, and from their early immersion in the neo-Kantian atmosphere which pervaded their intellectual youth. It was through his personal association with Émile Boutroux, who introduced him to Comte, with Charles Renouvier, whom he regarded as the 'greatest rationalist of our time', and with his colleague at Bordeaux imbued with epistemology, Octave Hamelin (whom he describes nicely as an 'austere lover of right reason'), that Durkheim was led to inscribe his thought in the Kantian lineage. As for Bourdieu, his rationalism is rooted in his assiduous relations with that 'philosophy of the concept' (associated with the names of Georges Canguilhem and Gaston Bachelard, whose student he was) that offered a refuge and recourse against the 'philosophy of the subject' that reigned over the French intellectual field during the years of his intellectual apprenticeship, but also with the German tradition of the philosophy of 'symbolic forms' personified by Ernst Cassirer (whose main works he had translated by Éditions de Minuit, and whose affinities with Durkheimian theory he perceived very early).[6] And if the two are, at a distance of almost a century, deeply marked by Kantianism, it is because, as Durkheim noted on his return from a sojourn of studies across the Rhine, 'of all the philosophies which Germany has produced, [it is] this one that, properly interpreted, can still best be reconciled with the demands of science'.[7]

For the uncompromising 'empirical rationalism' that gives impetus to the sociologies of Durkheim and Bourdieu is deployed and bolstered in *scientific practice* more than in professions of epistemological faith – even if both perpetrated, in their youth, manifestos of a methodological character. It is in the 'acts of research in the social sciences', to take up the title, which is not innocent, of the journal founded by Bourdieu in 1975 [*Actes de la recherche en sciences sociales*], that its postulates are affirmed and tested. Such is the case with the notion of the 'non-transparency' of the social world and with the priority given to the problematization of the ordinary sense of the social world: 'Rigorous science presupposes decisive breaks with first-order perceptions' and should therefore not be afraid of 'offending common sense'.[8]

But, whereas Durkheim is content to make a clean sweep of the *praenotiones vulgares* that obstruct sociology, Bourdieu intends to repatriate them in an enlarged conception of objectivity that accords to the practical categories and competencies of agents a critical mediating role between 'the system of objective regularities' and the space 'of observable behaviours'. 'The moment of methodical objectivism, an inevitable but still abstract moment, demands its own transcendence,'[9] without which sociology is doomed to run aground on the reefs of the realism of the structure or to get stuck in mechanistic explanations unfit to grasp the practical logic that governs conduct. And it is against the neo-Kantian tradition and its vision of the transcendental thinking subject that Bourdieu (re)introduces the concept of habitus in order to restore to the socialized body its function as active operator of the construction of the real.

Impersonal science, undivided and im-pertinent

Social science is, for Bourdieu as for Durkheim, an eminently serious matter, grave even, because it is the bearer of a great historical 'burden'. Practicing it implies an austere scientific ethic, which is defined by a triple refusal.

Refusal of worldly seductions, first of all, to which Bourdieu attaches, more firmly yet than Durkheim had, the condemnation of the pliancies of intellectual and political prophetism. According to the theorist of anomie, sociology must imperatively 'renounce worldly success' and 'assume the esoteric character that is appropriate to all science'. Bourdieu goes further: the particular difficulty that the science of society encounters in grounding its authority derives from the fact that it is a fundamentally esoteric discipline that presents all appearances of being exoteric, in continuity with 'the vulgar'.[10] This makes of the sociology of the fields of cultural production and of the diffusion of their products, not one chapter among others, but an indispensable tool of sociological epistemology – and of sociological morality. Bourdieu maintains in addition that the analysis of the historical process whereby the scientific universe wrenched itself, however imperfectly, from the pull of history, furnishes the means for reinforcing the social bases of the rationalist commitment which entry into this universe presupposes and produces at the same time.[11]

If sociology owes itself to avoid all compromising with the world, it should not for that withdraw from it. Bourdieu makes entirely his Durkheim's formula according to which sociological inquiries would be worth 'not one hour of trouble if they were to have only a speculative interest' and to remain 'an expert knowledge reserved for experts'.[12] To be socially pertinent, in touch with the sociopolitical reality of its time, social science has a duty to be *im-pertinent*, in the double sense of irreverence to and distance from established powers and established ways of thinking. It must practise that 'ruthless criticism of everything existing' for which the young Marx called in a famous article in the *Rheinische Zeitung*, and first of all a criticism of itself, of its illusions and limitations. Bourdieu departs here from the Durkheimian framework to defend the idea that scientific autonomy and political engagement can grow more intense in concert and give each other mutual support, whenever intellectuals apply themselves to instituting *collective* forms of organization and intervention liable to put the authority of scientific reason in the service of the 'corporatism of the universal' which, whether they want it or not, is their legacy and for which they are accountable.[13]

This *refusal of confinement within the scholarly microcosm* is made possible by the reciprocal checks of which the scientific community is the support and locus. For Durkheim, science, 'because it is objective, is something essentially impersonal', which implies that it 'cannot progress except by a collective labour'.[14] Bourdieu extends this idea by arguing that the true subject of the scientific enterprise, if there is one, is not the individual-sociologist but the scientific field *in toto*, that is, the ensemble of the relations of collision-collusion that obtain between the protagonists who struggle in this 'world apart' wherein those strange historical animals called historical truths are born.

It is also within this collective practice embracing a multiplicity of objects, epochs, and analytic techniques that the *refusal of disciplinary fragmentation and of theoreticism*, as well as of the conceptual mummification fostered by the 'forced division' of scientific labor, is declared. Durkheim and Bourdieu exhibit the same disdain for the scholastic posture that leads those who adopt it – or who are adopted by it – to that cult of the 'concept for concept's sake' which periodically comes back into fashion on one or the other side of the Atlantic according to a pendulum-swing hardly disturbed by the acceleration of the international circulation of ideas.

The 'lack of taste' that Durkheim affected 'for that prolix and formal dialectic' which propels the sociologist into orbit in the pure heaven of ideas has not always been realized. The unequivocal condemnation of it that he proffers in the course of a review is worth citing *in extenso*:

> Here again is one of those books of philosophical generalities about the nature of society, and of generalities through which it is difficult to sense a very intimate and practical intercourse with social reality. Nowhere does the author give the impression that he has entered into direct contact with the facts about which he speaks ... However great the dialectical and literary talent of the authors, one could not go too far in denouncing the scandal of a method that so offends all our scientific habits and yet is still quite widely used. We no longer nowadays admit that one speculates about the nature of life without being first initiated into the techniques of biology. By what privilege could we permit the philosopher to speculate about society, without entering into commerce with the details of social facts?[15]

This is a formulation that would not be denied by Pierre Bourdieu, who has stated time and again his disapproval of that 'theoreticist theory', severed from all research activity and unduly reified as an academic specialty, which serves so often as a G-string to cover up scientific infirmity. Theory, as Bourdieu conceives it, is *praxis* and not *logos*; it is incarnated and actualized by the controlled implementation of the epistemic principles of construction of the object. Consequently, it feeds 'less on purely theoretical confrontation with other theories than on confrontation with ever-new empirical objects'.[16]

The key concepts that make up the hard core of Bourdieu's sociology – habitus, capital, field, social space, symbolic violence – are so many *programmes of organized questioning of the real* that serve to signpost the terrain of researches that must be all the more detailed and meticulous as one hopes to generalize their results via comparison. Accomplished theory, for the author of *Distinction*, takes after the chameleon more than the peacock: far from seeking to attract the eye to itself, it blends in with its empirical habitat; it borrows the colours, shades, and shapes of the concrete object, located in time and place, onto which it seems merely to hang but which it in fact *produces*.

History as a sociological still [*alambic*]

Durkheim and Bourdieu have in common the fact that they are commonly read as fundamentally ahistorical, if not anti-historical, authors. The 'functionalism' of the former, engrossed with theorizing the 'Hobbesian problem' of social order (if one believes Talcott Parsons's canonical exegesis), is alleged to be congenitally incapable of incorporating social change and the irruption of the event. The 'reproduction theory' commonly attributed to the latter is depicted as an infernal machine for abolishing history, and the notion of habitus a conceptual strait-jacket aimed at locking the individual in the eternal repetition of a present frozen in an order of domination at once undivided and inescapable. In brief, Bourdieu and Durkheim are supposed to leave us culpably disarmed in the face of historicity. Nothing, on closer look, could be further removed from both the intent and content of their thought. [17]

Émile Durkheim is an eminently historical sociologist, first, in that all of his investigations partake of a project *of current relevance* (*actualité*), which is to contribute, by way of scientific analysis, to resolving the crisis, diagnosed as 'moral', which is shaking the societies of Europe to their core right before his eyes. The theoretical issue that obsesses him is not to elaborate a conception of social order *in abstracto* but to identify the changing conditions and mechanisms of solidarity in the era of industrial modernity, and thereby to facilitate the maturation of the morality fit for the new social relations. Durkheimian sociology is also historical in the sense that it purports to catch hold of institutions in the movement of their becoming and that its harmonious development requires an active and reflective collaboration with historiography.

For Durkheim, history can and must play 'in the order of social realities a role analogous to that of the microscope in the order of physical realities'. [18] It captures in its nets the particular expressions of the social laws and types which sociology discerns. And only the 'genetic method', which compares the diverse incarnations of a given institution, allows one 'to follow its integral development through all social species', to distinguish the *efficient causes* that have brought it about from the social *functions* that it performs on the synchronic level, and, consequently, to establish its normal (or pathological) character. 'To my knowledge, there is no sociology worthy of the name which does not assume a historical character', Durkheim proclaims during a debate with Charles Seignobos. And he insists he is 'convinced' that sociology and history 'are destined to become ever more intimately related, and that a day will come when the historical spirit and the sociological spirit will differ only in nuances'. [19]

If Durkheim's sociology, judiciously interpreted, must be held to be historical by virtue of its make and its method, that of Bourdieu deserves the qualifier *historicist*. [20] It is no exaggeration to consider that, for Bourdieu, the social is nothing other than history – already made, in the making, or to be made. So much so that one could describe his intellectual project, which some might against his will call philosophical, but after all the label matters little, as a *historicization of the transcendental project of philosophy* (seen from this angle, Bourdieu would be a sort of anti-Heidegger, since as we know that Heidegger's ambition was to ontologize history). [21]

Here, again, Bourdieu leans on Durkheimian positions in order better to go beyond them, especially by bringing the historical dimension onto the territory of social ontology and social epistemology. He impugns first of all the distinction, on which the director of the *Année sociologique* sought to found the possibility of a 'true historical science', between 'historical events' and

110

'permanent social functions',[22] and the artificial antinomies which undergird it, between nomothetic and ideographic approaches, conjuncture and *longue durée*, the unique and the universal. And he calls for working towards a truly unified science of humans, 'where history would be a historical sociology of the past and sociology a social history of the present',[23] starting from the postulate that social action, social structure, and social knowledge are all equally the product of the work of history.

Such a science must, to fullfill its mission, effect a *triple historicization*. Historicization of the *agent*, to begin with, by dismantling the socially constituted system of embodied schemata of judgement and action (habitus) that govern her conduct and representations and orients her strategies. Historicization of the various *social worlds* (fields) in which socialized individuals invest their desires and energies and abandon themselves to that endless race for recognition that is social existence. For, according to Bourdieu, practice no more results from the agent's subjective intentions alone than they flow directly from the objective constraints of the structure. It emerges, rather, in the turbulences of their confluence, from 'the more or less 'successful' encounter between positions and dispositions'; it is born from the obscure relation of 'ontological proximity' that weaves itself between these 'two modes of existence of the social' that are field and habitus, 'history objectified in things' and 'history incarnate in bodies'.[24]

Once the subterranean connections between embodied history and reified history have been elucidated, it remains finally to carry out the historicization of the *knowing subject and of the instruments of knowledge* by means of which she constructs her object, as well as of the universe in which the knowledge under consideration is produced and circulates (in this, Bourdieu is infinitely closer to Foucault than to Lévi-Strauss). To summarize:

> If one is convinced that being is history, which has no beyond, and that one must thus ask biological history (with the theory of evolution) and sociological history (with the analysis of the collective and individual sociogenesis of forms of thought) for the truth of a reason that is historical through and through and yet irreducible to history, then one must admit also that it is by historicization (and not by the decisive dehistoricization of a sort of theoretical 'escapism') that one may try to wrench reason more completely from historicity.[25]

Such a sociology, simultaneously and *inseparably structural and genetic*, can envisage explaining (and not only describing) the unforeseen advent of crisis, the sudden breakthrough of 'genius', the transformational unfolding of action that make for the great social and symbolic revolutions whereby history abruptly redraws its course. Thus 'it is by historicizing him completely that one can understand completely how [Flaubert] wrests himself from the strict historicity of less heroic destinies', the originality of his enterprise emerging in full view only as 'one reinserts it in the historically constituted space within which it was constructed'.[26]

This historicizing sociology can also purport to bring to light, and thus better to curb, the historical determinisms to which, as every historical practice, it is necessarily submitted. Durkheim asks history to *nourish* sociology; Bourdieu expects it to *liberate* sociology from the historical subconscious, scientific as well as social, of past generations that weighs with all its dead weight on the brain of the researcher. What is instituted by history can be 'restituted' only by history; historical sociology alone, therefore, offers to the sociologist, as historical agent and scholarly producer, 'the instruments of a true awakening of consciousness or, better, of a true *self-mastery*'. Free thinking, Bourdieu holds, comes at this price: it can 'be conquered [only] by a historical anamnesis capable of unveiling everything that, in thought, is the forgotten product of the work of history'.[27]

The 'indirect experimentations' of ethnology

Another methodological procedure equally prized by Durkheim and Bourdieu is one in which ethnology is typically entrusted with the lead role: the quest for the *experimentum crucis*, the test-phenomenon or the key-puzzle that will allow one, either to reformulate (and thus to resolve) the great questions bequeathed by philosophy in historical and empirical terms, or to effect a *demonstratio a fortiori*, bearing on the case presumed to be the least favourable, so as to win over the approval of even readers most restive to the model or to the mode of reasoning put forth.

Thus it is that, after having, in his dissertation thesis, climbed the rock of morality said to be impregnable by positive study, Durkheim chooses suicide as the object of a 'study in sociology'. This tragic march along the edge of one's interior abyss at the end of which the individual, through an intimate path inaccessible to the gaze 'from outside', comes to deprive herself of that most precious good which is her life, 'would seem to concern psychology alone'. To demonstrate that such an 'individual act which affects only the individual himself' – and which poses in concrete, measurable, terms two of philosophy's perennial enigmas, that of death and that of the will – is the resultant of social forces 'of great generality', is to demonstrate at the same time that there is no behaviour which is not 'the extension of a social state', and that sociological explanation can without harm leave aside 'the individual as individual, his motives and his ideas'.[28]

Bourdieu's 'suicide' is the aesthetic disposition, that 'love of art' that experiences itself as 'freed from conditions and conditionings', and that properly defines bourgeois culture, or, more generally, taste, that other, but more common, name for habitus.[29] Here again, what is more personal, more ineffable, more in-determinate (and thus seemingly undetermined) than that capacity for discernment which, to borrow the idiom of Kant, claims 'universal validity' although it arises out of that private reaction to the objects of the world which is the pleasure of the senses and seems by nature to exclude all 'decision by means of proof'? *Distinction* draws a vast ethnological tableau of the lifestyles and cultural propensities of social classes in order to establish the structural homology that links, through the mediation of the space of dispositions, the space of positions and the space of position-takings in such varied domains as food and music, cosmetics and politics, furniture and conjugal love. Whence it turns out that, far from being the inimitable signature of a free individual, taste is the form par excellence of submission to social destiny. Now, if things at first glance as insignificant as the manner of drinking one's coffee and wiping one's mouth at the table, the reading of a newspaper and one's favorite sport function as so many marks of distinction, exterior signs of (interior) wealth, (cultural) capitals, what practice can claim to escape this struggle over classifications that is the hidden face of the class struggle?

As Durkheim before him, Bourdieu is fond of supporting his theoretical schemas by means of binary comparisons between so-called 'traditional' or 'precapitalist' societies and 'highly differentiated' social formations (a furiously Durkheimian designation), wherein *recourse to ethnology serves as a technique of sociological quasi-experimentation.*[30] It is well known that Durkheim chose the Australian totemic system as the empirical basis for his quest for the collective foundations of religious belief and, beyond, the social origin of the frameworks of human understanding, because he saw in it 'the most primitive and simple religion that exists', thus the one most apt to 'reveal to us an essential and permanent aspect of humanity'. The 'very lack of refinement' of the so-called inferior religions, according to him, made of them 'convenient experiments, where the facts and their relations are easier to make out'.[31]

The Kabyle society which Bourdieu, as an ethnosociologist, studied at the height of the Algerian war of national liberation and, to a lesser degree (or less visibly, owing to a modesty that one suspects is both professional and personal), the Béarn villages of his childhood are for him what the totemic clans of inner Australia were for Durkheim: a sort of 'strategic research site' (as Robert Merton would say), capable of bringing to light in their 'purified' state, as if passed through a filter, mechanisms that it would be too difficult – or too painful– to bring into focus in a more familiar social environment. For Bourdieu, scrutinizing the practices and symbolic relations of weakly differentiated societies is the means for effecting a *radicalization of the socioanalytical intention*, i.e. for exposing the social unconscious nestled in the infolds of the body, cognitive categories, and institutions that seem most innocent and anecdotic.

This radicalizing function of ethnology is nowhere more noticeable than in the analysis to which Bourdieu submits 'masculine domination' in the course of a pivotal text that implicitly contains the core of his theory of symbolic violence as well as a paradigmatic illustration of the distinctive use to which he turns the comparative method.[32] The mythico-ritual practices of the Kabyle are distant enough that deciphering them allows for a rigorous objectivation; yet they are near enough to facilitate that 'participant objectivation' which alone can trigger the return of the repressed for which, as gendered beings, we are all depositories. Proof is found in those homologies, that one could not make up, between the purest categories of the purest philosophical and psychoanalytic thought (those of Kant, Sartre, and Lacan) and the paired oppositions that organize the ritual acts, myths, and oral tradition of the Berber-speaking mountain dwellers. 'Ethnology promotes astonishment before what passes most completely unnoticed, i.e. what is most profound and most profoundly unconscious in our ordinary experience'.[33] In that, it is, not an auxiliary, but an indispensable ingredient of the sociological method. Bourdieu's ethnological detour is not, properly speaking, a detour, but a *bypass* liable to clear for us an access to the social unthought that forms the invisible plinth of our ways of doing and being.

Appendix: Bourdieu's '*Suicide*'

I have entitled my remarks 'Bourdieu's *Suicide*' because *Distinction* is to Pierre Bourdieu what *Suicide* was to Emile Durkheim: what Francis Bacon calls an *experimentum crucis*, a 'critical experiment' designed to demonstrate, first, the generic potency of the sociological method – against the claims of philosophy – and, second, the fecundity of a distinctive theoretical schema – the theory of practice anchored by the conceptual triad of habitus, capital, and field.

When Bourdieu undertakes his 'critique of judgment' (the subtitle of *Distinction*, in reference to Immanuel Kant's famous three 'Critiques of judgment'), the notion of taste enjoys at best a marginal status in the social sciences. Apart from Max Weber's brief considerations on the 'stylization' of life, Thorstein Veblen's theory of conspicuous consumption, and Norbert Elias's (then little-known) study of the 'civilizing process', the notion has been abandoned to philosophers of mind and aesthetics, on the one side, and to biologists, on the other. It is deemed either too high or too lowly an object for the sociologist to bother with.

In *Distinction*, and in related studies of cultural practices upon which it builds (notably *Photography: A Middle-Brow Art*, 1965, and *The Love of Art: European Museums and their Public*, 1966), Bourdieu effects a Copernican revolution in the study of taste. He abolishes the sacred frontier that makes legitimate culture a separate realm and repatriates aesthetic consumption into everyday consumptions. He demonstrates that aesthetic judgment is a social ability by virtue of both its genesis and its functioning. In so doing, Bourdieu offers not only a radical 'social critique of judgement'. He also delivers a graphic account of the workings of culture and power in contemporary society. And he elaborates a theory of class that fuses the Marxian insistence on economic determination with the Weberian recognition of the distinctiveness of the cultural order and the Durkheimian concern for classification.

1 A theory of perception and judgment

First, Bourdieu shows that, far from expressing some unique inner sensibility of the individual, aesthetic judgement is an eminently *social faculty*, resulting from class upbringing and education. To appreciate a painting, a poem, or a symphony presupposes mastery of the specialized symbolic code of which it is a materialization, which in turn requires possession of the proper kind of cultural capital. Mastery of this code can be acquired by osmosis in one's milieu of origin or by explicit teaching. When it comes through native familiarity (as with the children of cultured upper-class families), this trained capacity is experienced as an individual gift, an innate inclination testifying to spiritual worth. The Kantian theory of 'pure aesthetic', which philosophy presents as universal, is but a stylized – and mystifying – account of this particular experience of the 'love of art' that the bourgeoisie owes to its privileged social position and condition (this point is revisited in historical fashion in *The Rules of Art*, in which Bourdieu retraces the historical genesis of the artistic field, which is the 'objective' counterpart to the emergence of the 'pure' aesthetic disposition among privileged classes).

2 Social judgement as a relational system of oppositions and complementarities

A second major argument of *Distinction* is that the aesthetic sense exhibited by different classes and class fractions, and the lifestyles associated with them, define themselves in opposition to one another: *taste is first and foremost the distaste of the tastes of others*. ('In matters of taste, more than anywhere else, any determination is negation; and tastes are no doubt first and foremost distastes, disgust provoked by horror or visceral intolerance ("sick-making") of the taste of others', Bourdieu 1984: 56). This is because any cultural practice – wearing tweed or jeans, playing golf or soccer, going to museums or to auto shows, listening to jazz or watching sitcoms, etc. – takes its social meaning, and its ability to signify social difference and distance, not from some intrinsic property it has but from its location in a system of like objects and practices. To uncover the social logic of consumption thus requires establishing, not a direct link between a given practice and a particular class category (e.g., horseback riding and the gentry), but the structural correspondences that obtain between two constellations of relations, the space of lifestyles and the space of social positions occupied by the different groups.

3 A theory of social space

Bourdieu reveals that this space of social positions is organized by *two cross-cutting principles of differentiation, economic capital and cultural capital*, whose distribution defines the two oppositions that underpin major lines of cleavage and conflict in advanced society. (We must note here that while Bourdieu's demonstration is carried out with French materials, his theoretical claims apply to all differentiated societies. For pointers on how to extract general propositions from Bourdieu's specific findings on France and to adapt his models to other countries and epochs, see 'A Japanese Reading of *Distinction*', Bourdieu, 1995).

The first, vertical, division pits agents holding large volumes of either capital – the dominant class – against those deprived of both – the dominated class. The second, horizontal, opposition arises among the dominant, between those who possess much economic capital but few cultural assets (business owners and managers, who form the dominant fraction of the dominant class), and those whose capital is preeminentaly cultural (intellectuals and artists, who anchor the dominated fraction of the dominant class). Individuals and families continually strive to maintain or improve their position in social space by pursuing strategies of reconversion whereby they transmute or exchange one species of capital into another. The conversion rate between the various species of capital, set by such institutional mechanisms as the school system, the labour market, and inheritance laws, turns out to be one of the central stakes of social struggles, as each class or class fraction seeks to impose the hierarchy of capital most favorable to its own endowment. (This is explored further by Bourdieu in *The State Nobility*.)

4 Distinction, necessity, and cultural goodwill: three kinds of class taste

Having mapped out the structure of social space, Bourdieu demonstrates that the *hierarchy of lifestyles is the misrecognized retranslation of the hierarchy of classes*. To each major social position, bourgeois, petty-bourgeois, and popular, corresponds a class habitus undergirding three broad kinds of tastes.

The 'sense of distinction' of the bourgeoisie is the manifestation, in the symbolic order, of the latter's distance from material necessity and long-standing monopoly over scarce cultural goods. It accords primacy to form over function, manner over matter, and celebrates the 'pure pleasure' of the mind over the 'coarse pleasure' of the senses (to use Kant's idiom). More importantly, bourgeois taste defines itself by negating the 'taste of necessity' of the working classes. The latter may indeed be described as an inversion of the Kantian aesthetic: it subordinates form to function and refuses to autonomize judgement from practical concerns, art from everyday life (for instance, workers use photography to solemnize the high points of collective life and prefer pictures that are faithful renditions of reality over photos that pursue visual effects for their own sake).

Caught in the intermediate zones of social space, the petty bourgeoisie displays a taste characterized by 'cultural goodwill': they know what the legitimate symbolic goods are but they do not know how to consume them in the proper manner – with the ease and insouciance that comes from familial habituation. They bow before the sanctity of bourgeois culture but, because they do not master its code, they are perpetually at risk of revealing their middling position in the very movement whereby they strive to hide it by aping the practices of those above them in the economic and cultural order.

116

5 Cultural consumption, the hidden dimension of class struggle

But Bourdieu does not stop at drawing a map of social positions, tastes, and their relationships. He shows that the *contention between groups in the space of lifestyles is a hidden, yet fundamental, dimension of class struggles.* For to impose one's art of living is to impose at the same time principles of vision of the world that legitimize inequality by making the divisions of social space appear rooted in the inclinations of individuals rather than the underlying distribution of capital. Against Marxist theory, which defines classes exclusively in the economic sphere, by their position in the relations of production, Bourdieu argues that classes arise in the conjunction of shared position in social space and shared dispositions actualized in the sphere of consumption: 'The *representations* that individuals and groups inevitably engage in their practices is part and parcel of their social reality. A class is defined as much by its *perceived being* as by its being' (Bourdieu, 1979/ 1984: 564). Insofar as they enter into the very constitution *of* class, social classifications are instruments of symbolic domination and constitute a central stake in the struggle *between* classes (and class fractions), as each tries to gain control over the classificatory schemata that command the power to conserve or change reality by preserving or altering the representation of reality.

To conclude: *Distinction* provides a sociological answer (i.e. a historical and empirical answer) to one of the grand questions of philosophy, the question of the origins and operations of judgment. It shows that, just as suicide varies according to social factors, taste, far from being the ultimate repository of spontaneous individuality, is a transfigured expression of social necessity. By revealing taste as simultaneously weapon and stake in the classification struggles whereby groups seek to maintain or improve their position in society by imposing their lifestyle as the sole legitimate *art de vivre*, Bourdieu brings *homo aestheticus* back into the world of the mundane, the common and the contested, that is, back into the heartland of social science.

In the course of this demonstration, *Distinction* puts forth and illustrates a historicist theory of knowledge (encapsulated by the idea of *practical sense*, which is the original title of *The Logic of Practice*, the companion volume to *Distinction*), a dispositional theory of action (anchored by the notion of habitus) and a relational and agonistic conception of social space (summed up by the concept of field). And it unties the vexed nexus of culture, power, and identity in modern society. All in all, not a bad recipe for attaining classical status.

Acknowledgement

L. Wacquant, 'Durkheim et Bourdieu: le socle commun et ses fissures', *Critique*, 51, 1995, pp. 646–660. Translation by Tarik Wareh. The Appendix 'Bourdieu's *Suicide*' was originally prepared for the Panel on Classics of the Twentieth Century, World Congress, International Sociological Association, Montréal, Canada, 28 July, 1999.

Notes

1 Bourdieu has warned against that 'classificatory functioning of academic thought' (*Choses dites*, Paris, Éditions de Minuit, 1987 [= *In Other Words* (1990)], p. 38) which inclines one to wield theoretical labels as so many weapons of intellectual terrorism ('X is a Durkheimian' can be taken to mean 'X is only a vulgar Durkheimian' or again 'X is already entirely contained in Durkheim'). The same caveat would apply to Bourdieu's relations to Marx, Weber, Husserl, Merleau-Ponty, or Wittgenstein.

2 É. Durkheim, 'Sociology', in Woff, K.H. (ed.), *Émile Durkheim: Essays On Sociology and Philosophy*, New York: Harper, 1964, p. 373.

3 É. Durkheim, *Les Règles de la méthode sociologique*, Paris, Presses Universitaires de France, 1895/1981, p. ix [= *The Rules of Sociological Method* (1982), p. 33].

4 P. Bourdieu, *Questions de sociologie*, Éditions de Minuit, 1980, p. 44 [= *Sociology in Question*, London: Sage Publications, 1994].

5 P. Bourdieu, *Leçon sur la leçon*, Paris, Éditions de Minuit, 1982, p. 32 [= 'Lecture on the Lecture,' in *In Other Words*, new edition, 1994]. On this point, see also *Raisons pratiques* [= *Practical Reasons* (1998)] (Paris: Seuil, 1994, esp. chap. 3 and 7), and the conference entitled 'La cause de la science' with which Bourdieu opens the debate in the issue of *Actes de la recherche en sciences sociales* devoted to 'The Social History of the Social Sciences' (106–107, March 1995, pp. 3–10).

6 Cf. P. Bourdieu, 'Sur le pouvoir symbolique', *Annales ESC*, 32: 3, 1977, pp. 405–411 [= 'On Symbolic Power', in *Language and Symbolic Power*, Cambridge: Harvard University Press, 1990]; *Choses dites*, pp. 13–15 and 53–54; (with J.-C. Passeron), 'Sociology and Philosophy in France Since 1945: Death and Resurrection of a Philosophy Without Subject', *Social Research*, 34: 1, 1968, pp. 162–212

7 É. Durkheim, 'L'enseignement de la philosophie dans les universités allemandes', *Revue internationale de l'enseignement*, 13, 1887, p. 330. For an interpretation of Durkheimism as 'sociologized Kantism', see D. Lacapra, *Émile Durkheim, Sociologist and Philosopher* (Ithaca, Cornell University Press, 1972); for a Kantian reading of Bourdieu, see P.R. Harrison, 'Bourdieu and the Possibility of a Postmodern Sociology', *Thesis Eleven*, 35, 1993, pp. 36–50.

8 The first citation is from Bourdieu (*Leçon sur la leçon*, p. 29), the second from Durkheim (*Le Suicide. Étude de sociologie*, Paris: Presses Universitaires de France, 1897/1930 [= *Suicide* (1951)], p. 349).

9 P. Bourdieu et al., *Un Art moyen*, Paris: Éditions de Minuit, 1965, p. 22 [= *Photography: A Middle-Brow Art*, Cambridge: Polity Press, 1994]; also on this point, 'The Three Forms of Theoretical Knowledge', *Social Science Information*, 12, 1973, pp. 53–80, and *Le Sens pratique*, Paris, Éditions de Minuit, 1980 [= *The Logic of Practice* (1990)], Book I.

10 É. Durkheim, *Les Règles de la méthode sociologique*, p. 144 [= *The Rules of Sociological Method*, p. 163], and P. Bourdieu, *Leçon sur la leçon*, p. 25.

11 P. Bourdieu, 'The Peculiar History of Scientific Reason', *Sociological Forum*, 5: 2, 1991, pp. 3–26.

12 The first part of the citation is drawn from Durkheim, *De la Division du travail social* (Paris, Presses Universitaires de France, 1883/1930, p. xxxix [= *The Division of Labor in Society* (1984), p. xxvi], the second from Bourdieu, *Questions de sociologie*, p. 7.

13 P. Bourdieu, 'The Corporatism of the Universal: The Role of Intellectuals in the Modern World', *Telos* 81, 1989, pp. 99–110, and 'Für eine Realpolitik der Vernunft' in S. Müller-Rolli (ed.), *Das Bildungswesen der Zukunft*, Stuttgart, Ernst Klett, 1987, pp. 229–234.

14 É. Durkheim, 'Préface', *Année sociologique* (1896–1897), reprinted in *Journal sociologique*, Paris, Presses Universitaires de France, 1969, p. 36.

15 É. Durkheim, *Année sociologique* (1905–1906), reprinted in *Journal sociologique*, p. 565.

16 P. Bourdieu, *Les Règles de l'art*, Paris, Seuil, 1992 [= *The Rules of Art* (1996)], p. 251, and 'The Genesis of the Concepts of "Habitus" and "Field"', *Sociocriticism* 2: 2, 1985, especially pp. 11–12.

17 An excellent discussion of Durkheim's relationship to history and historiography can be found in R.N. Bellah, 'Durkheim and History', *American Sociological Review*, 24: 4, 1958, pp. 447–461. For a partial inventory of Bourdieu's views on history, change, and time, see P. Bourdieu and L. Wacquant, *An Invitation to Reflexive Sociology*, Chicago: The University of Chicago Press, 1992, pp. 79–81, 89–94, 101, 132–140; *The Logic of Practice*, Chapter 6; *Choses dites*, pp. 56–61; *Raisons pratiques*, pp. 76–80 and 169–174; (with R. Chartier and R. Darnton), 'Dialogue à propos de l'histoire culturelle', *Actes de la recherche en sciences sociales*, 59, 1985, pp. 86–93; and 'Sur les rapports entre la sociologie et l'histoire en Allemagne et en France', *ibid.*, 106–107, 1995, pp. 108–122.

18 É. Durkheim, 'Sociologie et sciences sociales' (1909), in *La Science sociale et l'action*, Paris: Presses Universitaires de France, 1970, p. 154.

19 É. Durkheim, 'Préface', *Année sociologique* (1897–1898), reprinted in *Journal sociologique*, p. 139; *Les Règles de la méthode sociologique*, pp. 137–138 [= *The Rules of Sociological Method*, p. 157]; 'Débat sur l'explication en histoire et en sociologie' (1908), in *Textes*, Éditions de Minuit, 1968, vol. 1, p. 199; and *La Science sociale et l'action*, p. 157, respectively.

20 As Philip Abrams has rightly suggested in *Historical Sociology* (Ithaca: Cornell University Press, 1982).

21 P. Bourdieu, *L'Ontologie politique de Martin Heidegger*, Paris: Éditions de Minuit, 1988 [= *The Political Ontology of Martin Heidegger* (1991)]; as well as 'Les sciences sociales et la philosophie', *Actes de la recherche en sciences sociales*, 47–48, 1983, pp. 45–52; and *Raisons pratiques, passim*.

22 É. Durkheim, 'Débat sur l'explication en histoire et en sociologie', pp. 212–213.

23 P. Bourdieu, 'Sur les rapports entre la sociologie et l'histoire en Allemagne et en France', p. 111.

24 P. Bourdieu, 'Men and Machines', in K. Knorr-Cetina and A. Cicourel (eds), *Advances in Social Theory and Methodology*, London: Routledge and Kegan Paul, 1981, p. 313; *La Noblesse d'État*, Paris, Éditions de Minuit, 1989 [= *The State Nobility* (1996)], p. 59; and *Leçon sur la leçon*, p. 38, respectively.

25 P. Bourdieu, *Les Règles de l'art*, pp. 427–428.

26 P. Bourdieu, *Les Règles de l'art*, p. 145.

27 P. Bourdieu, 'Le mort saisit le vif. Les relations entre l'histoire incorporée et l'histoire réifiée', *Actes de la recherche en sciences sociales*, 32–33, 1980, p. 14, and *Les Règles de l'art*, p. 429.

28 É. Durkheim, *Le Suicide*, pp. 8, 33, 148.

29 P. Bourdieu, *Distinction*, Paris, Éditions de Minuit, 1979 [= *Distinction* (1984)], and (with A. Darbel and D. Schnapper) *L'Amour de l'art*, Paris: Éditions de Minuit, 1966. (See the analysis of *Distinction* as 'Bourdieu's *Suicide*' in the appendix)

30 Bourdieu says that he conceived his comparative investigations of the matrimonial customs of the peasants of Kabylia and of the Béarn as 'a sort of epistemological experimentation' (*Choses dites*, p. 75). See, e.g., P. Bourdieu, 'La société traditionelle: attitude à l'égard du temps et conduite économique', *Sociologie du travail*, 5: 1, 1963, pp. 24–44, and 'Les relations entre les sexes dans la société paysanne', *Les Temps modernes*, 195, 1962, pp. 307–331. On the Durkheimian uses of ethnology, see V. Karady, 'French Ethnology and the Durkheimian Breakthrough', *Journal of the Anthropological Society of Oxford*, 12: 3, 1981, pp. 166–176.

31 É. Durkheim, *Les Formes élémentaires de la vie religieuse*, Paris: Presses Universitaires de France, 1912/1960, pp. 2 and 11 [= *The Elementary Forms of Religious Life* (1995), pp. 1 and 8].

32 P. Bourdieu, 'La domination masculine', *Actes de la recherche en sciences sociales*, 84, 1990, pp. 2–31. One may read in the same vein the superb, if little read, article, 'Reproduction interdite. La dimension symbolique de la domination économique', *Études rurales*, 113–114, 1989, pp. 15–36.

33 P. Bourdieu, 'Division du travail, rapports sociaux de sexe et de pouvoir', *Cahiers du GEDISST*, 11, 1994, p. 94. The methodical 'ethnologization' of the familiar world can exercise a similar effect, cf. the 'Preface' to the English edition of *Homo academicus* (Cambridge, Polity Press, 1988) and the conclusion to *La misère du monde* (Paris: Editions du Seuil, 1993 [= *The Weight of the World*, Cambridge, Polity Press, 1999]).

Section III: The sociology of culture

Introduction to Section III

John Orr

John Orr's essay reassesses the theory of modernism found in Bourdieu (1996), in the light of Eagleton's argument concerning the historical distinctiveness of the Irish reactionary avant-garde (Yeats, Gomme, Markiewicz, etc.). It reveals that Bourdieu's analysis of the centre/periphery contrasts in literary space shows a potential for rupture at the periphery. In Ireland – England's graveyard – Eagleton shows the emergence of an Irish Renaissance, which, due to the absence of a realist tradition in Ireland, is a crucial exception to the centralizing tendency of the routinized modernism to which *The Rules of Art* allude. This is a fertile exploration of Marxist cultural theory and especially of Goldmann's *The Hidden God*, with its theory of the wager, as the concealed agenda behind the work of both Eagleton and Bourdieu. It illuminatingly examines the sociological conditions for a tragic modernist vision.

Nick Prior

Nick Prior, on the other hand, writes of the flourishing of middle-class culture in the city of Edinburgh and the emergence of new institutions which responded to this. One such was the civic or national art gallery. He studies in this essay the struggles between the older Royal Institution gallery, with its aristocratic patronage and slender facilities for living artists and the National Gallery of Scotland (1851), which aimed to free artists of their belief in the necessity for heteronomous control. In a situation of bitter conflict, the decisive move was the resiting of the Royal Scottish Academy within the new National Gallery. But the artists' 'purer' aesthetic went hand-in-hand with a more rigorous definition of art, excluding those forms which could be classified as possessing a craft element. Despite the expanding number of visitors and the greater degree of artists' control, the new gallery had an affinity with a more elevated and intellectualist conception of fine art. Prior thus provides an essential historical explanation of one gallery, which in turn is representative of the contemporary global pattern highlighted in Bourdieu's *The Love of Art*: the differentiated and unequal consumption of the museum's free symbolic goods.

Roger Cook

One of the very few Bourdieusian analyses of the transformations of the contemporary artistic field by a practising painter, Cook trenchantly assesses the recent configurations of culture with the rise of new forms of patronage, market intervention and media exposure. Portraying the whole field at a single moment of time through the *Sensations* exhibition, he contrasts this with the current Los Angeles' art-world, comparing the work of the young British Artists, especially Damien Hirst, Rachel Whiteread and (later) Tracy Emin, with the Los Angelinos artist, Lari Pittman. The essay concludes that the relative erosion of the boundaries in Britain between the expanded and restricted fields – or commercial and autonomous art – is less likely to increase democratic participation than to pose severe dangers for the survival of critical, experimental practices

Derek M. Robbins

To what extent does the sociological assessment of a literary movement depend on elective affinities between the sociologist and his object of study? If Bourdieu characterizes Flaubert as a heroic modernist and Heidegger as an irrationalist whose stance is concealed by his imposition of philosophical form, is this characterization a consequence of his own position-takings within the field? Robbins raises these questions, using Coleridge as a case-study, arguing that his current place within the British literary tradition invites his assessment purely in aesthetic terms. However, the meaning of his consecration was the outcome of struggles within the field, and especially within the new academic area of English, where Coleridge's religious ideas were translated by authoritative critics into a secular conception of the poetic imagination. Such a consecrated approach has neglected, and continues to resist, the earlier radical cosmological views which led Coleridge to associate with scientists and to turn to a heterodox unitarian ministry.

Philippe Marlière

This chapter addresses the most publicly controversial aspect of Bourdieu's writing. As Marlière reports, Bourdieu argues that television, which could have been an extraordinary instrument of democracy, is quickly becoming an instrument of symbolic violence. Marlière's analysis of the text sets it in the context of comparative research on British and French media. He is persuaded by many of Bourdieu's arguments in *On Television* ... including both the complicity of French TV with a relentless instrumental rationality, which favours the pursuit of high ratings for commercial and bureaucratic reasons, and the culture of 'fast-reading' commentators or philosopher-journalists, whose confrontation with experts possessing scholarly expertise threatens both the reputations of the latter and, indeed, the autonomy of the scientific field. Aspects of Marlière's critique are well-founded, such as the assessment that the study fails to consider the total range of journalists participating in television, including investigative journalists, and passes over the effectiveness of peer-assessment. It raises the question, however, as to whether sociologists such as Bourdieu are claiming a privileged understanding of the social world.

Richard Hooker, Dominic Paterson and Paul Stirton

Three art historians engage with Bourdieu in a chapter that provides a dissenting note within the whole collection and indeed suggests how fragile the sociological project still is. Bourdieu is accused of a range of misconceptions (with many of which this editor would take issue). The most specific objections are that Bourdieu has produced an over-totalizing description of art history that takes no account of its diversity; that he has vainly attempted to distinguish between the subject of art history and the cultural production occurring within the avant-garde (including Land Art, minimalism, installation art etc.); that he has been doctrinaire at the expense of the facts – thus failing to note the existence of a considerable degree of artistic autonomy which a socio-genetic method cannot acknowledge – and, not least, that his whole theory is based on misconstruing Panofsky's key distinction between pre-iconongraphic, iconographic and the iconological hermeneutic levels. He has thus misapplied an analysis which was intended to refer to deficiencies in interpretation of a specific style or period and applied it instead to an educationally-differentiated public, in the form of the 'naive gaze'. Bourdieu is thus compared detrimentally with Foucault, Marin and Panofsky himself.

Hidden agenda: Pierre Bourdieu and Terry Eagleton

John Orr

I

On the face of it, Pierre Bourdieu and Terry Eagleton are worlds apart, coming from very different traditions, French sociology and English literary criticism. While both admire the work of the other and they have appeared together publicly in 1991 at the ICA in mutual discussion, that discourse highlights a clear degree of philosophical difference. (Bourdieu and Eagleton, 1992) Eagleton has staked much on his intellectual renewal of ideology-critique, yet Bourdieu firmly rejects ideology as a primary concept in favour of the concepts of 'doxa' and 'symbolic power' (Bourdieu, 1991). The stand-off has affected in particular their respective work on literature and culture which they barely discuss at the ICA meeting at all. Absurdly Bourdieu does not even appear in Eagleton's reader on Marxist literary theory (Eagleton and Milne, 1995). Yet if we look more closely there are key affinities. The intellectual range of both writers has always been vast but of the two, Bourdieu's is more immense. He is, among other things, art historian, anthropologist, philosopher of language, connoisseur of Flaubert, empirical researcher and finally in *Distinction* expert in the nuanced class differences of French cuisine (Bourdieu, 1984). Eagleton's expansion out of the narrow frame of English literary criticism has been achieved partly in the shadow of the late Raymond Williams but now encompasses, at the very least, politics, sociology, history and the philosophy of aesthetics. In literature itself, Eagleton's interest are by far the broader. Whereas Bourdieu is distinctly Francophile, Eagleton has always used, like Franco Moretti, a broad comparative and European frame for literary analysis. Bourdieu's analysis is largely contextual. Eagleton combines context with close reading. Despite this Eagleton is closer to the revision of the Marxian tradition undertaken by Bourdieu than Williams who for many might provide a more natural yardstick of comparison. After Williams's death, that affinity has crystallized but gone unnoticed. In understanding the radical post-Soviet revision of the Marxian analysis of culture, however, the link is crucial.

In the 1990s a post-Soviet Europe and the official end of the Cold War have created a major crisis in Marxian analysis which Williams did not live to experience and yet out of this, I want to argue, both Eagleton and Bourdieu have published their most important work on culture and modernity.

© The Editorial Board of The Sociological Review 2000. Published by Blackwell Publishers, 108 Cowley Road, Oxford OX4 1JF, UK and 350 Main Street, Malden, MA 02148, USA.

Bourdieu's *The Rules of Art* was published in 1992, Eagleton's *Heathcliff and the Great Hunger* in 1995. In the same period, other striking similarities have emerged through the English translations of Bourdieu's work in the 1970s and 1980s. Both engage in a neo-Marxian critique of aesthetics which is implacably hostile to Kant and to his twentieth century successor, Hans Georg Gadamer (Bourdieu, 1984: 250–1, 485f; Eagleton, 1990: 70–100; 1996: 61–7). Both sustain a radical critique which confronts Heidegger and his modishness, Bourdieu voraciously tearing apart the German's political ontology (Bourdieu, 1988; Eagleton, 1990: 288–315). Both have transformed their critique of literature by reading, in complementary ways, the essays of Walter Benjamin (Eagleton, 1981; Fowler, 1997: 89–92). Yet Benjamin's importance in the delicate process of rewriting cannot be understood without the extent of an earlier imprint on their sociology of literature – that of Lucien Goldmann. It is an imprint which both would now be reluctant to acknowledge, but *The Hidden God*, Goldmann's study of Pascal, Racine and Jansenism in the birth of Absolutist France is a crucial marker for their transformed visions of late nineteenth century culture and more crucially, of modernity itself.

Of course an immediate *caveat* can be issued, stressing differences which appear to be vital. In the late 1970s Eagleton nurtured a Leninist infatuation with the philosophy of Louis Althusser and the criticism of Pierre Macherey while Bourdieu was engaged in keeping his distance from Althusser's militant anti-humanism through his original theorizing of the *habitus* as a structural and organizing principle of existence which reinstates the subject within framework of an objectified social world (Bourdieu, 1990; Brubaker, 1993). Despite this early divergence Goldmann remained a driving force behind both writers. Bourdieu's genetic sociology is clearly indebted, as Bridget Fowler has noted, to Goldmann's genetic structuralism. (1997: 87–9) Eagleton's early literary monograph on the Brontes, to whom he returns at the start of *Heathcliff and the Great Hunger* is inspired by Goldmann's conceptualizing of the bourgeois world-vision in modern writing. We might want to say therefore that the hidden agenda of both is Goldmann's *The Hidden God* (Goldmann,1964). For sure, its dissection of philosophy and drama in the early bourgeois age underpins their respective discourses of literary writing at the inception of bourgeois modernity. For Bourdieu, Baudelaire, Flaubert and Manet are the heroic modernists working against the grain of an industralizing and modernizing France. For Eagleton, the Irish Renaissance is not purely literary but overtly cultural and political, giving birth to an 'archaic avant-garde', a living contradiction which signals impending national uprising and the breakdown of British rule. Seen this way the mature Irish movement undermines received definitions of high-modernism and the avant-garde. But there is a more fundamental point of contact. In both instances, French and Irish, artistic opposition to the polity embodies two key elements of Goldmann's vision. These two elements operate not only through the artwork both also the critical discourse which takes the artwork as its object. In both cases, it is a Pascalian *wager* on the future coupled with an aesthetic of *refusal*,

refusal of the living present within the oppositional group, the Jansenists of Port-Royal, the circles of the Irish avant-garde. This fusion of wager and refusal also appears in the critical theorist who always wishes to reject the present and stake a wager on the future. The world of the detached artist is mirrored in the world of the radical critic.

Let us look once more at Goldmann in his study of Pascal and Racine. Pascal's belief in God is at once a wager on a Being both absent and present at the same time, a necessary salvation from the sustained terror of infinite spaces. The world's catastrophes show no evidence of his Existence, and yet his power is source of all epistemology and piety in the human realm. The Pascalian wager is an activated form of faith, of acting as if God exists in spite of his absence from the daily world but it leads in the Jansenist circles to a pronounced ascesis in the search for Grace. Goldmann faces here the same dilemma as Weber in his reading of Calvinist fundamentalism. At origin the rejection of the present world is so fundamental it seems to provide no basis for an embryonic world-vision of a emergent group or class. This happens only through the progressive moderation of the foundational belief. Mediations are vital components of alteration, the compromise with emergent class interests the intrigues of power. Jansenism must change or die, as Calvinism also found out. Yet what entranced Goldmann was the historic point of purity of the refusal of the world, embodied in the tragic refusal of Racine's heroines to face the world of profane husbands and lovers or submit to their political power. Despite Goldmann's concern with the antagonisms between the intendants and the *noblesse de robe*, and that nuanced reading of class fractions which recalls Marx's writings on the 1848 revolutions, the more unmediated relationship is surely with the field of political power. Religious heresy is above all political, and what makes Goldmann's reading of tragedy more germane than ever is recent speculation on Marlowe and Shakespeare's links to the Catholic Recusants of late Elizabethan England. Heresy becomes a vantage-point for glossing the complex relationships of perfidy and power. (Nicholl, 1992; Wilson, 1997) Where Racine's open poetics are those of refusal and finality, Shakespeare's hidden agenda contains disguise, banishment, exile, the trading of identities and in *Hamlet* the active powers of indecision. The tragic repudiation of the game had as it were already been superseded by new dramatic forms of tragic game-playing, positing the choice of relationship to the field of power in post-classical tragedy. Either you played to lose, or you did not play at all.

Eagleton finds his English equivalent of tragic refusal initially in novel form. That refusal is equally coloured by religious heresy, this time by the Puritan subtext of Samuel Richardson's *Clarissa*. (Eagleton, 1982) Anachronistically underwritten by the militant feminism of the 1980s, this both limits and recharges Eagleton's discourse after the polemical impasse of Althusser. On the one hand, his Clarissa too is informed by female resistance to patriarchy, although of a different kind. On the other hand, feminism helps to crystallize a key point of gender resistance in the rise of the English novel which has much wider implications. Just as Phaedra and Andromaque are female allegories of tragic refusal, so Eagleton's Clarissa is a re-enactment of the topos of refusal at the start of a new literary form, an evolutionary narrative of unsuccessful resistance to rape, a sublimation in the style of Goldmann's ironic reverse appropriation of Freud, of the politico-religious into the intimate-erotic, a sexualization of faith and power, rather than empowerment of sexuality. For Eagleton in the late twentieth century it became possible to read it as a sexual politics *avant la lettre*, the novel as a genre of positive moralizing which can assume the ethical high-ground. An exemplary narrative, however, is no longer a tragic one so that paradoxically Clarissa's defensive but righteous virtue vitiates the tragic element in her fate, as does the unconvincing ending to the novel.

By the same token, Bourdieu takes on the topos of tragic refusal but in a later age and in a more ambitious way. For Richardson in the mid-seventeenth century, refusal would have been a subterranean strategy sublated in Clarissa's predicament but in Flaubert in the mid-nineteenth it becomes an open slogan and an aesthetic philosophy as well as a literary conceit. Here Bourdieu simultaneously recreates Flaubert and his quasi-biographical hero of *Sentimental Education*, Frédéric Moreau, in the image of Goldmann's Andromaque. At the same time, this is a *post-tragic* refusal of the world. Frédéric enters that world and plays its social games with distance and disdain. Likewise he survives the revolutionary turmoil of 1848 which he witnesses so assiduously in self-conscious echo of his author's own witnessing. Survival and disdain mark out not reaction or betrayal, the knee-jerk reaction of the orthodox Lukàcs, but a new aesthetic of disengagement. In Flaubert the writer's aesthetic is ascetic or it is nothing. For Bourdieu, 1848 is the genesis of modernity signified by the subversions of its Artistic other, modernism, which does *not* reflect the immanent tendencies of the bouregois world-vision in artistic terms, as it would in Goldmann's formula which he rejects (1993: 140). Rather it challenges the very self-constitution of such a vision, clawing away at its foundations in the key period before all forms of modern art in France become prone to consumption by their bourgeois patrons as indispensable forms of cultural capital. That is to say, before they become constituted by a discriminating bourgeois public as aesthetic objects of desire. Viewed in terms of cultural production, Baudelaire and Flaubert have the same historic function for Bourdieu in the evolution of French society as the Irish Revival has for Eagleton in the context of the British state. They generate a maverick modernism which perversely opposes the doxa of a progressive modernity, which signifies a localized but decisive rupture within the bourgeois world. In each case the terms upon which it does so are radically opposed. In Eagleton it is national rupture premised on cultural periphery and the division of landmass. In Bourdieu it is metropolitan in the centralizing tradition of French polity and culture. The struggle over modernity is also a struggle over the soul and topography of Paris.

Goldmann's 'wager' was unexpectedly made topical by the spontaneous uprisings of '68, which Lyotard has recently termed 'the last great historic adventure' of modernity. In New Wave cinema, *les événéments* marked the emergence of a new Maoist Jean-Luc Godard, but one of the most fascinating postscripts came from his more conservative associate, Eric Rohmer. In Rohmer's 1969 film *My Night with Maud*, Goldmann's thesis is cryptically invoked in drunken cafe conversation by the Marxist friend of Jean-Louis Trintignant, a prim Catholic hypocrite whom Rohmer gently mocks. The pair manage to argue over Pascal and Marx in Goldmannesque terms without mentioning Goldmann or the political events of the previous year. Rohmer's conscious double omission of Paris – for the film is set in Clermont-Ferrand not on the Left Bank – is far from obvious since for the viewer the pair are also arguing over the same woman, Maud, doctor and divorced mother who is the object of their erotic attention. Conversation thus becomes power discourse and it is apt for Rohmer, the Catholic director ironizing the search for Grace, that Trintignant, the Catholic *faux naif*, should win both battles, the sexual and the ideological, so unconvincingly. '68 thus becomes a marker of rise and fall of a revolutionary discourse, of the seamless interplay of its vitality and entropy. In the wake of that abortive wager on history Eagleton and Bourdieu both sought out earlier revolutionary situations as a yardstick by which to measure the adventures of the subversive artwork, situations whose revolutionary natures, 1848 Paris, 1916 Dublin, are shrouded in ambiguity. Of course time and place are different, and the choice of different histories is in part biographical. Bourdieu was the provincial son who came from the rural South-West to metropolitan Paris. Eagleton was born in the north of England to Irish Catholic parents. Yet for both '68 is the shadow which still haunts and prompts in the 1990s their readings of culture as a passage out of Marxism still indebted to Marx himself.

II

In the age of an impure aesthetic when writing has a greater academic cachet than fiction or philosophy, when the novel appears to be a consumer's feast and not a producer's art, when the Western canon is proclaimed under threat but is not really under threat, and when most writing anyway has become a poor sibling of the moving image, it seems strange that Bourdieu persists in unmasking the conceit of a pure aesthetic which no longer exists. In the decade before *The Rules of Art* it seemed indeed that Bourdieu's fixated unmasking of the pure artwork was in danger of succumbing to petit-bourgeois *Schaden-freude*. Moreover, it posed more questions than it answered. Once he has exposed the charisma of the great artist as a glaring act of consecration by adoring critics, by connoisseurs trading in the stock-exchange of cultural capital, does it get us any further in our understanding of the artwork itself? The answer is yes and no. In *The Rules of Art* Bourdieu decisively modulates his argument, and in doing so snatches victory, it can be argued out of the jaws of a reductionist defeat. Here the fragile equation of Durkheim with Weber works for once and kickstarts his discourse into new dimensions. For just as the aesthetic object of desire is changed and changed utterly by the collective act of consecrating (Durkheim), so the charisma of the creative 'genius' must endure the temporal curse of evanescence (Weber). For Bourdieu, perversely, the artist consecrated is the artist desacralized, and the artwork stripped of its aura by its retro-celebrity. At its most extreme, this new pattern is imprinted on the passage of all cultural destinies in the modern age. Critical rapture is the kiss of death and for that very reason critical criticism must return to source.

There are previous echoes of this, very strong ones, in Adorno and Benjamin whose work feeds into Bourdieu's radical aesthetic. Yet historical evanescence, which becomes the model of what happens to the heroic modernism of Baudelaire, Flaubert and Manet in following generations, is framed differently. When the art trio are finally found acceptable, they quickly become big cultural commodities. Consequently their aesthetic refusal of modernity is recuperated through cultural acclaim in which the connoisseurs of art stage-manage the games amateur consumers are teased into playing. This is a radical shift of focus from the previous work where the artist is often seen as little more than a structural sign, a pivotal point in the artistic field where all extraneous factors – social, cultural, political, converge. The act of endowment which he calls, quoting Benjamin, 'the fetish of the name of the master', was a ritual naming of that which is distinctive, a conferring of personal signature upon a collective product. To write of someone as distinctive – and Bourdieu has analysed in detail the many social meanings of distinction – is to endow a work with cultural capital which can be circulated among potential consumers. It may celebrate art but it also opens up the market for symbolic goods. In *The Rules of Art*, however, the discourse shifts the balance back towards the author of the artwork, but only under key conditions. In France those conditions constitute the genesis of modernism out of modernity as its monstrous artistic Other. They begin with the trials and tribulations of the Three Figures on the Cross, Baudelaire as Poetry, Flaubert as Fiction and Manet as Painting who are censored, tried in court or out of it, and greeted in their lifetime by public opprobrium. Bourdieu thus reconstitutes the artwork by historicizing it. If New Testament crucifixion is invoked it is because Old Testament parable underlies it. The Terrible Three emerge at that very moment when history offers up the chance of parallel celebration and deformation, recognition and transmutation into base commodity. If crucifixion signifies redemption, it also invokes the Fall. 1848 is the start of the modernist heroic made possible by an autonomous field of art, but also the parable of its Fall since it is the start of a system of cultural capital which devours it. In the seeds of its autonomy lies its own destruction.

Bourdieu here shows his debt to Goldmann and his rejection of him. In reading Flaubert's *Sentimental Education* he links the text to the literary field and then to the field of power much as Goldmann had done in his study of Port-Royal, but subversive writing is no longer the reflection of a world-vision of an emergent social class. Rather it is a refraction of a complex field of social possibilities which marks out the aesthetic of the *illusio* as the dominant (and genetically Flaubertian) form of modern fiction. Here placing Flaubert in history as Bourdieu does, by placing *Sentimental Education* within the socio-spatial topography of 1840s Paris is to rescue Flaubert from the impasse of the pure aesthetic which Flaubert himself had propagated, by placing himself squarely within the realm of the social. Durkheim famously suggested that in worshipping God we worship society. Here Bourdieu shows his Durkheimian credentials. For he implies that in worshipping Flaubert we do much the same thing.

Bourdieu's fascination with Flaubert as heroic modernist is a fascination with the material legacy of a creator of imaginary worlds who reproduces in vivid detail the illusion of the real, a sense of time and place both autonomous and unique. That he should chose the one major text of Flaubert which is both contemporary and Parisian, which combines the panoramic canvas of the city with the lure of illusory social ascent, speaks volumes about his own method of textual reading. If context is inherently social, which is how he looks at the active heresies of Baudelaire in Paris at the same time, then the textual reading which he finds most comforting is the one which readily opens out onto key elements of modernity, which charts movement not stasis and explores intersecting social networks rather than Flaubert's other literary worlds of the reclusive, the ascetic and the exotic. The moves that he makes here are conscious ploys in the critical arena. He moves against the fashion of seeing in Flaubert the purity of literary form or his work enacting, as Sartre claims, the psychodrama of his own provincial life as 'the idiot of the family', neurotically refusing his father's ambitions for him and consciously failing to emulate the conformist trajectory of his older brother. (Sartre, 1981) While Sartre considered Flaubert's impersonality aesthetic to be a form of bourgeois bad faith illuminated in the trial of the book of *Madame Bovary* Bourdieu sees as it a profound springboard for the artistic confrontation with the social at the moment of modernity.

Equally Bourdieu stakes out a version of the social artwork which differs from two the opposed versions of mimesis in Erich Auerbach and René Girard (Auerbach, 1968; Girard, 1976). Highlighting the role of the *illusio* in Flaubertian narrative as opposed to representational perspective, he argues that Flaubert's singularity arises because 'he produces writings taken to be "realistic" (no doubt by virtue of their object), which contradict the tacit definition of "realism" in that they are written, they have "style".' This stylistic framing is echoed in Bourdieu's attraction to one of Flaubert's most intriguing aphorisms turned oxymoron 'Write the mediocre well' (1992: 91–4). There is a case for saying Flaubert writes the mediocre better in *Madame Bovary* than he does in *Sentimental Education*. In the former the aesthetic is not treated as object since in Emma's circle there are few would-be aesthetes. Yet Bourdieu critiques the aesthetic as necessarily reflexive, occurring simultaneously inside and outside the text, in the play-off between Flaubert's letters and his fiction, for example, as contiguous forms of writing. Aesthetic aspirations and illusions are incorporated reflexively in the Parisian novel precisely because of the firm hold upon the social which lies in its diurnal detail. The fusion of style and banality is crucial, for it creates the possibility of a 'realist formalism' which both transcends and destroys a binary opposition inhibiting the modernistic impulse and which he attributes to the doxa of the dominant culture. Here one can reread through Flaubert the cultural formation of the modern bourgeois world-view as a schizoid mind-set where there is little ideological consensus, in which the cultural is seen exclusively as a useful artefact or exclusively as a pure aesthetic.

The break with the homogenizing Goldmann could not be clearer as Bourdieu meticulously charts the cultural histories of these polarizing movements, of utilitarians demanding a purely social function out of the artwork, romantics claiming its pure transcendence of the social. Flaubert consciously steers between both extremes to make the literary form an artistic challenge to the conventions of tradition and the ideals of progress. In that respect, Bourdieu's reading builds upon Girard's formidable theory of the modern novel. For Girard the dilemma of the modern heroic self lay in the delirium of mimesis, of imitation of the desired and desirable other, the role-model to which one strives much as Don Quixote had strived absurdly to uphold the fiction of chivalry in a world bereft of it. Mimetic desire lies in imitation of the world past but also of the present other. Just as *Sentimental Education* imitates and surpasses Rousseau's *Confessions* and Stendhal's *Red and Black* so Frédéric mimics the fate of Rousseau and Stendhal's young ambitious males by falling in love, as they do, with an older woman who also acts as a surrogate for the absent mother. As Girard shows, such literary tropes here are common throughout European fiction of the period and they are linked to the ambitions of social ascent and material success (1976: 21–220). Flaubert takes this one stage further in Bourdieu's reading. The forms of mimesis lead on to rivalry not only in love, with the contest between husband and lover, but also in the social variations of mimetic desire. Not only does Frédéric fall in love with Madame Arnoux, he belongs to a male social circle where rivalry is linked to political belief and social ambition. Girard's formal rendering of mimetic rivalry is here fleshed out by Bourdieu's readings of social variation as each rival in the circle, always looking over his shoulder the others, undergoes his own 'sentimental education' which cathects different ideals, pathologies, aspirations and fates in the force-field of the narrative. This lateral spread of rival associates who are all in some respect versions of the hero but also at odds with him dovetails with the intrigues of passion where the key amours of Moreau's life, Madame Arnoux, Rosanette and Madame Dambreuse form an eternal triangle on which the points are interchangeable. Vain and brittle, Morea, confuses in his imagination the image and residence of the courtesan he possesses with those of the married women he desires as social acquisitions.

Rather than just forging a specific representation of reality through innovation in style, Flaubert forges a specific *illusio*, or fundamental belief in reality, where language structures the *illusio* itself (1992: 227–31). Here writer, hero and reader form a tight reflexive circle. At the start this is mimetic. One author copies another, one hero moulds himself upon the past heroes of literature or of history while the reader, in the act of reading, simulates simultaneously both the actions of the heroine and the author's act of writing her into the texture of the tale. Bourdieu concludes his argument thus:

> ... In coming back tirelessly from *Madame Bovary* to *Bouvard and Pecuchet* via *Sentimental Education* to characters who live life as a novel because they take fiction too seriously, for lack of being able to take the real seriously, and who commit a 'category error' totally similar to that of the realist novelist and his reader, Flaubert reminds us that the propensity to grant the status of reality to fictions (to the point of wanting the reality of existence to conform to fiction, as do Don Quixote, Emma or Frédéric) perhaps finds its foundation in a sort of detachment, an indifference, a passive variant of the stoical ataxaria, which leads to seeing reality as illusion and to perceiving the *illusio* in its truthfulness as a well-founded illusion, to take up once more the expression Durkheim uses about religion. (1992: 334–5.)

The *illusio* is profound in Flaubert, he contends, because like William Faulkner he mobilizes the most profound structures of the social world which correspond to the mental structures of reading, structures which are not explicit as in scientific discourse but implicit in a story where they are veiled and unveiled at the same time. In the way that fiction as an imaginary conceals, so the critique as materiality must unveil, but it can do so only under certain conditions. The critic's task is not to consecrate the work as act of genius but to expose its complex powers of dissimulating. Here there is a crucial homology. In *Sentimental Education* it lies in the game-playing dissimulation of Flaubert, the author, who seeks the reality of the Second Empire as a vain illusion and takes refuge in the ascetic detachment of the radical aesthete, and his fictional anti-hero Frédéric who pursues the imitation of life by living it out as self-conscious repetition of the passion of great fictions, since the endless game-playing in his own circle is seen by him an exercise in futility. Yet this conceit of fiction-as-detachment empowers him precisely in that game-playing of every-day life whose futility otherwise makes him feel impotent. Flaubert's authorial detachment leads to the modernist art of the next century and the impersonality of the Joycean writer paring his fingernails where Frédéric's emotional detachment had led to social paralysis. The split is later preserved reflexively in Joyce's doubling of Dedalus, the future artist destined to leave dirty Dublin with Bloom the entropic bricoleur doomed to remain there. Finally the moment of impersonality founded in the figure of Flaubert and his writing is also, reflexively, the model of scientific impartiality for the modern observer, including Bourdieu himself. The analytical precision and refusal of value-judgment necessary for the launching of modern science, both natural and social, during the Second Empire resides for Bourdieu in Flaubert as much as it does in Comte, Taine or Durkheim. In his reprise of this myth of genesis Flaubert is the founding figure of the discourse of modernity, its veiling as fiction and its unveiling as science. Conveniently, Bourdieu as polymathic sociologist then becomes a future beneficiary. In the world according to Bourdieu, Bourdieu in effect is Flaubert's future double.

III

For Terry Eagleton, fiction's constellations of tragic refusal are pointers to the transformation of British society and the field of power in the United Kingdom. Three dominate his culture critique. In 1748 the rape of Clarissa highlights the ironies of the historic alliance between landed aristocracy and new bourgeoisie which Clarissa's rejection of Lovelace fictionally subverts. This, in turn is the Puritan author's symbolic discharge of the defeat of his religion's radical promise which had foundered on the collapse of Cromwell's Commonwealth one hundred years earlier. A hundred years after *Clarissa* the contradictions of rural class form the tragic bedrock of *Wuthering Heights*, and here sexual status is reversed, Cathy as the yeoman's daughter, Heathcliff as the dark-skinned orphan found on the streets of Liverpool. Heathcliff's destructive ascent marks out social mobility not as a vessel of the civilizing influence of bourgeois society but the laying bare of capitalist brutality which begins exploiting cultural capital and ends by sending it into reverse. Finally the Bronte's Irish connection is self-consciously mythologized as the launching pad for Eagleton's own critical wager, his reading of Irish fiction's omission of the Great Hunger from its pages as an aporia which paradoxically fuels cultural transformation in the colony within-the Kingdom.

Eagleton's fracturing of Goldmann's world-vision had begun in his earlier reading of *Wuthering Heights*, but in a curious way. He pointed rightly to the fragile nature of Goldmann's Lukàcsian distinction between partial vision as a falsely conscious ideology and the coherent, structured and totalizing belief-system he calls world-vision. Yet the Anglo-Irish critic uses that distinction to divide the two Brontes, attributing to Charlotte's texts an ideological function of mythically resolving contradictory interests at the pragmatic level of daily coherence while crediting Emily's novel with the power of a universalizing text transcending the conflicts it portrays in the creation of a timeless myth of nature (49). That transcendence is only achieved, however, by exhausting in its narrative form the endless possibilities of class hatred (Eagleton, 1975: 49). *Wuthering Heights* becomes an artistic *Aufhebung*, a fictional transcendence of history almost by default. Just as Goldmann had attributed the power of Racine's vision to the transmutation of the hidden Jansenist God into the field of the Pagan deities of classical tragedy, in particular the figure of the Sun, so Eagleton connects the romantic structure of feeling in *Wuthering Heights* to a primal pre-modern source, antedating the nineteenth century opposition noted by Williams of pastoral rebel and English commercial society. This clears the way for the entry of Benjamin's cryptic philosophy of history where *constellation* is the call to a buried past obliquely signifying a future which cannot be fully imagined. The Anglo-Irish critic sees this very differently from Bourdieu's homing in on the diurnal metropolis, itself inspired by Benjamin's arcades project and his reading of Baudelaire. It entails, by contrast, a radical displacement to the cultural margin which deconstructs the myth of the 'primitive', which is precisely how Ireland was then perceived in the late Victorian mind-set. The Irish revival is not only a symbolic riposte to the clichés of backwardness, but a swift overtaking of English metropolitan culture itself.

Concern with myths of the primitive lies at the heart of Eagleton's Pascalian wager in *Heathcliff and the Great Hunger* which crudely put, can be called taking a chance on Emily. If Bramwell Bronte *had* discovered an Irish orphan on the streets of Liverpool in August 1845 who was a victim of the Hunger, then the trauma of the Bronte's Irish heritage would be invoked as an unexpected return of the repressed charging the force-field of Emily's tragic text. Eagleton admits, however, that the dating was all wrong (1995: 3). Moreover, if an orphan was found, even if he was Irish, how can it be proved that Heathcliff was Irish any more than we can prove that Lady Macbeth had sixteen children? As a close reader of Milan Kundera's reflexive poetics of irony and estrangement, Eagleton is surely setting up here his critical gamble on the historical meaning of Irish art. It *has* to signify in order that he can theorize, that is, on the metanarrative level to which Marxist theory categorically commanded him. In Bourdieu's strategy of reading, Flaubert emerges organically from previous discourses on modernity in general, while Eagleton is still haunted by implicit hiatus, the tell-tale gap between eclectic theorizing which surfs between ideological positions, and the drive of practical criticism which provides crucial override. Having seen the weakness in Goldmann but failed to ingest the productionist metaphysic of Althusser and Macherey, he turned to Benjamin to find a way out of the impasse. Yet the 'Marxist rabbi', as he called him, was too elliptical, Talmudic and figurative to provide the magic cornerstone of revolutionary critique which eluded him. He is thus driven to fuse Benjamin's historical anti-historicizing of art with Goldmann's critique which he never abandoned, in a specific context which calls up his own ancestry. Summoning up all the traces of complex reading in his Oxbridge career, Eagleton seeks final resolution in the Irishness of the Irish. But through the vital wager on Emily Bronte the connection to English writing remains as an allegory of openness. It is a tactical allegory to ensure the door is never closed.

The Irish Revival is a double displacement in time and space, its tragic vision very different from either the Jansenist vision of Racine or the petrified allegories of baroque German drama, the *Trauerspiel* which obsessed Benjamin, the one emerging at the start of absolutist rule, the other towards its end (Benjamin, 1977). By contrast Ireland's anomalous position in the politics of the modern European state is deceptively decentred. It was a backward economic colony incorporated within the Union, its oddity highlighted in the Victorian age by the sheer volume of British colonies being firmed up or added on in distant continents. This unique situation fuels theoretic device. The wager, the refusal and the constellation all coalesce in a theory of cultural overtaking too vast in detail and complexity to summarize here. Suffice to say, its key moments of discourse are those of the Great Hunger, the persistent anti-realism of the Irish novel and the art and politics which spring from 1916. All are deeply interconnected. The durée of the novel links the Hunger it predates to the Uprising it outlasts while the Uprising itself can be construed as oblique payback for the earlier ravages of famine, just as Trotsky saw the October revolution as part revenge for the destruction of the Paris Commune.

The paucity of the Hunger in Irish writing until 1950 echoes a more recent trauma which still engages us. Adorno's famous dictum 'No poetry after Auschwitz' is surely a key model for the Irish discourse. Eagleton is quick to dismiss the propaganda of the Hunger-as-Genocide and patient in his sifting of its complex causality without absolving the British of blame (1995: 13–14, 61–3). Yet the trauma of the Hunger, as too unspeakable and too horrible to portray, echoes debates on the representation of the Holocaust, a debate still very much alive in Claude Lanzmann's film *Shoah*. Eagleton claims the ambiguous response to the Hunger left a permanent mark on Irish writing. There was no Irish *Middlemarch* because stable living and total seeing did not coincide, as they did in George Eliot's England (1995: 150f). Instead sudden catastrophe, which returns in 1916 under a different guise, may have had the opposite effect sending writers into a defensive posture where they idealize Irish peasant life in response to external stereotypes of barbarism. At this point, one senses Eagleton is far happier with Irish literature in this period than he is with its English counterpart. His strident yet confused readings of Eliot and Dickens in *Criticism and Ideology* (1976) had previously suffered from an Althusserian fixation on finding ideology in every literary sign. Such weakness invariably put paid to his ideological project, grandiose and self-deluding, of displacing not only the Leavisite Great Tradition but in true Oedipal mode *its* replacement, the critical theory of his mentor Raymond Williams. Thankfully, despite the odd polemical blast, he never went back. To be admiring we could say that he had discovered something more powerful. To be cruel we could say this earlier wager, the ideology critique, had failure written all over it, something the critic tacitly confirms in his later plural readings of ideology (1996: 11). In other words the wager on Ireland is the *second wager* because the wager on England had failed.

In his ambitious overview of Irish anti-realism, Eagleton foregrounds two key factors. Firstly he situates narrative form in the life-worlds of the Anglo-Protestant diaspora through the very fact of colonial predicament. Cultural isolation bespeaks absurd perspective, the multiple obsessions with the Gothic and the fantastic, for instance in Bram Stoker's *Dracula*, and finally with the esoteric reaches of theosophy which entranced Shaw and Yeats. In Ireland the colonial and the divine became fatally fused. By contrast, it would make little sense for Bourdieu to foreground the Protestant ambience in the provincial setting of the French novel north of Paris, an equation neatly taking in Flaubert, Gide, Proust and Romain Rolland. The second factor is more fundamental. The Anglo-Protestant diaspora paves the way for an avant-garde formation in Irish writing which is anti-mimetic, a 'curiously hybrid artistic form, *non-realist* representation, art faithful to an action which is itself realistically improbable ...' (1995: 305). The linking of politics and form which follows is breathtaking but the suspicion lingers that Eagleton has got the equation the wrong way round. True the very idiom of Hiberno-English, as many critics have noted, centres in the play upon language prompted by the impulse of buried translation where the joke, the exaggeration and the tall tale readily take over as surplus signifying, in other words as humorous blether. But though this violates strict mimesis in every day discourse, in art it becomes the basis for something more profound, the rupture with representational form. In this instance the key violation is not of mimesis – everyone sees through Christy Mahon's boasting in the end – but of perspective itself.

Let us take some key instances. Joyce, Synge, Yeats and O'Casey can all be mimetic to a precise point. In all his fiction, Joyce's Dublin is reproduced with exact topographies of time and place while Synge's stage directions for *Riders to the Sea* exactly reproduced the size of a fishing family's cottage on the West Coast. O'Casey's intimate knowledge of the North Dublin tenement is impacted into the design of its dramatic space and the body language of its stage inhabitants. In his famous poem on the Uprising 'Easter 1916' Yeats attempts, as Eagleton is well aware, to forge the creation of myth of an immediate present by reiterating the names of its dead leaders (1998: 351–2). At the same time the poem intends a mythic perspective and not, as Eagleton notes, an analytic commentary. Through its resort to tragedy and myth, the archaic avant-garde breaks down representational perspective as much as their surrealist or expressionist counterparts in Europe. But it does so only through the epiphanic nature of its mimetic powers (Orr, 1987: 13–16, 163–8). That Eagleton gets things the wrong way round matters less because at least he sees the vital separation of mimesis and representation other critics wrongly conflate, and also sees the rupture in a particular perceptive way which echoes the reading by Raymond Williams of modern tragedy. Irish writing foregrounds an impossible idealism which splinters under the pressures of an unbearable history in two opposing directions. In passing, it itemizes precise aspects of its own history in a pure, incandescent language but in the long run seeks out national totality in myth, ancestry and the endowment of the diurnal voice with the sacredness of poetic style. Yet still, in spite of such schizoid tendencies, it creates unity of form. This minor miracle can lead us to only one conclusion. The Irish Renaissance has its own, very Irish, Renaissance perspective. Eagleton mistakenly sees the Irish avant-garde as soldiers in 'the war ... between naturalism and Nietzsche' (1995: 305–9). In fact they make that war redundant.

138

IV

The shift from Goldmann to Benjamin is also a loop since the key terms in *The Hidden God* are to be found, less theorized, in Lukacs's early *Soul and Form* which parallels Benjamin's search for an authentic route out of the impasse of German idealism in the twentieth century. The wager and the constellation thus ran in tandem without knowing it until they became linked more self-consciously in the current decade. This realignment in cultural method also provides a crucial encounter at the crossroads of contemporary theory. It is a key alternative to the myth of postmodernity, dehistoricizing Marx without forgetting his legacy, refusing to throw the baby out with the bathwater. Eagleton sees 1916 much as Bourdieu sees 1848. In fact he sets the dates side by side when he says of the Uprising and the civil war that its vivid intertextualities of politics, belief and art were like the events of 1848 and after as seen through the eyes of Marx ' ... Inherently fictive and theatrical, full of panache and breathless rhetoric and historical cross-dressing rising to an exuberant crescendo before sinking back, like some prolonged binge, into the crapulousness of daily life' (1995: 305). This is also the verdict, *en passant*, of Federic Moreau whose subsequent disdain for revolution in general matched Marx's disdain for this revolution in particular. This in a word is the pathos of tragic farce diagnosed as a structure of experience in the *18th Brumaire* and stylized as a structure of feeling in *Sentimental Education*. That history should repeat itself in this way is both tragic and farcical at the same time.

Yet tragic farce is what gives birth and then rebirth to modernist form. This of course is plural form, casting Baudelaire and Yeats as poets, Flaubert and Joyce as novelists, Manet as painter, Synge and O'Casey as playwrights. While Bourdieu's assiduous contextualizing of Baudelaire's contemptuous desecration of good taste fills out Benjamin's textual reading of Baudelaire as the poet of '48 who simultaneously sees himself as revolutionary and reactionary, perpetrator and victim, torturer and tortured, Eagleton's reading of Yeat's 'Easter, 1916' places that same contradiction at a mythopoetic level where Yeatsian revolutionaries can be heroes and villains, flesh and ghost, in the same breath. Bourdieu, while contextualizing Benjamin also displaces him and for good reason. Baudelaire is the poet of the fragment, Flaubert the novelist of the metatext whose ironizing of history can parallel the deadpan discourse of the sociologue. One feels too that Bourdieu would also have plenty to say about the James Joyce T-shirts now littering the trails of literary Dublin, just as De Valera would be left speechless as he turned in his grave. The period of opprobrium followed by the age of consecration applies as much to Irish and it does to French art. Yet of the two critics, Bourdieu is perhaps more exact in assessing the consequences. The feature of bourgeois autonomy in the field of art is this. The modern artist must desecrate the world in order to be consecrated in art. Here Benjamin is put into reverse. Aura is inseparable from desecration, its liquidation inseparable from consecration. Flaubert-Joyce – what's in a name? – imprimatur of genius becomes an icon among commodities in a world where cultural tourism is not so much a pilgrimage as a state of mind.

Both critics challenge the myth of postmodernity but in different ways, Bourdieu by largely ignoring it, Eagleton by excoriating it. For Bourdieu it can only be an attenuation of cultural capital in a consumerist age, an inflation of the market for symbolic goods he had already identified. Perhaps his weakness here is to ignore what Adorno spotted so astutely much earlier, the predilection among the highly educated for sophisticated kitsch which has increased rather decreased in the last three decades. His strength is in spotting however the narrower intellectual fix on Gadamerian 'hermeneutic narcissism' in which both author and reader are largely mirrored versions of academic critics talking to other academic critics (1992: 306–9). By contrast, his readings of Flaubert and Faulkner see the reflexive game-playing element in the author-reader relationship not as the mere vanity of a depthless ludic pursuit, but as a fundament of style, the artistic means by which the reader is drawn into a created history with its own mythologizing of origin, the *illusio* which it is the reader's challenging task to unmask (1992: 333–6). The reader-critic must use a different but complementary language to show both the power and limit of artistic invention. This is surely to be preferred, say in looking at the work of Toni Morrison, to the postmodern double-shuffle where most of the time style is a matter of depthless game-playing in which nothing is said, but all of a sudden if an author is female or black or both, the authenticity of experience is invoked by magic incantation to explain the text away.

Eagleton is brilliantly polemical in his denunciation of the sloppy habits of postmodernist life-style. In reviling the worst excesses of this pseudo-culture, however, Eagleton makes an unnecessary compromise. He grants to postmodernity the status of the era of the present. This goes much further than his ideology-critique which sees in the rhetoric of postmodern decentring a key homology with the amoral hedonism of the market or, taking the rhetorics one by one, a set of vacuous modish forms which signify the dumbing-down of present culture. The question then is, why is postmodernity a key concept for understanding our culture while self-proclaimed postmodernists are incapable of its defining critique? The subtext here is of course, the crisis of Marxism. Eagleton's generosity towards Fredric Jameson as a Marxist who rescues postmodern critique for the critical Marxist project contrasts with his absolute dismissal of the prevalent forms of postmodernism which do anything but. Sometimes the petulant tone of *The Illusions of Postmodernism* (1996) gives the impression of an anxious guru rapidly chasing after disciples who are busy deserting him. Reading between the lines one senses that for Eagleton, as for Habermas, modernity remains an incomplete project. The further truth, less palatable, is that since the fast changing world of capital is here to stay and not to be overthrown except by itself, or by nuclear catastrophe, it will always be incomplete. Here the wager, the constellation and the refusal dramatize the plight of incompleteness in new and powerful ways for any discourse. The legacy of Benjamin and Goldmann remains. But equally the artworks which are part of such discourse and define it, derive their tragic structures of feeling less from the pathos of lost opportunities than from a more primal recognition. Completion is itself a myth, but one which will never go away.

Bibliography

Anderson, P., (1988), *The Origins of Postmodernity*, London: Verso.
Auerbach, E., (1968), *Mimesis: The Representation of Reality in Western Literature*, Princeton, NJ: Princeton University Press.
Benjamin, W., (1973), *Illuminations*, London: Fontana.
Benjamin, W., (1979), *One-Way Street*, London: Verso.
Benjamin, W., (1977), *The Origins of German Tragic Drama*, London: NLB.
Bourdieu, P., (1984), *Distinction*, London: Routledge.
Bourdieu, P., (1988), *The Political Ontology of Martin Heidegger*, Cambridge: Polity.
Bourdieu, P., (1990), *The Logic of Practice*, Cambridge: Polity.
Bourdieu, P., (1991), *Language and Symbolic Power*, Cambridge: Polity.
Bourdieu, P., (1992), 'Doxa and the Common Life'. (In Conversation, Pierre Bourdieu and Terry Eagleton) *New Left Review*, 191: 111–121.
Bourdieu, P., (1993), *The Field of Cultural Production*, Cambridge: Polity.
Bourdieu, P., (1996), *The Rules of Art*, Cambridge: Polity.
Brubaker, R. (1993), 'Social Theory as Habitus', in Calhoun, C., Lipuma, M. and Posante, E. (eds), *Bourdieu: Critical Perspectives*, Cambridge: Polity.
Eagleton, T., (1975), *Myths of Power: A Marxist Study of the Brontes*, London: Macmillan.
Eagleton, T., (1976), *Criticism and Ideology: A Study in Marxist Literary Theory*, London: NLB.
Eagleton, T., (1981), *Walter Benjamin, or Towards a Revolutionary Criticism*, London: Verso.
Eagleton, T., (1982), *The Rape of Clarissa: Writing, Sexuality and Class Struggle in Samuel Richardson*, Oxford: Blackwell.
Eagleton, T., (1990), *The Ideology of the Aesthetic*, Oxford: Blackwell.
Eagleton, T., (1991), *Ideology*, London: Verso.
Eagleton, T., (1995), *Heathcliff and the Great Hunger: Studies in Irish Culture*, London: Verso.
Eagleton, T., (1996), *The Illusions of Postmodernism*, Oxford: Blackwell.
Eagleton, T., (1998), *The Eagleton Reader*, (ed. Stephen Regan) Oxford: Blackwell.
Eagleton, T. and Milne, Drew, (eds) (1995), *Marxist Literary Theory*, Oxford: Blackwell.
Fowler, B., (1997), *Pierre Bourdieu and Cultural Theory*, London: Sage.
Girard, R., (1976), *Deceit, Desire and the Novel*, Baltimore: The Johns Hopkins University Press.
Goldmann, L., (1964), *The Hidden God*, London: Routledge.
Nicholl, C., (1992), *The Reckoning: The Murder of Christopher Marlowe*, London: Jonathan Cape.
Wilson, R., (1997), 'Shakespeare and the Jesuits', *TLS*, 19 December, 1997.

A different field of vision: gentlemen and players in Edinburgh, 1826–1851

Nick Prior

'The interference of patrons, in the character of guardians, is no longer admissible, and would therefore be impertinent. The arts have come of age, and can manage themselves' (Monro, 1846: 113).

Introduction

The idea that art is an embedded social activity is neither new nor particularly remarkable. It forms the starting point for any sociology or history of art worthy of the name. While ideologies of cultural transcendence and romantic isolation still undergird popular and élite delineations of the artistic object (revealing, indeed, the extent to which the former has taken on, or 'misrecognized' the discourse of culture as nature), they no longer rest so easily in the firmament of scholarly and artistic life. Both the 'critical' and 'empirical' traditions of writings on art (Chaplin, 1994) have steered analysis towards extra-aesthetic factors that reside in the art-society problematic – whether they be the effects of capitalism, class and dominant ideology in the writings of Lukàcs, Hauser, Max Raphael and T.J. Clark, the mundane practices of the artist's 'support personnel' in Becker's (1982) institutional ethnography, or the sophisticated and cross-cutting influences of gender, race, language and power in the work of the 'new art historians' (Wolff, 1981; Zolberg, 1990; Pollock, 1988; Rees and Borzello, 1986).

Bourdieu's contribution to this problematic, whilst clearly indebted to the art historians Erwin Panofsky and Michael Baxandall and the 'genetic structuralism' of Lucien Goldmann (see Bourdieu, 1996: 313, 179; 1992: 69) is both *sui generis* and *nullis secundus*. It provides the most wide-ranging, analytically sophisticated and empirically productive set of concepts available, to represent the intricate mediations between artistic practice and social space. The concept of field (*champ*), in particular, marks the development of a 'science of the sacred' (see Swartz, 1997: 47), of artistic practice, that takes analysis beyond fuzzy references to 'context', 'art world' and 'institution' (Danto, 1999).[1] Field, instead, suggests the existence of partially independent regions of social activity, such as artistic practice, structured according to a relational set of struggles that take place over currencies or resources particular to that field. If an adequate sociology of art must cover the dynamic range of practices, agents and forces that cohere around art, it is the notion of field that is most able to reveal what is relational and conflictual about these forces.

Inspired by Weber's sociological analysis of the scrimmage between priests and prophets, field developed out of Bourdieu's desire to put the habitus concept to work in a more structured setting, without reducing practical sense to a one-dimensional carrier of structure. By dint of its own historical trajectory, the field acts, for Bourdieu, as a prism, refracting external forces, or converting demands from the broader field of power (the state, dominant economic classes) into a logic and currency befitting its own social topology. The more developed the field (and there is a definite theory of modern social change implicit in Bourdieu's work (Lash, 1990)) the greater the movement of refraction. In contrast to Althusser's half-hearted notion of 'relative autonomy', in other words, Bourdieu's field mechanism directs our attention to the general and the particular by taking both terms, 'relative' and 'autonomy', seriously.

Fields, then, are competitive arenas, social networks of conflict in which players manoeuvre to conserve or augment their address in relation to others in the same space. The social geography of the field is a function of the distribution of occupied positions and, by homology, the position-takings of the residents. Here, we might find the metaphor of a game of chess useful, where players possessed of specific capabilities (or in Bourdieu's terminology, a sum of capital, composed chiefly of economic and/or cultural resources which energize the habitus) engage in strategies appropriate to their location in the game. Agents in a position of dominance will tactically deploy their capital in order to *conserve* their position, whereas agents looking to outflank, displace or over-take those in a dominant position (*arrivistes*, avant-gardistes, heretics – the 'dominated fraction of the dominant social class') will attempt strategies of *succession* or *subversion* (Bourdieu and Wacquant, 1992: 98–99). Indeed, this on-going battle between orthodoxy and heresy – which in the artistic field has been drawn between defenders of traditional, aristocratic or centralized structures of patronage and defenders of an unfettered modern art – constitutes the driving dialectic of change in all cultural fields:

> the process that carries works along is the product of the struggle among agents who, as a function of their position in the field, of their specified capital, have a stake in conservation, that is routine and routinization, or in subversion, ie, a return to sources, to an original purity, to heretical criticism, and so forth (Bourdieu, 1993: 183).

Here, struggles which often take the form of demands for recognition, just as easily become struggles over the dominant criteria of legitimacy. In the field of artistic production, orthodox artists, connoisseurs or patrons endorse existing definitions, whereas heterodox artists, critics or patrons explicitly challenge the dominant standards and actively set out to revise the criteria that underpins the distribution of artistic capital. In turn, the attempt to impose a definition of legitimate practice – what is worthy art – often overlays questions regarding the limits of the field itself and the movement symbolically to exclude practices and members from the game. In this sense, as Bourdieu explains, struggles over definitions between poets, novelists, ancients and moderns, are more than mere conflicts with words, they are actually 'experienced by the protagonists as questions of life or death' (Bourdieu, 1993: 184).

Bourdieu's use of the concept is clearly most effective when dealing with those relatively developed fields, education, art, literature, in a state of high autonomy. His writings on the French literary field in the late nineteenth century, in particular, constitute a wonderfully detailed map of a 'chiastic' space of cultural effervescence that fizzed with altercations, symbolic struggles and artistic innovations.[2] Indeed, Bourdieu likens the genesis of the 'heroic rupture' from academic absolutism in France to a dance, 'a sort of well-regulated ballet in which individuals and groups dance their own steps, always contrasting themselves with each other, sometimes clashing, sometimes dancing to the same tune, then turning their backs on each other in often explosive separations' (1996: 113). What gives this dance its sociological co-ordinates is the fact that struggles over classification or legitimacy are codified expressions of a location in a *social space*, immediately raising the role that culture plays as a mediator of social class. Indeed, the success of Bourdieu's *Rules of Art* (1996) is precisely its ability to take in the repertory of organizations, institutions and agents, known and lesser known, that determine the shape of the field, and reflect upon the objective sociological origins and constraints that mark themselves in the trajectories of these agents, without relying on a reductionist calculation.[3]

All of which gives the field concept particular allure for the active researcher. Not only are we given methodological postulates on how to study the totality of agents that contribute to the symbolic production, distribution and reception of the art work, but also a neat set of sub-concepts – *nomos*, recognition, *illusio*, *doxa*, capital – that grasp the ways in which agents who appear to be at loggerheads, are actually contributing to the reproduction of the field itself. But the field concept's analytical strength, its ability to take in a broad range of processes, is perhaps also its principal weakness: it remains a somewhat vague and elastic idea. The concept has an almost chameleon-like quality in that it can mean all things to all people: determined and determining, structured and structuring, strong and weak, modern and postmodern, promoting reproduction and change, Marxist and Weberian. Moreover, as Fornäs (1995) suggests, it is not always clear what the metaphor of field, with its Germanic origins, actually implies, denoting as it does either a bounded space where cattle graze, (suggesting little horizontal movement, and therefore reproduction), a battle-field with its masculine tropes of trench warfare, or a magnetic field, in which agents (particles) are attracted towards one pole and repelled from the other (Bourdieu and Wacquant, 1992: 106).

One way in which conceptual clarity might be promoted is to follow Bourdieu's call to 'put the concept to work' and assess the resultant empirical productions (Bourdieu and Wacquant, 1992: 104). And while this might actually serve to intensify the plasticity of the concept, it is clearly one way to test the field's heuristic value. Indeed, despite the fact that field is a relatively recent concept in Bourdieu's work (especially compared to habitus) it is beginning to capture the attention of researchers seeking to understand the complex ways in which given fields (literary, legal, scientific, educational) operate (Marliere, 1998; Peillon, 1998; Calhoun, 1993; Pinto, 1996; Ringer, 1990; Ringer, 1991). Moreover, in the context of art, the field has been used effectively by scholars to investigate the ways patrons, collectors, critics, artists, museums and galleries, contribute to the modernization of the field, working up the value of art and struggling for cultural authority (Gerhards and Anheier, 1989; Forbes, 1997; Fowler, 1997; Fyfe, 1996; Pointon, 1994; Prior, 2000, 1998; Canclini, 1995; Collier and Lethbridge, 1994; Swingewood, 1997).

A socio-genesis of the National Gallery of Scotland

The following, then, should be read as an instance of the endeavour to operationalize the field concept. It is an attempt to unravel the stakes and tools used in the struggles to augment the interests of Edinburgh's art institutions by the early decades of the nineteenth century and the resultant construction of a modern space for art. The movement towards a *purer* aesthetic, of the belief in setting art apart from other value spheres or forms of activity, was the manifestation of a cluster of ideas, personnel and institutions that marked the onset of conflict and fragmentation in Edinburgh's art field. This movement was tied up, in turn, with changes in the composition and power of Scotland's upper classes and the resources that certain factions could draw upon to affirm their own cultural interests. A desire to professionalize the field and encourage the market were the most visible aspects of this movement; but so was the re-profiling, by the 1840s, of the city's art field to accommodate the interests of its most powerful art institution, the Royal Scottish Academy. The specifics of this struggle point to a profile that is relatively unique to Scotland, but which fit with Bourdieu's concern to follow Bachelard's advice and plot the variant in the common (Bourdieu, 1998: 2). The new National Gallery of Scotland (1851), in this view, emerged in particular conditions of a finite space of possibilities and can be differentiated structurally, from the Louvre (1793) and the National Gallery in London (1824).

By the early nineteenth century, Scotland's aristocracy was a relatively small, but powerful social constituency, integrated into modern sites of political power and able to secure its influence in a mature system of patronage and personal influence (Fry, 1987; Phillipson, 1973; 1975; Devine, 1990; Devine, 1994). In Edinburgh's nascent field of art, aristocratic interests were served by the Institution for the Encouragement of Fine Arts in Scotland. The Institution was comprised of around one hundred and fifty members, drawn from the nobility and aristocracy, and set up in 1819 in the image of London's British Institution. Members made available their private 'old master' paintings and exhibited them in local galleries, such as Henry Raeburn's York Place gallery (NG3/1/1). Born of a private, aristocratic culture, the show's commercial failure appeared to be tempered by the Institution's pleasure at the more exclusive private evening viewings, and 'by the attention of the higher classes' (NG3/1/1:10). A year later, attendance was further depleted, and, according to the sixpence catalogue, only twelve pictures were exhibited. These included a mix of seventeenth and eighteenth century 'generalized' landscapes, portraits, religious and classical scenes by the likes of Ruysdael, Titian, Rubens and Gavin Hamilton (EUL: Institution Catalogues and Misc. Pamphlets, 10/42–44: 7).

Clearly, the Institution's social position (owners of inherited landed capital) disposed them towards a set of traditional aesthetic values that pointed up its position as guardian of patrician culture. It spoke fondly of the old Royal Academy, of the works of Reynolds, Gainsborough and Richard Wilson, spent time canvassing for the 'interest of the nobility and gentry of Scotland in the objects of the Institution' (NG3/1/1: 48) and received the patronage of Prince George, as Regent, in 1819. Core members such as the Earl of Elgin, the Marquis of Queensberry and the Duke of Hamilton comprised a group of aristocratic patrons in the classical sense. Using the rhetoric of civic humanism and 'disinterestedness', this coterie of amateur collectors was disposed to preserve the shape of the field as it was, and to resist any attempt by artists to modernize structures of artistic production.

However, by 1820 the Institution was proposing the substitution of the work of 'ancient masters' with that of living artists in the light of the lack of a steady, varied and popular supply of older works to the city. This was expedient for both parties: the artists, who by this time had formed themselves into the first artist-led institution of its kind in Scotland (the Associated Society of Artists), gained exhibition space and potential patrons at a time when the market was still in its infancy; and the patrons exploited the growing popularity of modern art in Edinburgh to convey their self-perceived status as the field's chief sponsors, despite their allegiance to a more antiquated system of patronage. That the artists themselves were growing increasingly wary of the Institution's control is indicated by the gradual divide between the two constituencies from the late 1820s. For now, however, patrons and artists had little choice but to use each other in order to bolster their own relative positions within the field.

From 1820 until 1831, then, Edinburgh played host to modern exhibitions on a scale unmatched in Scotland up to that point. During the years 1821–6, the venue was changed to galleries at Waterloo Place in order to make room for larger audiences and for the growing number of modern works submitted (around two hundred by the mid-1820s). The exhibitions were a success, attracting local art buyers and proving to be somewhat of a shop-window for portraitists, landscapists and genre artists. Many painted accessible subjects – local views, commissioned portraits, cottage scenes, 'sleeping girls' – in a direct style that suited the growing middle class audience. But exhibitions were still run under the Institution's auspices, so whilst sixteen artists were admitted as associate members in 1823, these were excluded from any form of management or control, such as hanging procedures. Professional men, suggested the Institution, could not be trusted to wield voting rights with the requisite 'disinterestedness' that connoted aristocratic conduct.

Control of the Institution's affairs, instead, resided in an inner circle of aristocratic directors, whose confidence, wealth and connections with the Board of Manufacturers[4] served to place the Institution in a position of dominance in the field in the 1820s. Indeed by 1826 the Institution was calling for the reintroduction of annual shows that displayed 'pictures preserved in private collections country halls or colleges' (NG3/1/1: 134). For it was in the display and judgement of ancient art, the Institution asserted, a practice 'more generally inherent in the well educated class of society', that higher and 'purer' standards of taste could be reached ('pure', meaning, here, divested of the kinds of 'gratuitous', pecuniary, impulses that drove artists). Predictably, when modern Scottish artists were praised, it was the likes of Jacob More, Gavin Hamilton and Alexander Runciman, with their classical abstractions and connections to 'the most esteemed masters of the ancient and foreign schools' who were singled out (EUL: Institution Catalogues and Misc. Pamphlets: 10).

By 1825 the Institution's position was further buttressed by an application for a Royal Charter and the implementation of a purchasing policy for old masters through dealers in London and Paris. Since the French invasions of Italy, some important works had become available, and the Institution wasted no time in procuring pictures such as van Dyck's *Lomellini Family*. Talk was of fostering a 'Gallery of National Importance' under the dominion of the Institution and of raising the taste of artists by providing them with traditional examples that would inspire history painting (Thompson, 1972). Further success was achieved in 1827 with Royal incorporation and work begun on the construction of a new dedicated building, designed by William Henry Playfair, built at the head of the Mound and named after the new 'Royal Institution'.

Built in Doric style, with eight front columns and a portico, the building was eventually to house several semi-national institutions of learning and commerce in the city, including the Society of Antiquaries and the Royal Society. The Board of Manufactures, whose responsibilities had been re-defined by directives in 1828 to include the fine arts, was given overall charge of the building, which was completed in time for the Royal Institution's fifth exhibition of modern pictures in February 1826. The Board also footed what amounted to a £47,000 bill and took residence in the building. Accommodation for exhibitions and the Board's Trustee's Academy was provided in the double-storey building and additional rooms for a library and committee room built. It was the Royal Institution's galleries, however, which took centre stage.

The self-congratulatory tempo of the Royal Institution's reports at this time indicates an organization at the height of its powers in the art field. It wasted no time in clarifying its intention 'not as a Society of Artists, but for

Figure 1 *The Royal Institution Building, designed by William Henry Playfair, completed 1826, engraving by S. Lacy*

their benefit' (EUL: Catalogues and Misc. Pamphlets, Vol. 10, 10/42–44), reiterating its desire to set up a permanent gallery and academy to train artists in its own image. Meanwhile, the artists' own energies towards independence and power were bearing less official fruit with the news that their application for Incorporation had been scuppered, in turn fuelling rumours that the Board of Manufactures and Royal Institution had short-circuited their application in order to retain a monopoly over the art field in the city. In fact, the ties between the Royal Institution and the Board of Manufactures were particularly strong. The Institution received its grant from the Board and cross-membership between them was high. While the Board was not merely a one-dimensional vehicle for classical aristocratic power (the encouragement of Scotland's economic infrastructure and its design school indicated a more commercially aware compact civil élite, and at times the Board acted more like a pendulum, swinging expediently between the state, the artists and the patrons) it was very much open to the influence of the Institution. Furthermore, social trends suggested that landed power in Scotland – based on inheritance, old ties, land rights and property – was still significant by the second decade of the nineteenth century (Devine, 1990).

A further affront to the artists took the form of an exclusion from free access to the new galleries built on the Mound, reserving such privileges for the Life Governors only. All of which was topped by the inconsistencies over the status and whereabouts of proceeds taken from the previous modern exhibitions that were to be injected into a separate fund for artists.[5] From 1826 a series of memos and letters circulated between the three institutions that heralded the onset of overt conflict in Edinburgh and mobilized the artists into a more cohesive and offensive position in the field.

For a while, public battle had been joined in the city's newspapers between the patrons and artists: both claimed rights to the exhibition funds, and cast aspersions on the taste and propriety of the other. As far back as 1825, a letter signed by artists such as Hugh William Williams, William Allan and Alexander Nasmyth, raised 'doubts whether the Institution, in its present state, is of any material advantage to the Fine Arts in Scotland ... there is no inducement held out to Scotch Artists, to send their works to the Institution, more than to any other Exhibition in which they have no concern' (NG3/7/3/18: 11). Henceforth, the layered antagonisms of social class, aesthetics and institutional conduct had ceased to be latent, and spilled copiously into the city's public sphere.

1826–1834: the birth of the Scottish Academy and the Royal Institution in decline

The great upheavals arise from the eruption of newcomers who, by the sole effect of their number and their social quality, import innovation regarding products or techniques of production, and try to claim to impose on the field of production, which is itself its own market, a new mode of evaluation of products' (Bourdieu, 1996: 225).

Galvanized by the perceived injustice enacted on the faction, a breakaway group of twenty-four artists tendered their resignation from the Institution and canvassed others to withhold pictures from the Institution's modern exhibitions in order to gain independence from aristocratic tutelage. In May 1826, the first general meeting of 'The Scottish Academy of Painting, Sculpture and Architecture' was held. Academicians were to pay twenty-five guineas for membership and governance of the institution was to rest in the hands of a central council, the President and the collective body of the Academicians.[6] As the Scottish Academy was attempting to hive off a professional sphere of artistic value that would recognize art *qua* art, certain guidelines were laid down in order to restrict the kinds of objects that would be exhibited. This represented a concerted lurch away from the pre-modern conception of art, as a dedicated and functional activity or craft, and pointed up the Academy's authority to name, judge and categorize legitimate artistic practice. As long as art was attached to the imperatives of a patronal system of demand, art was presumed to 'sink to the level of the mechanic trades and handicrafts' (Roundrobin, 1826: 47). The new principles of 'vision and division' that accompanied the Academy's *nomos* (Bourdieu, 1996: 236) excluded from exhibition needle-work, shell-work, artificial flowers, cut paper and models in coloured wax, much to the consternation of the Board of Manufactures, whose remit had been to encourage the 'useful arts' and 'artisans' (NG1/2/8).

The Academy's inaugural exhibition of 1827, held at the Waterloo Place gallery, was a success, raising over £900 in entrance fees and picture sales (RSA catalogue, 1827). By 1828 this sum had increased markedly, prompting the

Figure 2 *Waterloo Place, Calton Hill, c. 1830, drawn by T.H. Shepherd*

Academy to claim it to be 'the most numerous Exhibition of Works of Art which has ever taken place in Scotland.' (RSA Annual Report, 1828). Predictably, the catalogue attacked the Royal Institution as an 'auxiliary' that 'ought not to supersede or repress the combined efforts of the artists themselves'; and reiterated professional autonomy as a cause worthy of struggle (quoted in Holme, 1907: x). Now, however, the Academy was emphasizing the distinction of its own social position in relation to the possession of specialized knowledge and taste. The artists' symbolic capital, in Bourdieu's terminology, resided in their mastery of a newer game of art that had growing currency throughout Britain: of art as a specialized realm of meaning and classification and of artists as a distinct category of producers of symbolic goods. In the Academy's view this necessitated lectures in aspects of painting, drawing, perspective and anatomy, a library and a school for aspiring professional artists, all for which the academy petitioned money from the Board of Manufactures.

Clearly, power in the capital's artistic field was slowly shifting towards the Academy. Artists who previously had sought patronage under the auspices of the aristocratic Royal Institution now flocked to the Academy and its desire to replace the culture of an aristocracy (by birth) with an 'aristocracy of culture' (through knowledge) (Fyfe, 1993). For painting, in the Academy's eyes, could no longer reside in the sphere of the 'unpractised amateur' – the task would therefore be to reconceptualize art in terms of pictorial meaning and the artist's own authority (RSA Annual Report, 1825: 9). Unlike France, however, this wasn't to be achieved centrally, through strict procedures of training and normalization laid down by an official state-backed institution, but by a steady professionalization in civic-artistic life that grew out of a struggle for recognition and autonomy. In this sense, Academy artists in Scotland were the most 'radical' in the field – not yet the epitome of conservative academicism, nor artistic representatives of aristocratic ascription (like the Royal Academy up to the mid-nineteenth century) but members of a popular, urban, artistic assembly whose attacks on the traditional Royal Institution were assertions of an almost romantic conception of the artist (Prior, 1995).

Such a conception was increasingly homologous with the sensibilities of Edinburgh's own growing middle-rank audience. Hence, enthusiastic acclaim greeted the Scottish Academy's annual exhibitions in the city's press and in art journalism. One critic enthused in later years

> Our Art and Exhibitions are unquestionably the best things our country can boast. Put together our yearly crop of books, forensic speeches, and pulpit preachments, consider them, and then pass into the Academy's exhibition, and admit that the artists are clearly our best and cleverest of men (Iconoclast, 1860: 4).

In contrast, the Royal Institution's civic popularity was being undermined by the growing antipathy towards aristocratic grandeur and older vestiges of patronal control. Certain newspapers, in particular, attacked the pomp of the Institution: 'To find such a body pluming itself upon its high honours and lofty position, and insulting the individuals to whom it is indebted for all that it possesses, is, indeed, a marvellous and somewhat revolting spectacle' (Monro, 1846: 110–11). *The Scotsman*, in addition, charged the Institution with exploiting public amenities – the gaslight which lit their evening promenades – for private purposes (*The Scotsman*, 25th March, 1826). With the weight of this tide against them, the Royal Institution rescinded claims to the profits from the modern exhibitions in the summer of 1829, promising to make the library, life academy and collection available to the artists, and agreed in principle to provide exhibition space for the Academy. By the following year the Institution was requesting assurances from the Academy that some members would still be sending works to the Institution's annual exhibitions, lest the whole event would collapse. The Academy's reply – 'they could not support the ensuing exhibition at the Royal Institution, without materially injuring the establishment with which they are more immediately connected' (cited in Holme, 1907: xii) – indicated an inversion of positions between patrons and artists.

The growing strength of the Academy, therefore, fed off the flowering confidence of the artists as a coherent social interest group, or a fraction in the field, whose position-takings appeared more and more to be supported by social trends in other fields, including the field of power as a whole.[7] A distinct middle-class culture was increasingly detectable in religion, politics, law as well as intellectual thought, cultural consumption and education (Nenadic, 1988); while the general expansion of middle-class occupations was secured by the expansion in domestic and overseas trade and the growth in urban manufacturing in Scotland's central belt.[8] In short, aristocratic traditions were being gradually chipped away by the vicissitudes of an increasingly urban society. Art itself was a site of competing class allegiances and used to facilitate the constitution of a more distinct sphere of professional, bourgeois values. Hence Cockburn's laconic attack on the Royal Institution can be read as a broader declaration of confidence in a progressive constellation of values in distinction to the vestiges of aristocratic control in the spheres of politics *and* culture:

> Begun under great names, it had one defect and one vice. The defect was that it did, and was calculated to do, little or nothing for art except by its exhibitions of ancient pictures which could not possibly be kept up for long, for the supply of pictures was soon exhausted. A rooted jealousy of our living artists as a body (not individually) by the few persons who led the institution was its vice. These persons were fond of art no doubt, but fonder of power, and tried indirectly to crush all living art, and its professors, that ventured to flourish except under their sunshine. The result was that in a few years they had not a living artist connected with them. Their tyranny produced the Academy; and then having disgusted the only persons on whose living merit they could depend, the institution itself sank into obscurity and uselessness (Cockburn, 1854: 49).

This was the beginning of the end of the aristocratic Institution. Its 1832 exhibition of old masters at the Royal Institution galleries was conspicuous defiance in the light of the Academy's new-found success, but only thirty nine pictures are listed in the catalogue and the whole event was far less popular in the city than the Academy's efforts. The Academy was even outshining the Institution with respect to the purchase of high profile pictures. Its acquisition of a Rubens and several pictures by William Etty indicated the Academy's symbolic achievements in the field. Etty's *Judith and Holofernes* and *The Combat*, in particular, were significant guarantors of permanence and success in the Academy's eyes, given Etty's renown and professional standing at the time.[9] The Institution's position, on the other hand, waned, despite its connections and possession of a £500 annual state grant.

So, where once the pact between *literati* and landed had melded Enlightenment culture, now the relative divergences between the older vestiges of a lesser and middling aristocracy and a newer more progressive bourgeois class were apparent. In effect, the key stimulant for motoring the art field in the early nineteenth century was conflict between two fractions previously co-existing in harmony. Certainly the pointed struggles between orthodoxy and heresy, subversion and conservation, which, for Bourdieu (1993), represents a critical force in the evolution of the art field in France was really the principal factor in the development of national art institutions in Scotland. In particular, the accelerated move away from an outmoded conception of art as craft, symbol of aristocratic virtue or handmaiden to patrician living was subject increasingly to the attacks of artists and critics who were aiming to insert art into a more professional field made possible by the market and an increasingly complex art world. All of which was given a final twist in pointed conflicts over the Royal Institution's artistic space and the resultant foundation of a national gallery for Scotland.

1834–1847: the 'Royal' Scottish Academy, altercations over space and the foundation of the National Gallery

From 1834 to 1847 artistic aspirations towards independence were heavily implicit in the Academy's continuing struggles for cultural authority. On the grounds that art could only be furthered with the specialized knowledge of professional agents, the Scottish Academy petitioned the Board of Manufactures for public money, permanent exhibition space and the possibility of a life academy (a more relevant form of training in the 'higher arts'). After all, declared the Academy, the Royal Institution continued to receive a £500 annual grant and yet possessed no 'professional experience' (NG 1/73/13/ 1: 10). Furthermore, both the Royal Academy in London and the Royal Hibernian Academy received public funds, the latter an annual sum of £300. The Board's reply to the Academy was tepid: access was granted to the Board's 'Statue Gallery' on four days a week and agreement to have the Royal Institution's south octagon room for the annual exhibition was given, but no guarantees of official backing or any degree of permanence to these arrangements were made (NG1/73/13/2).

Despite being extended by sixty feet, space in Playfair's Royal Institution building was becoming increasingly scarce by the late 1830s. The rooms were used by the Royal Society, the Society of Antiquaries, as well as the Board of Manufactures, the Royal Institution and their respective collections. The Board's design school – the Trustees Academy – was also resident in the building, its head being chosen from the ranks of academicians. The acquisition of casts of part of the Elgin marbles from the British Museum in 1837 (the Earl being an active member of the Board) and two hundred and fifty casts of Greek and Roman portrait busts from Fillipo Albacini (1777–1858) heightened tensions over space in the building.

Clearly, the possession of exhibition space in Edinburgh was a principal stake in the field by the late 1830s because it was emblematic of the power to 'name', classify and divide art, to consecrate favoured artists and to have a series of symbolic goods recognized as legitimate by an audience. Disharmony, therefore, increasingly revolved around who had access and control over dedicated art rooms. On the one hand, the Academy's position in the struggles over space was supported by the official apparatus of governance in London in the movement away from aristocratic control. In 1838 the Academy was finally successful in its application for a Royal Charter which fixed its constitution and laws. On the other hand, however, the Royal Institution and Board of Manufactures had residual hold over accommodation in the Royal Institution building and used their official standing in the field to make the Royal Scottish Academy's position uncertain.

In 1844, for instance, a picture by the son of Thomas Dick Lauder, secretary of the Board of Manufactures and the Royal Institution, was moved by the Academy council to a less visible position in the annual exhibition. This set in train a series of disputes over who had control of the building and command of the knowledge of hanging procedures. For the Academy defended their decision with respect to the 'nature of the colouring throughout the picture, which seriously injured the effect of the exhibition at that place ... its discordance with the surrounding pictures' (reprinted in Monro, 1846: 11); and thereby revealed their territories to be based upon art-knowledge. The Academy, in other words, claimed the right to exclude Board and Royal Institution members from access to their exhibition space before exhibition, in order to 'purify' the art space and retain independence.[10]

The Board on the other hand, claimed that the Academy had acted interestedly and that: 'no public confidence can be placed in future in a council which can allow ... the judgment of its Hanging Committee ... to be swayed and overturned by every unworthy intrigue that may be originated by selfish individuals in the body which it ought to govern' (quoted in Gordon, 1976: 100). Sir Thomas Dick Lauder, in particular, argued that access to the galleries must be constant since the Board could not surrender control of the building to a 'series of individuals changed every year, and of whose habits and even names they are ignorant!' (quoted in Maxwell, 1913: 239). As the Board's position in the field had been dislodged by an attempt to exclude them symbolically and physically from the Academy's exhibitions, a show of strength was chosen by the Board's traditional members to reaffirm its status as landlord, official treasury for the fine arts and institutional gatekeeper. The Board's impulse towards conservation translated as an attack on the artist's impulse towards autonomy and modernity – 'ungrateful rebels' who were changing the rules of art forever.

The most controversial disagreement, however, was reached with the Board's final broadside at the Academy in the guise of an effective 'notice to quit' from the galleries of the Royal Institution. In 1845 the Board took custody of the Torrie collection of 'ancient masters' (mainly Dutch and Flemish seventeenth century pieces) from Edinburgh Town Council and vowed to place the collection on permanent display in the exhibition rooms at that time used by the Academy for the annual shows. This was to be exhibited *gratis* to the public at least two days a week, to become the nucleus, in the Board's view, 'of a kind of national Gallery of paintings ... which may be daily expected to increase without any expense to the public' (NG1/1/38: 137). The work of the 'Ancient Masters', in other words, was being deployed as a symbolic resource by the Board and Royal Institution to displace the incursions of the modern artists and the increasing popularity of the Association for the Promotion of Fine Arts – set up in 1834 as an art union to disseminate prints and pictures amongst its 4,000 or so members (see Forbes, 1997; Prior, 1995, 1998).[11]

The ensuing legal battle between artists and patrons over accommodation was compounded by a series of public disputes in the city's press and in the correspondence between the various institutions. From the artists' perspective, the very purpose of the building was to hold modern exhibitions, and that it was partly the success of these that provided the Royal Institution with the means to buy the old masters and to acquire a library. However, the way the affairs of the Board and the Royal Institution had been co-ordinated under the auspices of a small coterie of traditionalists had undermined the rights of the Academy. The appearance of separateness was indeed a favourite device employed by the Board and the Institution to use in official representations and in grant applications. 'In reality' wrote David Scott, RSA, the Royal Institution was 'a mere appendage of the Trustees; and in this transaction the one is so mixed up with the other, that each may be considered to represent the other' (Scott, 1845: 8). Nothing less than a thorough investigation of the accounts and minutes of the Royal Institution would reveal the injustices enacted on the artists, declared the Academy, who wrote to the Treasury and the Board of Manufactures to such an effect.

Precisely because of the Academy's growing influence amongst a widening art public, its interests were taken up by key institutions and individuals, including Edinburgh's Lord Provost, Henry Cockburn (Solicitor General), the London Art Union and influential newspapers such as the *Edinburgh Evening Post*. It was the Provost and Sheriff of Edinburgh, for instance, who modified the agreement under which the Torrie collection was to be displayed in order to allow the RSA requisite space during exhibition season. Moreover, key members of the Board itself were gradually moving towards the Academy's position, and new appointments made to the Board by the Treasury included Academy members in key posts. The public's general sympathy with the Academy was clearly evident in the series of articles and letters that appealed for public support and defended the artists against the 'eviction order' served to them in 1845. Sheriff Monro's summaries of the conflict were in fact so popular that a collection of the essays, with appended documents, was published in Edinburgh in 1846.

More symbolic power accrued to the Academy with the results of the accountant's report into the whereabouts of the profits of the Royal Institution's modern exhibitions. Concrete documentation had been supplied by the RSA to show how the Royal Institution had creamed off profits from these shows in order to build up their own library and collection of old masters. The Institution's response to this was to publicly charge the artists with 'wilful and deliberate falsehood'. Now they had to retract this charge and the imputations made against the President and the Council, and accepted inconsistencies in their handling of the profits. The violations of the Royal Institution were now publicly aired, placing the Board itself in a very precarious position. By this time, news of the growing conflicts north of the border had reached state offices in London, whose response to the growing mess was the ordering of an official inquiry into the positions, histories and claims of Edinburgh's various art institutions and the search for a solution.

As it stood, the report into the affairs of Edinburgh's art world by the secretary of the Board of Trade, Sir John Shaw Lefevre, was extensive and far-reaching. The Academy was to label the report 'one of the most important documents which have ever come under the Scottish Academy, and may be said to constitute an era in the history of Scottish Art'. (Committee Annual Report, 1847: 9). Not surprisingly, it was the Academy which came out of the report the best. £10,000 was to be ear-marked out of the Board's funds to be given to the RSA for them to build their own galleries. The RSA was to have its own life academy, for its own pupils, and given a brief to teach those of the Trustees Academy. The separation between 'design' and 'fine art' was sanctioned by the state in the recommendation that the RSA's life class was to stick to painting and drawing from the model, whereas the Trustees Academy was to concentrate on craft, the antique and commercial design. In the meantime, until the building had been erected, the RSA was to have use of the galleries in the Royal Institution building for its exhibitions and teaching (Government Report, 1847).

In effect, the inquiry executed the *coup de grace* on the Royal Institution, taking away its grant and declaring its private collection to be national and public. All of its power was devolved to the Board of Manufactures, and its collection of old masters given to the Scottish nation to comprise part of a new National Gallery of Scotland collection. This was to be permanently displayed in the Royal Institution building until such a time when the RSA had been re-housed in their new building.

As for the Board of Manufactures itself, the social composition of its membership and its brief had been slowly re-shaped in favour of closer alliance with the RSA. By 1850, D.O. Hill, Lord Cockburn, John Watson Gordon and John Steel, all RSA members, had been appointed to the Board, which was no longer comprised of upper and middling aristocracy (Lord, Dukes, Earls), but of the baronetcy, professionals and financiers. Indeed, the Treasury had written to the Board asking it to appoint artists to its membership in order to include an 'artistic element' within the Board's affairs (NG1/73/23/11).[12] The Board was henceforth entrusted with the foundation and development of the National Gallery of Scotland, its status flattened to guardian of a collection forged in the struggles between various institutions over which it adjudicated.

Eventually, Lefevre's proposals were applied, but with some notable modifications. For the purposes of rationalization, the building was to be shared between the Academy and the National Gallery collection, as it was for a time at Trafalgar Square and at the Louvre. William Henry Playfair was to build the edifice in neo-classical style on the Mound, to the south of the Royal Institution building, from 1850, with funds provided by the Board, but also a £30,000 government grant. Despite being voted down on grounds of expense, Parliament eventually ratified the foundation of the gallery, to provide 'opportunities, which cannot be over-estimated, of rational amusement, mental cultivation, and refinement of taste' (Government Report, 1847: 15). No rent was to be charged to the Academy and the curator of the National Gallery was

Figure 3 *Side-view of the National Gallery of Scotland, completed 1851, and the Royal Scottish Academy*

to be chosen from a short-list of Academy members, 'for the beneficial and harmonious working of the National Gallery, and for securing the confidence of the public' (NG1/1/41: 327). All of which, in effect, delivered a kind of art world monopoly to the Academy.[13]

The gallery's foundation stone was laid in August 1850 by Prince Albert in an elaborate civic-national ceremony. A bottle was buried at the site, into which were put mementos from the relevant institutions. So very aptly squeezed together in a fragile space were placed objects from the RSA, the Royal Institution, the Board of Trustees, the Lord Provost of Edinburgh and the Edinburgh Art Union. Prince Albert's speech praised the 'rigour' and 'independence' of industry, and reinforced the practical advantages of extending the scope of the 'younger and weaker sisters, the Fine Arts' to a broader population and the improvement of the British nation as a whole (NG1/1/39: 212). That such rhetorics of nationhood and universal access, however, veiled the gallery's operation as a space that served to elevate the 'refined' *habitus* is evident in the subsequent development of the gallery and the ideo-logics of its guardians.

Precisely because the gallery had been carved out as a space of rank, hierarchy and professional distinction, bourgeois subject positions and identities were clearly marked out for preference and fulfilment. The gallery's layers of spatial effect, particularly the décor, layout, catalogue and informal codes of conduct, comprised an argot through which Edinburgh's superintendents of high art collectively established a familiar zone of consecrated culture. The catalogue, for instance, was patterned according to a relational set of knowledges that privileged the cultivated gaze and its ability to decipher the invisible codes and make them coherent – that could place works and artists into recognisable movements, schools and styles. On the other hand, in an act of 'symbolic

157

violence', that body of the unpalatable 'other' – drunks, criminals, children, the lower classes – was either kept at one remove or controlled in the gallery space itself. The Board of Trustees regularly directed its guards to check for any 'misconduct', while officers were empowered to 'refuse admittance to suspicious characters' (NG1/1/44). The possible inclusion of the 'masses' gave itself to caution, for the potential escape of transgressive, disruptive or 'eccentric' behaviour might undermine the respectable foundations of the space (Prior, 1996).

Conclusion

The National Gallery of Scotland, then, was the summation of pointed struggles for recognition amongst a modern group of artists whose claims to space, coupled with a desire for autonomy, placed an incendiary in the field. Such struggles between the 'ancients and the moderns' mirrored those elsewhere, and in this sense the broad game of conflict was universal.[14] As Bourdieu notes in 'The Market for Symbolic Goods' (1993), the enduring friction between artists/intellectuals and aristocrats/patrons over legitimacy is one correlative with the growing complexity of the field and therefore with the growth of consumers, agencies and other modern art institutions. To this extent, the conflict in Edinburgh's art field matched those of modernizing fields elsewhere.

If the fact of struggle was universal, however, the details were distinct, local and particular to Edinburgh. The gallery, especially, was less a centralized, state-run organization of the continental type, a space of republican or nationalist victory, and more of a fragmented patchwork of influences with a Trustee-based management. To the extent that 'national' is understood in its limited meaning of relating to a state, then the gallery was 'non-national'.[15] The collection itself reflected this: not based on a state purchase (like, eventually, the National Gallery in London) but made up of the Torrie Collection, the Royal Institution's collection of ancient masters, pictures acquired by the Edinburgh Art Union, Academy pictures and the casts and pictures owned by the Board itself.

This is certainly not to claim that the concept of field is inappropriate to the sociology of art; merely that it must be 'put to work' in a way that reveals what is specific about the trajectory and morphology of individual fields. Indeed, what is useful in the field concept is its promotion of a detailed understanding divested of the distortions of excessive national feeling that is better placed to deal with 'the particularities of different *collective histories*' (Bourdieu, 1998: 3).[16] Indeed, while 'truculent exceptionalism' might be a useful corrective to over-generalized accounts of 'British history', it too easily becomes incommensurate with a properly *relational* understanding of development (Wrightson, 1989). If Scottish culture is viewed too long through the lens of 'particularism', questions of historical genealogy begin to take on the search for an internal national essence. This distorts the thrust of comparative social history and narrows the scope of inquiry to a selective excavation of a national *sine qua non* or style. What the notion of the field does, instead, is steer between the Scylla of particularism and the Charybdis of universalism – a matter of recognizing Scottish development in terms of parallels and divergences concentrated in the 'same as/different to' calculation (McCrone, 1992: 74). Where distinctions can and should be made (for instance between French, English, Scottish and American fields of cultural production) is in the nuanced differences of pace, chronology and the detailed profile of the key social agents involved.

If, as Bourdieu suggests, the 'sociology of culture is the sociology of religion of our time' (quoted in Bourdieu and Wacquant, 1992: n.32) then it is surely Bourdieu himself who takes Weber's mantle as the interlocutor of the conditions of the sacrosanct. Despite its relatively loose set of connotations and, perhaps, its greater adequacy to map fields in historical *genesis*, the pay-offs from using the field as a research tool are considerable. The range of apposite forces taken in by the concept, from everyday 'petty' struggles amongst artists, to audience perception, patronage and power, extend way beyond the practical and intellectual constraints of the present paper; but it constitutes, at least, an aspirational target. Displacing the 'fetish of the master' for the sake of a 'materialist art history' (Doy, 1998) is not a mere matter of social history but of an appreciation of the totality of forces and relations that construct the *illusio*, or collective belief, of art itself – the way a field accumulates its own history. By entering a plane of analysis inspired by the field concept it becomes possible to render fine-grained sociologies of art that transcend the mistakes of formalism and determinism. Bourdieu's 'labour of objectification' (1996: 207) is indeed producing the goods.

Notes

1 Indeed, Danto seems to have distanced himself from the very 'institutional' theory of art associated with his own work and that of George Dickie, in the light of Bourdieu's observation that such a theory fails to consider 'the historical and sociological analysis of the genesis and structure of the institution (the artistic field) which is capable of accomplishing such an act of institution' (Bourdieu, 1996: 287). In particular, the question of 'who creates the creator?', for Danto, is one that cannot be answered without recourse to 'an historical science of cultural fields' (Danto, 1999: 216).

2 The chiastic principle of ordering fields is based on Bourdieu's differentiation between economic and cultural capital. Within mature cultural fields, the fundamental opposition, for Bourdieu, is between a restricted, pure pole of production, whose protagonists possess high levels of cultural capital and low levels of economic capital, and a large-scale pole, ordered through the satisfaction of a large audience, and championed by agents with high levels of economic capital and lower levels of cultural capital. This division mirrors and reproduces the founding autonomy of the cultural field, itself, from the field of power (1996: 121).

3 One might argue that Bourdieu's analytic sits more readily with the more intricate writings of Marx, such as *The Eighteenth Brumaire of Louis Bonaparte*. In particular, the unravelling of intricate webs of allegiance and symbolic power, irreducible to a simplistic bipartite model of class, is a feature of both.

4 This was a body of lesser nobility and gentry set up by the British state in 1727, as a political concession, to administer a £2,000 annual development grant. The Board engaged in the modernization of agriculture, purchasing machinery, distributing funds to farmers, encouraging inventions and, later, promoting commercial design. It eventually took over the running of the National Gallery of Scotland in the 1850s.

5 According to the artists the Royal Institution had promised support for Scottish artists and in the 1826 catalogue of modern pictures the possibility of an amelioration fund for artists and their families was raised (SRO, Catalogues and Misc. Pamphlets, 10/42–44). From the artists' perspective, this proposal was reneged, despite the popularity and commercial success of the modern exhibitions comprised of their works. In fact, the Royal Institution had decided to pool all profits made in the modern exhibitions into a general fund, without separation, to be expended 'in whatever manner shall seem advisable to the directors' (NG 3/1/1: 155).

6 Three categories of membership were announced, as with the Royal Academy in London: academicians, associates and associate engravers, although the Scottish Academy was significantly different from the London institution in terms of social composition, power and aesthetic motivation: it was certainly less patrician.

7 This is to recognize that 'the internal struggles always depend, *in outcome*, on the correspondence that they maintain with the external struggles – whether struggles at the core of the field of power or at the core of the social field as a whole' (Bourdieu, 1996: 127). In fact, in a field like Edinburgh's, which only set out on its journey to autonomy in the late eighteenth century, the 'space of possibles' was still heavily reliant on developments in the broader field of power. For instance, many of the Academy's most powerful members were also lawyers, doctors, academics and MPs who wielded their economic capital alongside their cultural capital. Indeed, Bourdieu identifies the existence of agents who occupy 'median positions, almost equally rich in economic capital and cultural capital (the liberal professions like doctors, lawyers and so on)' (1996: 259–60) and whose field strategies tend to be 'transversal'.

8 This was validated politically, of course, by the Great Reform Act of 1832, the Scottish version of which was drawn up by Henry Cockburn, legal champion of the Academy (Cockburn, 1854).

9 Indeed, William Etty visited the Academy in 1844 and praised the artists for their 'independent exertion of mind unawed by fear and uninfluenced by favour ... the Artists ... are undoubtedly the best judges of what Art requires' (reprinted in Monro, 1846: appendix XXII: 110).

10 The defence of a 'pure aesthetic' was fast becoming the Academy's *raison d'etre*: they were defending a 'disinterested view for the promotion of Art which are [sic] inwoven with its existence ... and that an ardent devotion to the cause of Art on the part of the Academy, as a body, is the only effectual and permanent mode of securing the interests of the Artists themselves' (Annual Report, 1844: 8).

11 The Association for the Promotion of Fine Arts in Scotland was in fact crucial to the intensification of the art market and the freeing of the artist from the aristocratic commission. Based on England's Art Union, the Association extended the patronage principle to a more widespread audience for art by making available engravings of famous modern Scottish pictures. Members were also given the chance to win a painting in the annual lottery and helped the artists gain prime position in the field by buying Academy pictures and distributing them by lot to subscribers. Indeed, it was the Association that helped to sponsor an emerging vision of the professional Scottish artist and of landscape painting especially, in and through the idiom of Romanticism (Prior, 1995).

12 Still, the dual purpose that had always characterized the Board (the promotion of fine arts and commercial design) was intact inasmuch as the Trustees' Academy continued to instruct in 'practical skill', 'industrial design' and the principles of 'decorative and ornamental art' (Government Report, 1847: 10). For the time being the state was content to sanction this dual role, although by 1858 the autonomy of the Trustees' Academy was further dissolved when it was affiliated with the Department of Science and Art in London as a government school of design.

13 As the field developed, however, Academy members were to become conservers of an outmoded aesthetic attacked by a new breed of modernists, the 'Glasgow Boys'. The unfolding of this logic of succession in the field unfortunately lies outside the present chapter.

14 In England, for instance, the split in the Society of Artists between the inner aristocratic élite and ordinary members; and in Ireland a divergence between the Dublin Society, comprised of aristocratic patrons, and the Royal Irish Academy, who were artists striving for artistic authority.

15 However, that the relevant institutions saw themselves as progenitors of both civic and national ideals is emblematic of the currency of eighteenth century ideals of civil society – of provincial government, national improvement and (semi) autonomous cultural organization (Paterson, 1994, Prior, 1998).

16 Indeed, in Scotland, the search for core national attributes – the emphasis on a 'democratic intellect', intransigent Kirk or unique empiricism, has a tendency to morph into an introspective search for a national *geist* that says more about a historiographical and political present than it does a social history of the past.

Bibliography

A Primary archive sources

Records of the Royal Institution for the Encouragement of Fine Arts, the Board of Manufactures and the National Gallery of Scotland, Scottish Records Office.

NG 1/1/35 – 44	1824 – 1873 (minutes)
NG 1/2/8	1828 – 1837 (index to minutes)
NG 1/3/24 – 33	1829 – 1869 (letters)
NG 1/73/13	1835 (misc. papers)
NG 1/73/23	1847 – 1848 (misc. papers)
NG 3/1/1	1819 – 1867 (letters)
NG 3/7/3	1820 – 1845 (misc. correspondence)
NG 6/1/1 – 4	1858 – 1906 (minutes)
NG 6/6/1 – 22	1849 – 1930 (building records)
NG 6/7/1 – 29	1850 – 1866 (misc. papers)

Royal Institution for the Encouragement of Fine Arts in Scotland, Catalogues and Misc. Pamphlets Vol. 10: ATT. 80, pp. 10/42–44, University of Edinburgh Library.

Royal Scottish Academy Annual Reports, (1828–1849), Royal Scottish Academy.

Catalogues of the Royal Scottish Academy, (1827–1832), Royal Scottish Academy.

Iconoclast (1860), *Fine Art Pamphlets – Scottish*, 4: Royal Scottish Academy.

Lefevre, Sir J.S., (1850), Report to Treasury Respecting the Erection of Galleries of Art in Edinburgh, *Parliamentary Papers 1800–1900*, Vol. VII: 1845, (612).

Monro, A., (1846), *Scottish Art and National Encouragement*, Edinburgh: Blackwood and Sons.

Roundrobin, R., (1826), 'A Letter to the Directors and Members of the Institution for the Encouragement of the Fine Arts in Scotland and other correspondence', Royal Scottish Academy.

Scott, D., (1845), 'Letter to the Right Honourary Duncan McNeill, Lord Advocate for Scotland on the Discussion betwixt the Honourary the Board of Trustees in connexion with the Royal Institution and the RSA regarding the Fine Arts in Scotland', *Annual Reports of the RSA*, Vol. 1826–49, Royal Scottish Academy.

B Secondary sources

Bourdieu, P., (1977), *Outline of a Theory of Practice*, Cambridge: Cambridge University Press.

Bourdieu, P., (1990), *In Other Words: Essays Towards a Reflexive Sociology*, Cambridge: Polity.

Bourdieu, P., (1993), *The Field of Cultural Production*, Cambridge: Polity Press.

Bourdieu, P., (1996), *The Rules of Art*, Cambridge: Polity Press.

Bourdieu, P., (1998), *Practical Reason*, Cambridge: Polity Press.

Bourdieu, P. and Wacquant, L., (1992), *An Invitation to Reflexive Sociology*, Cambridge: Polity Press.

Canclini, N., (1995), *Hybrid Cultures, Strategies for Entering and Leaving Modernity*, Minneapolis: University of Minnesota Press.

Calhoun, C., (1993), 'Habitus, field and capital; the question of historical specificity', in Bourdieu, *Critical Perspectives*, edited by Craig Calhoun, Edward LiPuma and Moishe Postone, Cambridge: Polity Press, 61–88.

Cockburn, H., (1854), *Journal of Henry Cockburn 1831–1854*, Vol. 1: Edinburgh: Edmonston and Douglas.

Collier, P. and Lethbridge, R., (eds) (1994), *Artistic Relations: Literature and the Visual Arts in Nineteenth Century France*, New Haven and London: Yale University Press.

Danto, A., (1999), 'Bourdieu on Art: Field and Individual', in Shusterman, R. (ed.), *Bourdieu: A Critical Reader*, Oxford: Blackwell.

Devine, T.M., (ed.) (1990), *Conflict and Stability in Scottish Society*, Edinburgh: John Donald.

Devine, T.M., (ed.) (1994), *Scottish Elites*, Edinburgh: John Donald.

Doy, G., (1998), *Materializing Art History*, Oxford: Berg.

Forbes, C., (1997), 'Artists, Patrons and the Power of Association: The Emergence of a Bourgeois Artistic Field in Edinburgh, c.1775–c.1840', unpublished PhD thesis, University of St Andrews.

Fowler, B., (1997), *Pierre Bourdieu and Cultural Theory*, London: Sage.

Fry, M., (1987), *Patronage and Principle: A Political History, 1832–1924*, Aberdeen: Aberdeen University Press.

Fyfe, G., (1993), 'Art Museums and the State', *University of Keele Working Papers*, no. 2, Keele.

Fyfe, G., (1996), 'A Trojan Horse at the Tate: theorizing the museum as agency and structure', in Macdonald, S. and Fyfe, G. (eds), *Theorizing Museums*, Oxford: Blackwell.

Gerhard, J. and Anheier, H., (1989), 'The Literary Field: An Empirical Investigation of Bourdieu's Sociology of Art', *International Sociology*, 4 (2): 131–146.

Gordon, E., (1976), *The Royal Scottish Academy 1826–1976*, Edinburgh: Charles Skilton.

Holme, Sir C., (1907), *Royal Scottish Academy 1826–1907*, London: The Studio.

Lash, S., (1990), *The Sociology of Postmodernism*, London: Routledge.

McCrone, D., (1992), *Understanding Scotland*, London: Routledge.

Marliere, P., (1998), 'The rules of the Journalistic Field; Pierre Bourdieu's contribution to the Sociology of the Media', *European Journal of Communication*, 13 (2): 221–236.

Maxwell, J.S., (1913), 'The Royal Scottish Academy', *Scottish Historical Review*, Vol. X, no. 39.

Nenadic, S., (1988), 'The Rise of the Urban Middle Classes', in Devine, T.M. and Mitchison, R. (eds), *People and Society in Scotland*, Vol. 1, 1760–1830, Edinburgh: John Donald.

Paterson, L., (1994), *The Autonomy of Modern Scotland*, Edinburgh: Edinburgh University Press.

Peillon, M., (1998), 'Bourdieu's Field and the Sociology of Welfare' *Journal of Social Policy*, 27 (2, Apr): 213–229.

Phillipson, N., (1973), 'Towards a Definition of the Scottish Enlightenment', in Fritz, P. And Williams, D. (eds), *City and Society in the Eighteenth Century*, Edinburgh: John Donald.

Phillipson, N., (1975), 'Culture and Society in the Eighteenth Century Province', in Stone, L. (ed.), *The University in Society*, Vol. II, London: Oxford University Press.

Pinto, L., (1996), 'The Theory of Fields and the Sociology of Literature; Reflections on the Work of Pierre Bourdieu', *International Journal of Contemporary Sociology*, 33 (2): 171–186.

Pointon, M., (ed.) (1994), *Art Apart: Museums in North America and Britain Since 1800*, Manchester: Manchester University Press.

Pollock, G., (1988), *Vision and Difference: Femininity, Feminism and the Histories of Art*, London: Routledge.

Prior, N., (1995), 'Edinburgh, Romanticism and the National Gallery of Scotland', *Urban History*, Vol. 22, pt. 2 (August 1995), 205–215.

Prior, N., (2000) 'The High Within and the Low Without. The Social Production of Aesthetic Space in the National Gallery of Scotland, 1859–70', *Cultural Logic: An Electronic Journal of Marxist Theory and Practice*, http://eserver.org/clogic/, Volume 2, Number 2, Spring 2000.

Prior, N., (1998), 'Taste, Nations and Strangers: A Socio-Cultural History of National Art Museums with Particular Reference to Scotland', unpublished PhD thesis, University of Edinburgh.

Rees, A.L. and Borzello, F., (eds) (1986), *The New Art History*, London: Camden Press.

Ringer, F., (1990), 'The Intellectual Field, Intellectual History and the Sociology of Knowledge', *Theory and Society*, 19, no. 3 (June): 269–294.

Ringer, F., (1991), Fields of Knowledge: French Academic Culture in Comparative Perspective, 1890–1920, Cambridge: Cambridge University Press.

Swartz, D., (1997), *Culture and Power: The Sociology of Pierre Bourdieu*, Chicago: University of Chicago Press.

Swingewood, A., (1997), 'Force Field, Socio-Biography and the Genesis of the English Musical Field: The Case of Benjamin Britten', conference paper, Bourdieu's Cultural Theory, University of Glasgow, 5th–7th September, 1997.

Thompson, (1972), *Pictures for Scotland: the National Gallery of Scotland and its Collection*, Edinburgh: Trustees of the National Galleries of Scotland.

Wolff, J., (1981), *The Social Production of Art*, Basingstoke: Macmillan.

Wrightson, K., (1989), 'Kindred Adjoining Kingdoms: An English Perspective on the Social and Economic History of Early Modern Scotland', in Houston, R. and White, I. (eds), *Scottish Society 1500–1800*, Cambridge: Cambridge University Press.

Zolberg, V., (1990), *Constructing a Sociology of the Arts*, Cambridge: Cambridge University Press.

The mediated manufacture of an 'avant-garde': a Bourdieusian analysis of the field of contemporary art in London, 1997–9.[1]

Roger Cook

one would need to construct a true chronicle of events to get a concrete appreciation of how this universe, anarchic and wilfully libertarian in appearance (which it also is, thanks in large part to the social mechanisms that authorize and favour autonomy), is the site of a sort of well-regulated ballet in which individuals and groups dance their own steps, always contrasting themselves with each other, sometimes clashing sometimes dancing to the same tune, then turning their backs on each other in often explosive separations, and so on, up until the present time ... (Bourdieu, 1996: 113).

Wherever you look, people are thinking in terms of market success. Only thirty years ago, and since the middle of the nineteenth century ... immediate market success was suspect. It was taken as a sign of compromise with the times, with money .... Today, on the contrary, the market is accepted more and more as a legitimate means of legitimation ... It is very disturbing to see this ... because it jeopardizes works that may not necessarily meet audience expectations but, in time, can create their own audience (Bourdieu, 1998b: 27–8).

Creating capital: Charles Saatchi, the Royal Academy and *Sensation*

Since its initial introduction, field (*champ*) has been a central concept in Pierre Bourdieu's work along with the earlier concepts of habitus, capital and practice (Swartz, 1997: 118). His analysis of the 'field of cultural production' provides a model with which to make 'site-specific' analyses of particular fields of cultural production (Bourdieu, 1993a). In this chapter I want to use it to make an analysis of transformations in a particular recent field of cultural production in the visual arts in London, the so-called young British artist ('yBa') phenomenon which climaxed in an exhibition of the work of forty-two artists purchased by the advertising mogul Charles Saatchi entitled *Sensation: Young*

British Artists from the Saatchi Collection shown at the Royal Academy of Arts in London between 18 September and 28 December 1997 (see Figures 1 and 2). It is perhaps worth noting that the ambivalent title of this exhibition, which has operated primarily as a marketing device to advertise the exhibition as *sensational*, originates from its very opposite meaning as used by Cèzanne and Francis Bacon who utilized the term to designate the specific action of sensory experience on the nervous system of artist and spectator.[2] *Sensation* has subsequently toured to Berlin and at the time of writing is at the centre of a storm of controversy as the Mayor of New York threatens to withhold funding if the exhibition goes ahead at the Brooklyn Museum of Art.[3] Next year it travels to Sydney and Tokyo. In July 1999, it was announced that Saatchi, in partnership with Chris Bodker, the chief executive of Moving Image Restaurants was planning 'to open an international chain of restaurants named Sensation after the exhibition ... said Mr. Bodker. "It combines Charles's creative genius, his art collection and the Saatchi brand with our flair for high-quality restaurants"' (Mills and Milner, 1999).

From the outset this exhibition received and continues to receive an enormous amount of publicity and has generated a large quantity of commentary in both the popular press and in the more specialized journals devoted to contemporary art. It provides a unique opportunity to make a socio-scientific analysis of a 'moment' in the concrete relations between power and culture at a specific time and place; a 'concretization of the universal' as Bourdieu would say, which, hopefully, by virtue of my own present and past position in the field, I may be in a practically productive place to explicate.[4] The significance of adopting this mode of analysis for those practically and critically engaged in contemporary art is a pragmatic one: that of avoiding the rhetoric germane to the journalistic field, a rhetoric, which as Bourdieu argued in *Television and Journalism* (Bourdieu, 1998b) is more tied to the economics of the market place than to the objective pursuit of truth. It therefore ultimately

Figure 1 Rachel Whiteread, *Untitled (One Hundred Spaces)* 1995. Courtesy Saatchi Gallery. Photo: Stephen White

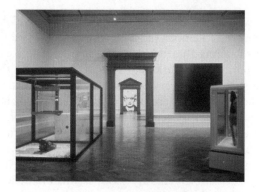

Figure 2 Left, Damien Hirst, *A Thousand Years, 1990*. Courtesy Saatchi
Gallery. Photo: Stephen White

fails to bring about any lasting transformation in our understanding of the social mechanisms, ('the rules of art') which, as Bourdieu has so amply shown, regulate the field of art and culture. The journalistic field tends simply to bat about the relativities of 'opinion' and cannot make a sufficiently intellectually and experientially grounded claim to objectivity, which is of course a *relatively* scientific, not *positivistic*, form of scientificity. It is unfortunate that so many in the field of art and culture, particularly the field of cultural studies, deny themselves the usefulness of this form of social-scientific analysis by mistaking it for a reductive form of scientific positivity. Bourdieu himself asks his readers to judge for themselves whether 'scientific analysis of the social conditions of the production and reception of a work of art' does not intensify rather than reduce or destroy the aesthetic experience (Bourdieu, 1996: xvii).

The autonomy of the artworld as a relatively independent social field was historically only gradually attained and was finally won in Paris in the latter half of the nineteenth century by the Impressionists who were emancipated from the French Academy system. Such is the long historical investment in the autonomous artworld that it is hardly surprising that it is jealously guarded by those social agents who have most at stake within it. For it was then that the mutually interdependent relationships between the Artist, the Critic, the Curator, the Historian, the Dealer and the Collector were established and modernism and the institutionalization of anomie and the notion of the 'avant-garde' were born.

Bourdieu has insisted that though produced by individual agents, the meaning of works of art are ultimately the collective product of the whole cultural field: the accumulated, historically engendered products of all agents working within that field.

Thus, as the field is constituted as such, it becomes clear that the 'subject' of the production of the art-work – of its value but also of its meaning – is not the producer who actually creates the object in its materiality but rather the entire set of agents engaged in the field. Among these are the producers of works classified as artistic (great or minor, famous or unknown), critics of all persuasions (who themselves are established within the field), collectors, middlemen, curators, etc., in short, all those who have ties with art, who live for art and, to varying degrees, from it, and who confront each other in struggles where the imposition of not only a world view but also a vision of the artworld is at stake, and who through these struggles, participate in the production of the value of the artist and of art (Bourdieu, 1993a: 261).

In the light of this we might now take a closer look at Bourdieu's analysis of the field of cultural production, which he situates within the field of power, in a diagram based on Bourdieu's diagram on page 124 of *The Rules of Art*; a revision of his diagrams in *The Field of Cultural Production* (Bourdieu, 1993a: 38) (see Figure 3). As one can see the field of cultural production is situated in the dominant half of the field of social space. And within the field of power it is situated in a symbolically and economically dominated position. Artists and intellectuals are the dominated portion of the dominant class. The field of cultural production is stretched between two ends; the small-scale field and the large-scale field. The small-scale field is the restricted-field of avant-garde cultural production where the cultural producers produce primarily for each other and a small group of *aficionados* for the autonomously pure pursuit of 'art for art's sake' without any immediate concern for economic profit. As Bourdieu would say, who and what constitutes and legitimates an 'avant-garde' is one of the struggles of constitution and legitimation in the field of cultural production. It should be noted that Bourdieu does not, as many do, constitute the avant-garde as a transhistorical essence, 'a notion like the avant-garde, is *essentially* relational (in the same way as conservatism and progressivism are), and is definable only at the level of a field at a determined moment' (Bourdieu, 1996: 386–7). Historically, the notion of the 'avant-garde' was initially constituted as a restricted field of cultural production against bourgeois and mercantile art and culture in the late nineteenth century (Bourdieu, 1996). This restricted field is where the truly innovative advent of the new takes place; one might think of the artistic innovations of the Impressionists or Braque and Picasso inventing cubism together in the Bateau Lavoir. Such artistic innovations are, of course, eventually disseminated into the larger-field and the artists may then be symbolically and economically rewarded, as with Monet in later life, or their invention may never be recognized in their own lifetime (Van Gogh). At the other extremity to the small-scale restricted field, is the large-scale field of cultural production (where 'business is business') whose ultimate aim is to reach the largest audience possible for the sake of maximum economic profit. This is epitomized by the field of advertising, in which Charles Saatchi has been commercially invested, and to a different degree by the bourgeois artist Academians who once a year in the Royal Academy Summer Exhibition present their works for sale to their bourgeois public, along with a

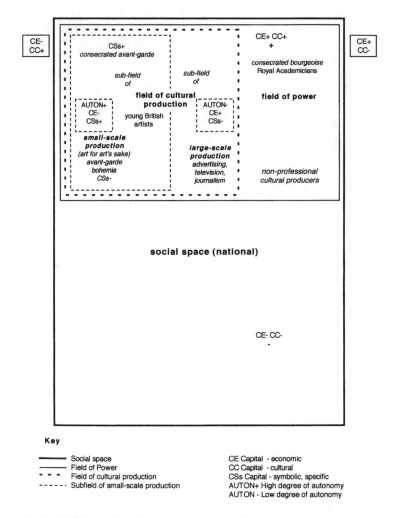

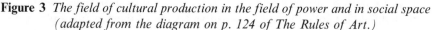

Figure 3 *The field of cultural production in the field of power and in social space (adapted from the diagram on p. 124 of The Rules of Art.)*

handbook listing prices and contact addresses. The whole enterprise is quaintly and disavowedly commercial, like a church bazaar.

In this chapter I will analyse, in the way that Bourdieu did for his own academic field (Bourdieu, 1988: 276) the 'space of positions and dispositions' in my own field, the field of contemporary art in London around the time of the *Sensation* exhibition (Bourdieu, 1993a: 30–1). It is somewhat ironic; to say the least, that the work of these 'young' artists should end up being shown in this venerable academic institution (founded by Sir Joshua Reynolds in the eighteenth century) at the heart of the British establishment.[5] It gives a wonderful opportunity to witness the mediation that disavowedly goes on in the field of cultural production ('the economic world reversed') (Bourdieu, 1993a: 29f.); a world in which there is the 'common misrecognition' (Bourdieu, 1997: 232) of the 'logic of the gift' that operates in an 'economy of symbolic goods' (Bourdieu, 1998d: 92f). The apparently gratuitously given gift, of necessity hides the fact that there may in time be a an economic or symbolic dividend, otherwise it would not be a gift but a calculated investment accruing interest. Disavowal of calculation is thus a necessity in the game of economic/symbolic negotiation. In this specific instance, this misrecognized mediation is carried on, on behalf of the Academicians by their exhibitions secretary Norman Rosenthal, a master player in such negotiations. The *Sensation* exhibition at the Royal Academy came about somewhat accidentally, when another exhibition 'Age of Modernism' from the Gropius Bau in Berlin failed to secure extended loans. Charles Saatchi stepped in, to the mutual benefit of all, thus saving the day with a selected show from his collection. Somewhat to the bemusement of those Academicians who had not resigned in protest, the packed opening was attended by numerous pop stars and supermodels. (A number of British popular music stars have purchased contemporary art since the sixties.) By the time the show closed at the end of December it had had 284,734 visitors, a weekly average of 2,800, making it one of the Academy's most popular shows in the last 10 years. The full price admission was £7.50. Prior to this exhibition, the Academy, England's oldest art institution, had a public image of being out of touch, and had amassed a deficit of two million pounds plus, thanks in part to embezzlement on the part of its former Treasurer. Added to this there is Charles Saatchi who has a controlling interest in the field of contemporary art in Britain by virtue of his economic capital. His symbolic capital, ie his ability to command respect in the long term as a symbolically viable patron, is another matter. By profession, as an advertising executive, he belongs to Bourdieu's large-scale field of cultural production and whilst possessing the economic capital endemic to that field, it is an open question as to whether he possesses the symbolic capital in terms of educational and cultural capital to enable him to join the ranks of the great dealers and collectors of modern art; those who through an intimate and embodied aesthetic connoisseurship are able to collect 'ahead of the game'.

Interests and investments

Along with his brother Maurice, Charles Saatchi was the founder of the worldwide advertising agencies, Saatchi & Saatchi and M & C Saatchi, which became the largest and most powerful advertising agencies in the world.[6] It is rumoured that he has now abandoned the world of advertising, and has become a speculative dealer in contemporary art. He has been a central, though rarely visible, figure on the English art scene for many years.[7] He began collecting art in the 1970s and bought his first work; a Sol LeWitt drawing, for £100; prior to this he collected jukeboxes. In 1984 he resigned from the Trustees of the Whitechapel Gallery following speculation that 'he profited from insider information about the gallery's exhibition plans, which allowed him to buy works ... at a favourable moment' and from the select band of collectors and dealers known as the Patrons of New Art at the Tate Gallery, London (the government controlled national gallery of contemporary art), following the exhibition of Hans Haacke's work *Taking Stock (unfinished)* 1983–1984, which satirized the Saatchi brothers' relation to Margaret Thatcher, whose Conservative Party advertising campaigns for the 1979 and 1983 elections Saatchi & Saatchi engineered. In a lengthy text accompanying the reproduction of *Taking Stock (unfinished)* 1983–4 in the catalogue for his 1986 New Museum of Contemporary Art exhibition in New York, Haacke details the 'global marketing' ambition of the Saatchis', stating that 'in London, the brothers are referred to as "Snatchit and Snatchit"' (Wallis 1986: 260–66, Haacke 1995: 134–39). In 1986 Haacke made a work entitled *Global Marketing*, a black minimalist cube sculpture measuring $80 \times 80 \times 80$ inches, whose text 'declares the Saatchis' involvement – through an affiliate agency – with the South African Nationalist party in helping to promote a change in the country's constitution that according to Haacke, would buttress apartheid (Glueck, 1993: 72–3).[8]

From the beginning Saatchi was a short term professional collector. Already in 1978, Saatchi & Saatchi, the company he had set up with his brother in 1970 reported sales of £380,000 for the year (the percentage ownership of the Collection by the company and its shareholders has never been made clear but the growth factor of the company was reflected by its escalating share prices which rose from 48p in 1972 to £41 in 1986). In 1979, the year of the Saatchis' infamous slogan, 'Labour isn't working!' that helped bring in Margaret Thatcher's Government, both the company and the Collection were riding high. Portentously, in 1984 the Collection was catalogued in four volumes as *Art of Our Time*. This Collection has long since been sold. Among the first to go were all the works of Sandro Chia which Saatchi had shed by 1985, thereby reputedly damaging the artist's career (Bickers, 1997).

To this day, Saatchi remains an unabashed admirer of Margaret Thatcher. When asked in a recent interview with the *New York Times* to explain why the London art scene had generated so much interest, he replied:

Margaret Thatcher .... She created an environment in Britain where people felt they could escape the role they had been pushed into. They no longer had to be dropouts and failures. Students like Damien Hirst felt they could do absolutely anything (Solomon, 1999).

Though my purpose here is not to engage in political polemic but rather to allow the facts to speak for themselves, one can see that Charles Saatchi is very much part of the creation of the capitulation to the economic model, to what

Bourdieu has called the 'economic fatalism' of the neo-liberal and conservative restoration, even of the Left (Bourdieu, 1998a, 1988c: 94–105). From this one can garner something of Charles Saatchi's position in the 'space of positions and dispositions' within the field of contemporary art in London. It is hardly surprising, that one critic in a review of the *Sensation* show for *Art in America* wrote:

> Had this been an advertising campaign, Saatchi could not have organized it better. And, as one notes which artists were not included in the show (the relatively low-key and less controversial), it is difficult to escape the suspicion that an advertising campaign, for himself, for the yBa's and, by association, for the RA, was just what *Sensation* was (Macritchie, 1998).

Over the years Saatchi has been constantly on the look out for the most advanced and cutting edge young 'avant-garde' producers in this field, not only in Britain but also in Europe and America.[9] Since he opened his private museum in north London in 1985 he has mounted a succession of exhibitions of what he considers advanced art. In the early 1990s Saatchi switched his emphasis to young British artists; this, at over 875 works, now eclipses all other aspects of the collection, including young German and American art. The collection now stands at around 1500 artworks in all media, including video and photography.

Following Bourdieu's understanding of the nature of practice it is important to assert that Saatchi is not necessarily involved in any kind of conscious conspiracy to control British art (Bourdieu, 1988: 246). Rather, he is, by virtue of his own particular habitus a practically engaged player in the game, and as a practically engaged player he may unknowingly *seek control*. 'Intellectual or artistic position takings are also always semi-conscious *strategies* in a game in which the conquest of cultural legitimacy and the concomitant power of legitimate symbolic violence is at stake' (Bourdieu, 1993a: 137). For the field of contemporary art is a prime example of a 'field of struggles' in which players fight to impose their own legitimation strategies upon the game. As an individual agent, Saatchi is one important, player in this game. Practically, as Bourdieu would no doubt remind us, though he does not necessarily act with conscious guile, nevertheless, he plays a highly strategic game by virtue of his position in the large-scale field. Bourdieu sums up the kind of misrecognitions and double games ('*double jeu*') engaged with in the field of culture:

> Culture is the site, par excellence, of misrecognition, because, in generating strategies objectively adapted to the objective chances of profit of which it is the product, the sense of investment secures profits which do not need to be pursued as profits, and so it brings to those who have a legitimate culture as second nature the supplementary profit of being seen (and seeing themselves) as perfectly disinterested, unblemished by any cynical or mercenary use of culture. This means that the term 'investment', for

171

example, must be understood in the dual sense of economic investment – which it objectively always is, though misrecognized – and the sense of affective investment which it has in psychoanalysis, or, more exactly, in the sense of *illusio*, belief, an involvement in the game which produces the game. The art-lover knows no other guide than his love of art, and when he moves, as if by instinct, towards what is, at each moment, the thing to be loved, like some businessmen who make money even when they are not trying to, he is not pursuing a cynical calculation, but his own pleasure, the sincere enthusiasm which, in such matters, is one of the preconditions of successful investment (Bourdieu, 1984: 86).

Saatchi may well be genuinely aggrieved at the suggestion that his *interest* in art is primarily an economic one, but one wonders just how aware he is of the *double jeu* that goes on between interests and investments in the cultural field. Whilst the blind sincerity of his interest, symbolic and economic, in contemporary British art might not be questioned, what may be challenged is the exact extent, and therefore legitimacy, of his cultural capital; his understanding of the autonomous workings of the practically embodied 'field of struggles' – as to what constitutes advanced art. It is worth repeating that his expertise is in the analogous but *not* homologous field of advertising, and it leaves an uncomfortable doubt as to the true nature of his skills which may be more in the field of marketing than in the specialized and autonomous field of art. [10]

Hopefully, there are agents (I count myself as one) who challenge his cultural capital as a legitimating agent. Hopefully there are others, those (gallery directors, curators, critics etc.) in the established field who do not inevitably submit to the symbolic violence of his economic capital; though, for some, it must be difficult to resist. [11] As Bourdieu says:

The threats to autonomy result from the increasingly greater interpenetration between the world of art and the world of money. I am thinking of new forms of sponsorship, of new alliances being established between certain economic enterprises ... and cultural producers. I am thinking too, of the more and more frequent recourse of university research to sponsorship, and of the creation of educational institutions directly subordinated to business ... But the grip or empire of the economy over artistic or scientific research is also exercised inside the field itself, through the control of the means of cultural production and distribution, and even of the instances of consecration. Producers attached to the major cultural bureaucracies (newspapers, radio, television) are increasingly forced to accept and adopt norms and constraints linked to the requirements of the market and, especially, to pressure exerted more or less strongly and directly by advertisers; and they tend more or less unconsciously to constitute as a universal measure of intellectual accomplishment those forms of intellectual activity to which they are condemned by their conditions of work (I am thinking, for example of *fast writing* and *fast reading*, [one might add *fast looking* as well!] which are often the rule in journalistic production and criticism) (Bourdieu, 1996: 344).

Positions and dispositions

I will now briefly examine the different relative positions of two of the leading artists (both Turner Prize [12] winners) in the exhibition: Damien Hirst (b.1965) and Rachel Whiteread (b.1963). Hirst is described in the catalogue as having 'become the most famous living British artist after David Hockney.' In 1988, whilst still a student at Goldsmiths College, he curated the 'Freeze' exhibition, which launched the careers of many successful young British artists, including his own. Hirst represents a new kind of entrepreneurial market orientated artist, fostered by the socio-political climate of Margaret Thatcher's Tory governments. The model for this kind of artist was initiated in the Reaganite 1980s by American artists who followed the lead of Marcel Duchamp and the artist Andy Warhol who named his studio the 'Factory' in the 60s, and later called it the 'Office'; both, along with his idea of 'Business Art' represent his witty and candid *outing* of the placement of the artist within the capitalist mode of production. The 60s Pop artists were interested in referencing the large-scale field of cultural production in their work; the world of quotidian culture; advertising, fashion and package design. Hirst is no exception and has acknowledged the influence of the world of advertising. The problematic aspects of this on his practice as an artist have been noted by the critics (Corris, 1997). [13] Hirst has also been involved, along with the nephew of the artist Lucian Freud, Matthew Freud, the founder of the public relations firm Freud Communications, in the opening of two restaurants in London and has had other involvements in the commercial world.

Rachel Whiteread, on the other hand is a very different type of artist, coming from a different 'pedigree'. Whilst her work references the quotidian world of everyday objects (she makes casts from these objects) it can be seen as being more 'purely' sculptural than Hirst's. He, besides continuing the tradition of what has been called 'vitrinism' (in the wake of Joseph Beuys, another exemplary figure in the world of avant-garde art), makes, or rather manufactures, paintings ('spot' paintings and 'spin' paintings) in a factory production line method akin to Andy Warhol. Whiteread has drawn heavily on the example of another American artist of the 60s, Bruce Nauman (in particular his casts, especially, his *A Cast of the Space under My Chair* 1966–8 which was the model for her *Untitled (One-Hundred Spaces)* 1995 exhibited in *Sensation*) (Figure 1). In 1997 she was given a retrospective exhibition (*Rachel Whiteread: Shedding Life*) at the Tate Gallery Liverpool, which contained a catalogue essay by the doyenne of contemporary art history and criticism, Rosalind Krauss. [14] Whiteread is now represented by the major dealer of contemporary art in London, Antony D'Offay.

Hirst (born in Bristol) and Whiteread (born in London) represent a recent example of the dialectic of positions and dispositions which Bourdieu saw represented in nineteenth century Paris by Manet and Zola on the one hand, and Courbet and Champfleury on the other, which became two long standing and opposing poles of interest in the field of contemporary art (Bourdieu, (1992) 1996: 264f.). The one signifies the culturally subversive egalitarian engagement of the everyday as a challenge to the aristocratic distantiated autonomy of avant-garde art; the other re-asserts that autonomy, and challenges the dangerous dissolution of art into the large-scale field, or the collapse of art as an autonomous realm into the everyday. However we must be aware of the danger of over polarizing these autonomous-heteronomous positions. Their positions are always relative to each other. 'One should beware of seeing anything more than a limiting parameter construction in the opposition between the two modes of production of symbolic goods, which can only be defined in terms of their relations with each other' (Bourdieu, 1993a: 127).

The 1960s

Now, I shall turn briefly to the question of British art in the 1960s. Like the present time of so-called 'Cool Britannia' (linked with the Blair administration's modernization programme[15]), the so-called 'Swinging Sixties' seemed like a utopian period for some young British artists, when there was a rapid expansion in the field with the 'explosion of POP': pop art, pop music and popular colour magazine and television journalism, all of which have proliferated since. The 60s was the period when the relation of so-called high or avant-garde culture and popular everyday culture came to a head in Europe and the United States:

> Having developed amongst the avant-garde art intelligentsia and their students in the art schools, Pop Art's subversive techniques filtered into the realm of popular culture via the channels of rock music and youth culture ... this seepage from the academy into the mainstream was what 'was really new' about the 1960s and was a consequence first 'of the acceleration of cycles of stylistic change' and secondly of 'the determined violation of taboos against mixing vulgar commercialism with high art (Seago, 1995: 12).[16]

At this time, Bryan Robertson, then Director of the Whitechapel Gallery, put on a series of exhibitions of the work of young British artists entitled 'New Generation'. The most publicly visible artist in that period, comparable to Damien Hirst, who likewise shot into the relatively large-scale field, was David Hockney. However famous and endearing he might be, true cognoscenti of avant-garde art might not regard David Hockney as the significant avant-garde artist that he briefly seemed to be in the 60s; and sadly, if we compare the significant young avant-garde British artists of that period with their equivalents in Europe and the United States, they do not rate well. There are few British artists of that generation who can compare with German artists like Sigmar Polke, Gerhard Richter, or American artists of the stature of Bruce Nauman and Brice Marden.

If British artists of a future generation are to escape this fate then they will need to take more care in their reading of the history of contemporary art and culture and be less enthralled by the short term success and the immediacy of the publicity machine. As Bourdieu has pointed out cultural products age through 'the logic of change' – familiarization and an inevitable wearing down of innovative value (Bourdieu, 1996: 146–173). In the 60s, there was an important book circulating in the advanced field by the cultural historian George Kubler entitled *The Shape of Time: Remarks on the History of Things* (1962). It was a favourite of the *éminence grise* of American avant-garde art Ad Reinhardt. It deals with the cycles of time in which cultural goods circulate; from the shortest obsolescent cycles of fashion, to the longest *almost imperceptible* transformations of form and style in antiquity, such as in the long dynasties of Chinese painting or Egyptian funerary sculpture. Art, of course, has always been subject to the action of time. Nevertheless it has been, and is still, the hope of serious artists that they will produce cultural products that will have some long-term lasting value. Of course, all artists operate within the capitalist consumer system, yet it seems that there is the danger that some will allow the fast turnover of the capitalist 'culture of consumption' to cheapen their product for the sake of quicktime profit. In the long term, this is, of course, not a very smart strategy, economically or symbolically. It is ironic that Saatchi is on record as saying that '90% of the art I buy will be worthless in ten years' (Buck, 1997: 128). In the light of the post-Duchampian institutional theory of art, espoused by Danto (Danto, 1964) and Dickie (Dickie, 1974), one might accept that whatever is institutionally framed as 'art' is art, at least in the sense that it is a form of cultural production, but go on to ask the more precise Deleuzian question as to what level of intensity of aesthetic force of this particular 'art' embodies (Bogue, 1993).

There are some 'British' artists who are engaging with the best aspects of quotidian and popular culture, those who perhaps have the most to fight for, those other 'yBa's' ('young black artists') such as Chris Ofili and Yinka Shonibare, both of whom were included in the *Sensation exhibition*, and Sonia Boyce and Keith Piper, who were not.[17]

In the weeks when I was putting the final touches to the original version of this chapter, we had the good fortune to have in London (for his exhibition at the ICA) the Los Angelenos artist (painter) Lari Pittman (b.1952) whom I had previously interviewed in Manchester in May.[18] Pittman's paintings are assertively, transgressively and *anti-pejoratively* 'decorative', utilizing graphic motifs (clip art) borrowed from common culture, but formally reconstructed in such a way as to elevate them from their original source to the 'high' art of élite culture; in this way they are consonant with the avant-garde tradition of quotidian quotation, as in Cubist collage and Pop art. On one of his last days in London Pittman participated in a public discussion on the relative situations of the London and Los Angeles art worlds. Interestingly enough both are dominated by élite art institutions; Goldsmiths in London and Cal Arts, in Los Angeles. However, it would seem that in LA there is not the great divide between generations of artists that there is in London. Pittman told us that the LA art world is not, as has been the case in London, a 'scene' dominated by the cult of youth and personality. Furthermore it would seem that LA artists are more mature in their attitude to economic capital and the marketplace than artists have been in either London or New York. It seems that in the shadow of Hollywood there is a more open acknowledgment of the capitalist system which looms over all, a system in which they see room for honest investigations of the close relationship, so intimate that they often seem indistinguishable, between desire and critique, something that Pittman and I agreed that Andy Warhol had keenly uncovered in his art practice. Also LA is not dominated by one power hungry dealer/collector, there are a number of serious collectors of contemporary art and also (and Pittman stressed this) artists in LA were consumers of each other's art (sometimes, but not always, economic consumers), something he believed to be very important. For out of this there emerged a level of investment (in Bourdieu's double sense) and a criticality that simply does not exist in London to anything like the same degree. It also seemed that because of the presence of the large-scale field represented by the movie industry, the cultural élite's interest in and use of forms of popular or quotidian culture did not get confused with that culture itself, the way it sometimes does in London.

It has seemed to me that Lari Pittman, who as far as I know has never read a single word of Pierre Bourdieu, has understood at the level of his own practice and long term investment in the art world, everything that Bourdieu makes so explicit at the theoretical level, ie: a profound understanding of the *illusio* and *collusio* (the individual and collective cultural construction and misrecognition) of the 'love of art' in which those of us 'in love' are so often unreflexively engaged; a practical grasp of the field of contemporary art as a complex 'field of struggles'; the relatively dominated position of the restricted-field of élite critical culture in relation to the large-scale field and the field of power; and finally; a complex and subtle grasp of the ways different forms of capital, economic and symbolic are (so often disavowedly) exchanged, and of the different kinds of profits to be obtained from their exchange. I suspect that Bourdieu would not be at all surprised by any of this and would see it as a practical ratification of his own struggles to elucidate the hidden operations of practice in the field of cultural production.

Conclusion

In 1996 Bourdieu published his social analysis of the effects of television and journalism on intellectual culture. It gives those with vested interests in art and culture the means to analyse the effects of television and journalism on contemporary art. In Britain, there is no better place to observe these effects than in the yearly controversies which surround the awarding of the Turner Prize, which is itself tied to a sponsorship deal with Channel 4. It is my belief, that far from aiding understanding of contemporary art in Britain, the Turner Prize is one of the factors that is in danger of handing over the British artworld to the entertainment industry. Surely, it is a very serious matter indeed when the leading government sponsored institution for contemporary art in Britain, the Tate Gallery, in the name of the misguided democratic idealism of engaging the interest of the greatest number of persons in contemporary art, disavowedly colludes with commercial enterprise. The Turner Prize, founded in 1984, was grounded in the growth of the enterprise culture of the Thatcher and Reagan years, when government support for the arts weakened and was increasingly supplemented by sponsorship deals with corporate business. Sponsorship, as Bourdieu has shown, and as the artist Hans Haacke has graphically uncovered, is a highly problematic form of gift exchange, of which there is far too little general understanding and discussion. As Bourdieu said in 1994, in his book of conversations with Haacke:

> Private patronage is in fashion. Some public relations firms, for example, are hired to help businesses choose the best place for their symbolic investments and to assist them in establishing contacts in the world of art or science.
>
> In the face of this, critical awareness is nil, or almost nil. People move along in a dispersed manner without collective reflection …. Lacking a collective strategy, researchers run the risk of having their objects of study, their problematics, and their methods imposed by their funding agency … Indeed, it may be feared that recourse to private patronage in order to finance art … will gradually place artists…in a relationship of material and mental dependence on economic powers and market constraints. In any case, private patronage may justify the abdication of public authorities, who use the pretext of the existence of private patrons to withdraw and suspend their assistance, with the extraordinary result that citizens still finance the arts … through tax exemptions. Furthermore, they finance the symbolic effect brought to bear on them to the extent that the funding appears as an example of the disinterested generosity of the corporations. There is, in this, an extremely perverse mechanism which operates in such a way that we contribute to our own mystifications …
>
> But it would be necessary to analyse the effects of the material and symbolic exchanges that are ever more frequently instituted between corporations and certain categories of intellectual producers …. It is not easy to measure the doubtlessly insidious effects of these kinds of practices, but it is improbable that they increase independence from economic powers and, more generally, from the values of money and profit, against which the literary and artistic worlds were, at least initially, constituted (Bourdieu and Haacke, 1995: 14–19).

177

This increasing emphasis on sponsorship in the arts is part of the slide into 'economic fatalism' of which Bourdieu spoke in his 1997 Ernst Bloch Prize speech (Bourdieu, 1998a). Bourdieu begins the prologue of his book *On Television and Journalism*, which is a transcription of a presentation of his ideas on the non-commercial television station of the Collège de France, with the following statement:

It should go without saying that to reveal the hidden constraints on journalists, which they in turn bring to bear on all cultural producers, is not to denounce those in charge or to point a finger at the guilty parties. Rather it is an attempt to offer to all sides a possibility of liberation, through a conscious effort, from the hold of these mechanisms, and to propose, perhaps, a programme for concerted action by artists, writers, scholars, and journalists – that is, by the holders of the (quasi) monopoly of the instruments of diffusion. Only through such a collaboration will it be possible to work effectively to share the most universal achievement of research and to begin, in practical terms, to universalize the conditions of access to the universal (Bourdieu, 1998: 1).

What exactly does Bourdieu mean by this notion of universalizing access to the universal? If one knows something of his work on the sociology of culture, then one knows that he has been vitally concerned to challenge the doxa of the *universality* of culture (which is what makes his statement so full of reverberating irony), demonstrating in earlier works such as *The Love of Art* (1969, 1991), *Photography: A Middle-brow Art* (1965, 1990); and *Distinction: A Social Critique of the Judgement of Taste* (1979, 1989), concern with exactly *who* has access to the 'love' and tasteful cultivation through education of art and culture. And in these analyses, he has been careful not to fall into that negatively reactive *ressentiment* that Nietzsche analysed so well, and even detected it in himself in his description of the tennis-playing President of France.[19] Bourdieu sincerely believes that everyone has the *right and capacity*, given the right social and educational conditions, to attain to the highest levels of cultivated experience: but he insists that such access is in no way natural or innate, as the socially dominant dilettantes of culture, reinforcing their social superiority, like to imagine. On the contrary, it is socially constructed, inculcated in family and education. In order to attain it one has to have the *leisure* (*skholè*), liberation from menial life tasks in order to make a living.[20] Social injustice ensures it *is few who attain such leisure*: so there is the urgent necessity, on the part of those who enjoy these conditions, of *politically* changing society in order for *all* to gain access to these universal conditions, the conditions of *education* (the time and means to cultivate tastes) that the dominant and privileged classes, *frequently* and, sometimes, *arrogantly* take for granted.

There is a great deal of confusion in relation to this subject of access to culture. It often seems that the dominant players in the world of contemporary art – critics, curators and museum directors – in the name of a misguided democratic idealism of engaging the interest of the largest number of persons in contemporary art, an apparently altruistic idealism which veils commercial interests, are engaged in a process of *dumbing down.*[21] Instead of raising the stakes and providing access for the public to the specialized knowledge and experience needed to enjoy the best of contemporary art, they are falling prey to the *populist trap* of showing less demanding and more sensational forms of art for the more immediate gratification of a fictional, market–researched notion of the 'public', and *what is worse,* artists themselves and the educational institutions that they hale from are colluding, even revelling, in the effects of media sensationalism and of the collapse of the autonomy of the research of the most advanced, and therefore difficult, forms of contemporary art, into the realm of the everyday.[22] One of this year's Turner Prize nominees, Tracey Emin, is a case in point.[23] However much her work was initiated by a genuine and entirely valid desire to confront her abject experience of sex and love as lived in the everyday, has she not dissolved the tension that must exist between art and life; the famous 'gap' that the American artist Robert Rauschenberg said he wished to act in? Relying on the now academically accepted notion of the 'ready-made' she presented her bed along with an assortment of abject accoutrements, within the four walls of the institutionalized white cube of the national gallery of contemporary art, the Tate, thus providing easy fodder for the lowest levels of television and journalism. Art may confront and certainly has confronted every imaginable kind of experience, no matter how extreme, but if it is to retain any autonomy and last, it must surely not collapse or suture itself into life, but retain the tension of its own autonomy, however fragile or ironic that autonomy might be. Emin seems to fail in this, to the detriment of her art and with the cultural consequence of patronizing her public.

At this point it might be wise to once again reiterate, with Bourdieu, that it is not so much a case of 'pointing fingers' or making accusations, as of understanding the mechanisms in which all players in the game of contemporary culture are caught. As Bourdieu says:

Sociological analysis often comes up against a misconception. Anyone involved as the object of the analysis...tends to think that the work of analysis, the revelation of mechanisms, is in fact a denunciation of individuals, part of an *ad hominem* polemic ... In general, people don't like to be turned into objects or objectified ... They feel under fire, singled out. But the further you get in the analysis of a given milieu, the more you are likely to let individuals off the hook (which doesn't mean justifying everything that happens). And the more you understand how things work, the more you come to understand that the people involved are manipulated as much as they manipulate. They manipulate even more effectively the more they are themselves manipulated and the more unconscious they are of this (Bourdieu, 1998b: 16–17).

179

Emin is a prime example of an artist caught in these mechanisms of manipulation with the journalistic and televisual field. Bourdieu has also articulated the difficult problem of the relation of popular to so-called high culture in his discussions with Löic Wacquant: and it is worth quoting him on this:

> To accuse me, as has sometimes been done, of consecrating the difference between so-called popular culture and 'high' culture, in sum of ratifying the superiority of bourgeois culture (or the opposite, depending on whether one purports to be 'revolutionary' or conservative) is to ignore the Weberian distinction between a judgement of value and a reference to values (Weber, 1949). It amounts to mistaking a reference to values that agents actually effect in objectivity for a value judgement passed by the scientist who studies them. We touch here on one of the great difficulties of sociological discourse. Most discourses on the social world aim at saying, not what the realities under consideration ... are, but what they are worth, whether they are good or bad. Any scientific discourse of simple enunciation is strongly liable to be perceived either as ratification or as denunciation .... Irrespective of what we think of this dichotomy, it exists in mechanism (such as the sanctions of the academic market) as well as in the subjectivity of schemata of classifications, systems of preferences, and tastes, which everybody knows (in practice) to be themselves hierarchized. Verbally to deny evaluative dichotomies is to pass a morality off for a politics. The dominated in the artistic and the intellectual fields have always practised that form of radical chic which consists in rehabilitating socially inferior cultures or the minor genres of legitimate culture ... To denounce hierarchy does not get us anywhere. What must be changed are the conditions that make this hierarchy exist, both in reality and in minds. We must – I have never stopped repeating it – work to universalize in reality the conditions of access to what the present offers us that is most universal, instead of talking about it (Bourdieu and Wacquant, 83–84).

Many of the problems of current (young) British art are engaged in these elisions of definition with regard to popular and high culture, and are tied to the slide into commercialism and banality that is sometimes shamelessly encouraged by some of those who consider themselves the guardians of British culture. It is hardly surprising, given Bourdieu's comments on the temptations open to academics, that academic historians, like Lisa Jardine, have been drawn into the fray by lending their academic capital to the Saatchi enterprise by providing an essay on art patronage in the catalogue of the 1997 *Sensation* exhibition, in which she describes Saatchi as a modern Medici, something which, ironically, maybe nearer the truth than she intended.

In *The Rules of Art* Bourdieu traces the genesis and structure of the field of avant-garde resistance to bourgeois mercantile culture in mid-nineteenth century Paris, and ends with a rousing call to intellectuals, as one of the last critical countervailing powers capable of opposing the forces of economic and political order, to mobilize in defense of their own autonomy, increasingly threatened by the strengthening forces of the market. Subsequently he has made similar appeals in his Ernst Bloch Prize acceptance speech (Bourdieu, 1998a) in *On Television and Journalism* (Bourdieu, 1998b) and *Acts of Resistance* (Bourdieu, 1998c). Bourdieu suggests that if the autonomy of culture is to survive and continue to thrive, then autonomous artists and intellectuals (those not solely motivated by market forces) need to organize themselves and unite in its defence. They can only do this, of course, if they first understand and accept that there is a threat to the autonomy and quality of their endeavours by the large-scale field. In view of its importance, to conclude, I will take the liberty of quoting Bourdieu at length on this:

> When we speak as intellectuals, that is, with the ambition to be universal, it is always, at any moment, the historical unconscious inscribed in the experience of a singular intellectual field which speaks through our mouths. I think that we only have a chance of achieving real communication when we objectify and master the various kinds of historical unconscious separating us, meaning the specific histories of intellectual universes which have produced our categories of perception and thought.
>
> I want to come now to an exposition of the particular reasons why it is especially urgent today that intellectuals mobilize and create a veritable *Internationale of intellectuals* committed to defending the autonomy of the universes of cultural production or, to parody a language now out of fashion, *the ownership by cultural producers of their instruments of production and circulation* (and hence of evaluation and consecration). I do not think I am succumbing to an apocalyptic vision of the state of the field of cultural production by saying that this autonomy is very severely threatened or, more precisely, that a threat of a totally new sort today hangs over its functioning; that artists, writers and scholars are more and more completely excluded from public debate, both because they are less inclined to intervene in it and because the possibility of an effective intervention is less and less frequently offered to them (Bourdieu, 1996: 344).
>
> The anarchic order reigning in an intellectual field which has achieved a high degree of autonomy is always fragile and threatened, to the extent that it constitutes a challenge to the laws of the ordinary economic world and to the rules of common sense. It is dangerous for it to depend on just the heroism of a few. It is not virtue which can found a free intellectual order; it is a free intellectual order which can found intellectual virtue (Bourdieu, 1996: 347).

And in his Ernst Bloch Prize acceptance speech Bourdieu had this to say:

> Let us acknowledge the fact that we are currently in a period of neo-conservative reconstruction ... It is a new type of conservative revolution

that claims connection with progress, reason and science – economics actually – to justify its own re-establishment, and by the same token tries to relegate progressive thought and action to archaic status. It erects into defining standards for all practices, and thus into ideal rules, the regularities of the economic world abandoned to its own logic: the law of the market, the law of the strongest. It ratifies and glorifies the rule of what we call the financial markets, a return to a sort of radical capitalism answering to no law except that of maximum profit; an undisguised, unrestrained capitalism, but one that has been rationalized, tuned to the limit of its economic efficiency through the introduction of modern forms of domination ('management') and manipulative techniques like market research, marketing and commercial advertising. (Bourdieu, 1998a: 125).

Notes

1 A version of this paper was originally given at the 1998 Midwest Modern Language Association Conference: 'Working the Fields: Bourdieu's Sociology of the Cultural Field' St. Louis, Missouri, November 5–7 1998.
2 For a profound discussion of this sense of sensation, see Deleuze's book on Francis Bacon *The Logic of Sense* (Deleuze, 1981, Boundas, 1993: 65–71). See also Daniel W. Smith 'Deleuze's Theory of Sensation: Overcoming the Kantian Duality' (Patton, 1996: 29–56).
3 Michael Ellison 'Checkmate at art show' *The Guardian*, 30 September 1999.
4 I was briefly a 'yBa' myself in the 1960s, when I exhibited in the structural equivalent of the exhibitions of young British artists at the Saatchi Gallery in London in the 90s; the 'New Generation' exhibitions at the Whitechapel Gallery. Though no longer participating in the field as a practising artist, I still have a stake and a long-term investment in the game. With the help of Bourdieu I hope to avoid falling into either a subjectivist or objectivist mode of analysis. We must also, as John Guillory has shown, guard against being either *determinists* or *voluntarists* when analysing the positions of agents in the field (Guillory, 1997).
5 The obsession with 'youth' is endemic to the large-scale field, where market success is openly avowed, especially in relation to the field of avant-garde production, which represents the youthful end of the field of cultural production. See Bourdieu ' "Youth" is just a word' (Bourdieu, 1993b): 94–102).
6 It is perhaps worth noting that Maurice Saatchi received a First Class Hons. from the London School of Economics.
7 He made a rare public appearance on television in 1994 when he presented the Turner Prize to Anthony Gormley (Buck, 1997: 128).
8 'The real Saatchis – masters of illusion', Channel Four, 10 July, a Laurel Productions film Produced by Bernadette O'Farrell; directed by Chris Oxley, (781,000 viewers) which dished some dirt on the rise and fall of the Saatchi's omnivorous acquisitions strategy during the 1980s, an unseemly saga of vanity, hedonism and reckless corporate leverage in which they set about consuming the global food-chain of advertising agencies and management consultancies. In the event it also turned out to be required viewing for those seeking a clearer understanding of Charles Saatchi's art-dealing activities.
   'Saatchi and Saatchi wasn't trying to be the best advertising agency in the world; it was just trying to be the biggest', said founding shareholder and former director Tim Bell, one of a procession of ad execs who queued up to trade anecdotes on the brothers and their modus operandi. The advertising philosophy clearly extended into Charles Saatchi's art buying which for a time conformed to a similar pattern of capricious adoption followed by unceremonious

dumping, Sean Scully, one of the many artists who felt the dead hand of Saatchi patronage, described it as more akin to commodity trading than collecting.

Chris Oxley's film exposed the brothers as corporate piranha, insensitive to the protocols that characterize certain types of creative activity, but it also revealed them as friable fish, for their master-plan for world domination ultimately came to naught. A revealing journey into the megalomaniac mindset, this documentary put into a fresh context the recent allegations that some current advertising from the New Saatchi Agency is parasitic upon the creative ideas of the artists Charles Saatchi patronizes' (Flynn, 1999).

9 The historical formation of the 'avant-garde' in nineteenth century Europe has now become a highly commodifiable idea in the large-scale field of cultural production equal in status to that of 'tradition' as can be observed in the field of fashion where styles are marketed in terms of the 'traditional' or the 'avant-garde'. Bourdieu has made some fruitful comparisons between the fields of culture and fashion (Bourdieu, 1993b: 132–38; Bourdieu, 1975).

10 A catalogue for his next 'production' was produced in advance; another new wave of artists marketed under the moniker *New Neurotic Realism* with an essay by the art columnist for the popular youth culture magazine *I–D*.

11 He is renowned for buying and selling in bulk.

12 The Turner Prize established in 1984, is a prize of £20,000 given to a contemporary artist for their contribution to the field in last twelve months. It is sponsored by the television company Channel 4 and, like its literary equivalent, the Booker Prize, receives a great deal of television and media coverage. It can be compared to the relatively low key Hamlyn Awards, in which artists receive from the Hamlyn Foundation, bursaries of £10,000 a year for three years, with no strings attached, to enable them to work without financial pressure.

13 Hirst has said: 'I get a lot of inspiration from ads in order to communicate my ideas as an artist and of course Charles is very close to all that' (Buck 1997: 127). This traffic works both ways, as Gillian Wearing discovered when she found that M & C Saatchi 'stole the idea of her video installation "10–16", a copy of which Saatchi bought for $30,000 and showed as part of the *Sensation* exhibition ...' (Greenberg, 1999).

14 The author of pioneering books on contemporary sculpture.

15 'It is worth noting that British prime minister Tony Blair was regarded as little more than an image manager on first taking office. He undertook a "style offensive" to give Britain a new avant-garde identity'. 'It was time to "rebrand" Britain as one of the world's pioneers rather than one of its museums', asserted 'Demos, a social policy research center close to Mr. Blair'. Quoted in Warren 'Blair's "Rebranded" Britain is no Museum' *The New York Times*, November 12, 1997, A1. Successful image-making or aesthetic rebranding adds to the power, authority, and wealth of the image maker, for he seems to be an efficient, competent, knowledgeable manager of reality, even if he is not' Kuspit, 1999).

16 The text in quotation marks is from Bernice Martin, *A Sociology of Contemporary Cultural Change*, Oxford, 1981, p. 94.

17 Kobena Mercer, 'Back to the Routes: A Postscript to the 80s' *Pictura Britannica: Art From Britain*, Sydney, 1997.

18 Unpublished interview with the artist.

19 Isn't the root of my revolt, my irony, my sarcasm, of the rhetorical vibration of my adjectives when I describe Giscard d'Estaing playing tennis (Bourdieu, 1984a: 210) the fact that, deep down, I envy what he is? *Ressentiment* is for me the form *par excellence* of human misery; it is the worst thing that the dominant impose on the dominated (perhaps the major privilege of the dominant, in any social universe, is to be structurally freed from *ressentiment*). (Bourdieu and Wacquant, 1994: 212).

20 The scholastic view is a very peculiar point of view on the social world, on language, on any possible object of thought that is made possible by the situation of *skholè* – is a particular form, as an institutionalized situation of studious leisure. Adoption of this scholastic point of view is the admission fee tacitly demanded by all scholarly fields: the neutralizing disposition ... implying the bracketing of all theses of existence and all practical intentions, is the condition – at least as much as the possession of a specific competence – for access to museums and works of art.

We should take Plato's reflections on *skholè* very seriously and even his famous expression, so often commented upon, *spoudaiôs paizein*, 'to play seriously'. The scholastic point of view is inseparable from the scholastic situation, a socially instituted situation in which one can defy or ignore the common alternative between playing (*pazein*), joking, and being serious (*spoudazein*) by playing seriously and taking ludic things seriously, busying oneself with problems that serious, and truly busy, people ignore – actively or passively. *Homo scholasticus* or *homo academicus* is someone who can play seriously because his or her state (or State) assures her the means to do so, that is, free time, outside the urgency of a practical situation, the necessary competence assured by a specific apprenticeship based on *skholè*, and, finally but most importantly, the disposition (understood as an aptitude and an inclination) to invest and to invest oneself in the futile stakes, at least in the eyes of serious people, which are generated in scholastic worlds ... (Bourdieu, 1998: 127–28).

21 See 'Dumb and dumber?' Chapter 4 of Julian Stallabrass' book on the yBa phenomenon (Stallabrass, 1999).

22 In fact there is no such totalizing entity as 'the public', only different 'publics' with tastes formed by the class fractions to which they belong, see Bourdieu's *Distinction: A Social Critique of the Judgement of Taste.*

23 It is not surprising to discover that she is the first choice of *Time Out* listings columnist, Sarah Kent, for the Turner Prize this year. Sarah Kent is also one of the writers that Charles Saatchi has employed for his leaflets and catalogues.

References

Bickers, P., (1997), 'Sense and Sensation', *Art Monthly*, no. 211, pp. 1–6 (London) November.

Boundas, C., (ed.), *The Deleuze Reader*, New York: Columbia University Press.

Bogue, R., 'Gilles Deleuze: The Aesthetics of Force', *Journal of the Society for Phenomenology*, vol. 24, no. 1, January 1993, reprinted in Paul Patton ed., *Deleuze: A Critical Reader*, Oxford: Blackwell.

Bourdieu, P., (1975), 'Le couturier et sa griffe, contribution à une théorie de la magie', *Actes de la recherche en sciences sociales*, 1: 7–36.

Bourdieu, P., (1984), *Distinction: A Social Critique of the Judgment of Taste*, London: Routledge.

Bourdieu, P., (1988), *Homo Academicus*, Cambridge: Polity.

Bourdieu, P., (1993a), *The Field of Cultural Production*, Cambridge: Polity.

Bourdieu, P., (1993b), *Sociology in Question*, London: Sage.

Bourdieu, P., (1996), *The Rules of Art*, Cambridge: Polity.

Bourdieu, P. and Haacke, H., (1995), *Free Exchange*, Cambridge: Polity.

Bourdieu, P., (1997), 'Marginalia – Some Additional Notes on the Gift', Schrift, A.D., *The Logic of the Gift: Toward an Ethic of Generosity*, London and New York: Routledge.

Bourdieu, P., (1998a), 'A Reasoned Utopia and Economic Fatalism', *New Left Review*, 227, Jan/Feb.

Bourdieu, P., (1998b), *On Television and Journalism*, London: Pluto.

Bourdieu, P., (1998c), *Acts of Resistance: against the new myths of our time*, Cambridge: Polity.

Bourdieu, P., (1998d), *Practical Reason: On the Theory of Action*, Cambridge: Polity.

Buck, L., (1997), *A User's Guide to British Art, Now*, London: Tate.

Corris, M., (1997), 'Pop Star Divided: Damien Hirst and the Ends of British Art', *Art + Text*, No. 58, Aug–Oct.

Danto, A., (1964), 'The artworld', *Journal of Philosophy*, 61, pp. 571–584.

Deleuze, G., (1981), *Francis Bacon: Logique de la Sensation*, Paris: Édition de la Différence.

Dickie, G., (1974), *Art and Aesthetic*, Ithaca: Cornell University Press.

Flynn, T., (1999), *The Art Newspaper*, No. 95, September.

Glueck, G., (1993), 'A kind of Public Service', *Hans Haacke: Bodenlos*, Stuttgart: Cantz.

Greenberg, S., (1999), 'Art and copyright: Gillian Wearing V. Saatchi', *The Art Newspaper*, Vol. X, No. 91, April.

Guillory, J., (1997), 'Bourdieu's refusal' in *MLQ* Volume 58, Number 4, December.

Haacke, H., *Obra Social/Hans Haacke*, Barcelona: La Fundació.

Kuspit, D., (1999), 'Art is Dead: Long Live Aesthetic Management', *New Art Examiner*, April.

Macritchie, L., (1998), 'Rude Britannia (Sensation)', *Art in America*, v. 86 no. 4 (Apr. '98) pp. 36–39.

Mills, L. and Milner, C., (1999), 'Saatchi puts shock-art on menu of planned Sensation restaurant', *The Sunday Telegraph*, 18 July.

Patton, P., ed., (1996), *Deleuze: A Critical Reader*, Oxford: Blackwell.

Seago, A., (1995), *Burning the Box of Beautiful Things*, Oxford: OUP.

Solomon, D., (1999), 'The Collector', *New York Times Magazine*, September 26.

Stallabrass, J., (1999), *High Art Lite*, London and New York: Verso.

Swartz, D., (1997), *Culture and Power: The Sociology of Pierre Bourdieu*, Chicago: The University of Chicago Press.

Wallis, B., (1986), *Hans Haacke: Unfinished Business*, Cambridge, Massachusetts: MIT.

Weber, M., (1949), *The Methodology of the Social Sciences*, Glencoe, Ill: The Free Press.

The English intellectual field in the 1790s and the creative project of Samuel Taylor Coleridge – an application of Bourdieu's cultural analysis

Derek M. Robbins

'Let us then go straight ahead', said the Captain, 'and connect this idea with what we have already defined and discussed. For example: what we call limestone is more or less pure calcium oxide intimately united with a thin acid known to us in a gaseous state. If you put a piece of this limestone into dilute sulphuric acid, the latter will seize on the lime and join with it to form calcium sulphate, or gypsum; that thin gaseous acid, on the other hand, escapes. Here there has occurred a separation and a new combination, and one then feels justified even in employing the term 'elective affinity', because it really does look as if one relationship was preferred to another and chosen instead of it'.

'Forgive me', said Charlotte, 'as I forgive the scientist, but I would never see a choice here but rather a natural necessity and indeed hardly that; for in the last resort it is perhaps only a matter of opportunity. Opportunity makes relationships just as much as it makes thieves; and where your natural substances are concerned, the choice seems to me to lie entirely in the hands of the chemist who brings these substances together. ... [1] (Johann Wolfgang von Goethe: *Elective Affinities* (1809).

The German title of Goethe's *Novelle, Die Wahlverwandtschaften* – is borrowed from a technical term in eighteenth-century chemistry which was first used in the German translation of Torbern Bergmann's *De attractionibus electivis*. The Latin emphasizes the choice of 'attraction' whilst the German rendering emphasizes the choice of relationships – 'Verwandschaften' are family 'relatives'. 'Affinity' has come to mean a 'common origin' but derives from the Latin which means the point at which boundaries touch each other. Through these various linguistic forms, however, the issue is clear. Goethe was deliberately using a terminology developed in the natural sciences to offer an explanation of the forces at play in human relationships. The characters who idly discuss whether the language of chemistry applies analogously or actually to human relations by so doing demonstrate that there is an uneasy tension between self-conscious choice and unconscious attraction as they become (inexorably?) drawn into a web of new relationships. It may not be a matter of an opposition between choice and necessity so much as that, in some reciprocal fashion, choices are determined whilst, also, determination is chosen. Or even, as Goethe makes his fictional Charlotte say, that the reciprocal process is dependent on the contrivance of an author.

'Elective affinity' is an extremely apt and suggestive phrase through which to understand Bourdieu's thinking – and it is a phrase which Bourdieu has himself used. Translated into Bourdieu's terminology, we can say that all individuals possess a 'habitus' – which is a set of manners and attitudes which amount to a disposition to act distinctively. Our tastes and interests – our choices of affinities, whether personal, aesthetic, or intellectual – are expressions of that disposition. But it is not a pre-disposition, in the sense of being fixed or intrinsic. We inherit dispositions which condition our social and moral choices, but we are able to modify this conditioning somewhat by making circumscribed, new choices. There are parameters within which our 'habitus' can be adjusted, just as there are parameters which enable a natural process to be both the consequence of affinity and of choice.

This tension exists in all of Bourdieu's thinking and is most clear if we transpose the insights of his *Distinction: towards a critique of the judgement of taste* to the English situation. Our inclinations to vote Labour rather than Conservative, to enjoy wine rather than beer, to prefer Mozart to Bowie, to worship in a Roman Catholic Church or in a 'charismatic' pentecostal church, to read Joanne Trollope or Milan Kundera, to live in Liverpool or in Orpington, to eat in McDonald's rather than at the Ritz, to play golf rather than soccer, to go to university at Durham rather than at South Bank, to take *The Guardian* rather than *The Sun*, and so on, are all complicatedly inter-related and are all the consequences of choices made within contexts which are varyingly constrained.

Bourdieu's own affinities cannot be detached from this complex nexus of tastes and attitudes. Certainly since the late 1960s he has consolidated a commitment to a philosophy of scientific method which is rooted in a particular French tradition of anti-positivist thought. As he writes in *Thinking About Limits* (1992):

What I now very quickly want to address is the epistemological tradition in which I have begun to work. This was for me like the air that we breathe, which is to say that it went unnoticed. It is a very local tradition tied to a number of French names; Koyré, Bachelard, Canguilhem and, if we go back a little, to Duhem. One should should study the historical reasons for its existence, since it was not at all a national miracle, but no doubt related to favourable conditions within the structure of the education system. This historical tradition of epistemology very strongly linked reflection on science with the history of science. Differently from the neo-positivist Anglo-Saxon tradition, it was from the history of science that it isolated the principles of knowledge of scientific thought.[2]

Equally, again since the late 1960s, Bourdieu has applied the philosophy of science which was the product of the social conditions of the French Third Republic to two artists who were also the product of the same social and political conditions – Flaubert and Manet. *Prima facie*, the possibility emerges that Bourdieu's method of analysis and the objects on which that method has been practised are mutually reinforcing – that the 'analytical' procedure may not generate 'criticism' so much as a consolidation of a community of personal affinities. The purpose of this paper, therefore, is to explore the extent to which the adoption of Bourdieu's concepts can assist in the interpretation of cultural production that might be ideologically alien to the basic thinking on which those concepts have been established. In carrying out this exploration – which can only be undertaken here in summary fashion – one further important point needs to be made. At the very beginning of the interview of April, 1985 with A. Honneth, H. Kocyba and B. Schwibs, published as 'Fieldwork in philosophy' in *In Other Words* (1990), Bourdieu was asked about the intellectual situation when he was a student, and, in particular, about his attitude towards Marxism and phenomenology. In relation to Marxism, Bourdieu replied:

> Marxism didn't really exist as an intellectual position, even if people like Tran-Duc-Thao managed to give it a certain profile by raising the question of its relation with phenomenology. However, I did read Marx at that time for academic reasons; I was especially interested in the young Marx, and I had been fascinated by the *Theses on Feuerbach*. But this was the period of Stalinist ascendancy. Many of my fellow students who these days have become violently anti-communist were then in the Communist Party.[3]

Almost unconsciously, Bourdieu makes a revealing distinction between forms of reading. Within an autonomous intellectual field, Marxism possessed no currency. There was no possibility of any intellectual position-taking vis-à-vis Marxism. The response to Marxism was dominated by issues related to *social* position-taking and, tacitly, Bourdieu states that he had no wish to be associated socially with those of his fellow students who were overtly Communist. Nevertheless, in the telling phrase, he did read Marx 'for academic reasons' and, within that reading, found that there were elements which 'interested' him or 'fascinated' him. In other words, Bourdieu distinguishes between reading which is part of an imposed academic exercise (within which interests may be identified or may emerge) and reading which relates to the cluster of affinities which shape the intellectual and social trajectories of individuals. It was beyond the scope of Bourdieu's 'habitus' to be socially aligned with Communists, but it was within the scope of his 'habitus' to engage with the work of Marx as one part of the process of acquiring cultural capital through educational attainment. This distinction between an existential response and an academic response will inform my discussion of what now should be our response to Bourdieu's own intellectual achievements.

The two emphases of this chapter – on the study of the creative activity of the poet Coleridge within the English intellectual field of the 1790s and on the social conditions in the present which construct the perspective to be adopted in undertaking that historical study – both derive from points made by Bourdieu in the opening paragraphs of the article from which my title is taken: *Intellectual field and creative project*. In the very first sentence, Bourdieu writes:

> In order that the sociology of intellectual and artistic creation be assigned its proper object and at the same time its limits, the principle must be perceived and stated that the relationship between a creative artist and his work, and therefore his work itself, is affected by the system of social relations within which creation as an act of communication takes place, or to be more precise, by the position of the creative artist in the structure of the intellectual field (which is itself, in part at any rate, a function of his past work and the reception it has met with).[4]

Bourdieu sought to make it clear that the construction of a sociological *understanding* of intellectual or artistic creation is dependent on a commitment to the view that art or thought are *produced* within a system of social relations. The sociological analysis of creativity is, in other words, dependent on a prior rejection of any supposedly 'Romantic' ideology of the artist or thinker as 'self-expressive', charismatic, a-social, transcendent creator.

Typically, Bourdieu went further in the opening sentence of his second paragraph:

> Obviously this approach can only be justified in so far as the object to which it is applied, that is, the intellectual field (and thus the cultural field) possesses the relative autonomy which authorizes the *methodological autonomization* operated by the structural method when it *treats* the intellectual field as a system which is governed by its own laws.[5]

He argued that it is only possible to carry out this kind of analysis if this *methodological autonomization* on the part of present consumers corresponds with an autonomization that was objectively produced within the historical period which is the object of analysis. By implication, in other words, it is, for Bourdieu, only legitimate to carry out sociological analyses of cultural activities which are involved in developing sociological self-understandings of their own production.

The difficulties inherent in the relationship between these two sentences relate to the point in Bourdieu's intellectual development when 'Intellectual field and creative project' was first published – in 1966. Bourdieu was wanting to adopt the methodological position which is derived from Bachelard and is fully articulated in *Le métier de sociologue* (1968). Following Bachelard, the objects of enquiry have to be constructed. They do not have objective existence. At the same time, Bourdieu was seeking a reconciliation of the ethnomethodological and structuralist approaches to social enquiry which he was to articulate in *Esquisse d'une théorie de la pratique* (1972) and, particularly, in *The three forms of theoretical knowledge* (1972). Bachelard's methodological constructivism could not be allowed to be a form of objectivism. It had to be subjected to a second epistemological break which would disclose the constructivism in the actions of agents.

In short, there was a tension between the theory of science that Bourdieu took from Bachelard and outlined in *Le métier de sociologue* and the more fundamental theory of knowledge which, I believe, had its origins in Husserl's phenomenology, particularly *Experience and Judgment*, and which Bourdieu articulated in an anthropological context in *Outline of a Theory of Practice*. That tension in relation to our present understanding of past creativity was latent in the opening sentences of 'Intellectual Field and Creative Project'. In order to produce a science of artistic production, we, as present intellectuals, have to construct a sociological analysis against, if necessary, the self-understandings of the artists. In order to liberate the self-understandings of the artistic agents, however, we have to analyse reflexively the historical origins of the conceptual framework which we apply. In taking artists such as Flaubert and Manet as the objects of his enquiries, however, I suggest that Bourdieu's work fudged the methodological tension. There was a pre-existent affinity between the conceptual framework that Bourdieu wished to adopt and the endeavours of those artists to whom the framework was applied. Just as the theory of science was articulated strategically to justify an institutional position *vis-à-vis* the French higher education system after the events of 1968, and just as the theory of knowledge was developed strategically to vindicate a position in relation to structuralism, so the analyses of Flaubert and Manet are not so much applications of prior methodologies as mobilizations of Third Republic, socialist approaches to art and society as elements in Bourdieu's post-1968 position-taking.

I have used the notions of 'strategy' and 'position-taking' here deliberately because, of course, we should not be disconcerted by the apparent tensions in Bourdieu's thinking. Those of us who are attracted to, sympathizers with, supporters of Bourdieu's thinking will be well aware that we are compelled by it to acknowledge that what Bourdieu substantively says about 'strategies' and 'soft logic' must pertain to his process of saying these things. It is part of Bourdieu's position that there is no coherent system of thought at the back of his individual concepts and interventions. We are all aware that Bourdieu's insistence that his thought is not exempted from his own analysis means that there is a mutually reinforcing coherence between his thinking and his actions which strategically places him beyond criticism. I think the small book on Bourdieu by Richard Jenkins demonstrates very clearly that you cannot simultaneously esteem Bourdieu's theory of practice and attempt to criticise his theory without reference to the practical contexts within which it has functioned, and continues to function. This means that any account of Bourdieu's work is likely to be absolute. You either reject what he says and how he says it or you accept his pragmatism and attempt simply to evaluate it in operation.

These are some of the problems I have experienced in trying to produce exegeses of Bourdieu's pragmatism in an academic context which seems to regard 'criticism' as the only appropriate form of 'interpretation'. These are not, however, the problems which I want to focus on to-day. Bourdieu can, after all, look after himself very well. We have different problems. I suggest that our difficulty in following Bourdieu is to establish precisely in what sense his work is paradigmatic for us. Briefly, if we accept that Bourdieu is a conceptual strategist, do we follow him best by adopting his intellectual style – which might lead to the negation of some of his concepts – or do we apply his de-contexted concepts in our work. Or thirdly, perhaps, do we most accurately follow Bourdieu by consciously reflecting on the cross-cultural transfer of his concepts within our own conceptual strategies. (As an aside, I think that even here the guidance which Bourdieu gives is ambiguous as a result of the pragmatically different situations in which it has been advanced. On the one hand, in *Le métier de sociologue*, Bourdieu tries to extrapolate common sociological procedures from the diverse ideological frameworks of, for instance, Marx, Comte, or Weber, seeking to isolate generally transferable, de-contexted procedures. On the other hand, when, more recently, it has been a question of the transferability of his own texts and concepts, he has argued, notably in the English preface to *Homo Academicus*, that, with the exception of that text itself, texts transfer without their contexts and that the appropriation of foreign texts requires a full understanding of their conditions of production and consumption.)

Having identified a tension or inconsistency in Bourdieu's methodological position, I want now to explore the ways in which Bourdieu's thought might be applied by reference to literary production which could be said to be alien to that thought. I chose to do this in relation to an interpretation of Samuel Taylor Coleridge for two reasons. The first is still exegetical. As I have already indicated, it seemed to me that Bourdieu's approach to literature has developed mainly in the context of the French literary tradition with which he feels affinity. I am not aware of any reference in his work to French romanticism. Partly, I suspect, under the influence of Jean Bollack, Bourdieu was responsible for the publication, by Editions de Minuit in 1974, of Peter Szondi's *Poésie et poétique de l'idéalisme allemand*. I think this probably coincided with the work for the 1975 article on 'L'ontologie politique de Martin Heidegger' and, hence, my hypothesis is that Bourdieu has always been inclined to identify romanticism with German romanticism and to see it as proto-idealist and, hence, to be opposed and exposed. I wanted to test out Bourdieu's procedures on literary practice which might be thought to be antipathetic to those procedures – in relation, for instance, to the romantic ideology of 'self-expression'. Secondly, I chose Coleridge for the simple reason that I did my doctorate on Coleridge under the supervision of Raymond Williams between 1966 and 1971 – at the same time, in other words, as Bourdieu was developing his concepts and before almost any of Bourdieu's work was known in the U.K. (I remember, for instance, that, in 1971, Williams was still just 'discovering' Lucien Goldmann.)

I want to map out two kinds of application of Bourdieu's work to thinking about Coleridge. For convenience, I shall call the first response 'academic' and the second 'existential'.

A Bourdieusian academic analysis of Coleridge would, I think, have three main components. It would involve using the concept of 'field' to analyse the field of Coleridge's production during his life-time from 1772 until 1834. It would involve using the same concept to analyse the intellectual field in which, post-mortem, Coleridge's persona and reputation were constructed during the remainder of the 19th century. Thirdly, the concept of field would also be used to analyse the field of transmission of Coleridge in the 20th century. Just to give some more detail of these elements, the first would involve the attempt to avoid reading current prenotions back into the historical context of Coleridge's life. It would involve constant vigilance to understand the social role that Coleridge was seeking to establish for himself. Did he see himself as a poet, a political thinker, a religious thinker, a philosopher, a journalist, or perhaps, a sage? Much sociological analysis of the romantic poets has argued that their writing was a manifestation of their social alienation and this interpretation has often had a vestigial Marxist nuance. A Bourdieusian analysis would be closer to the approach followed by Raymond Williams in his *Orwell* than in his *Culture and Society*. That is to say that it would be necessary to analyse what Coleridge and his context thought that it might have meant to 'be a poet' or 'be a philosopher' or, maybe, to 'be an intellectual'. There is a real sense, for instance, in which Coleridge wanted to write poetry but did not want to accept the social role of the poet which was the legacy of Augustan England. His early unitarianism and his short-lived ministry can be seen as related attempts to establish some kind of solidarity between private intellectual reflection and public social position.

Throughout Coleridge's own life-time there was, of course, always the possibility that the public identity was one which Coleridge might privately wish to disown. Even during his lifetime, the ambiguity of Coleridge's own aspirations generated a multiplicity of interpretative stereo-types. The Coleridgean 'label' was used, by a religious fanatic like Edward Irving for instance, to give intellectual legitimacy to a movement which Coleridge himself would not have wished to condone. From Coleridge's death onwards, the second object of analysis would be the tension between the post mortem endeavour to sustain the reality of Coleridge's objective presence – through the publication of collections and editions of hitherto unpublished work – and the attempt made by different groups to deploy Coleridge's reputation to assist them in their own strategic manoeuvring through the social structure of

Victorian England. The publication of unpublished Coleridgeana was itself either a selective activity or, if genuinely seeking to be purely scholarly, a different form of ideological intervention. There was also, through the activity of Coleridge's sons, daughter, and grand-children, a continuing commitment – arising from family loyalty – to sustaining the reputation of S.T. Coleridge throughout this period.

Between 1832 and 1914, two distinct phases in the reception of Coleridge's work can be identified. Initially it was harnessed to give intellectual force to Christian apologetics which were threatened by the challenge of Darwinism. Coleridge's reputation as a religious thinker reached a climax in J.H.Green's *Spiritual Philosophy* (1865) and it was soon established on a different, aesthetic basis by Walter Pater's essays in the Westminster Review in the late 1860s. The purpose of this research would be to offer a sociological explanation of this shift in the grounding of Coleridge's reputation. Bourdieu argued in 'Intellectual Field and Creative Project' that it was in the mid-nineteenth century in France that the intellectual field succeeded in achieving autonomy from the religious field that remained subservient to Roman Catholic dogma. Bourdieu did not differentiate between an emergent intellectual field dominated by positivistic science and an artistic field dominated by aestheticism. In the competition between fields in England, it seems likely that it is possible to suggest that the work of Coleridge was first appropriated by the religious field in opposition to emergent positivism and then appropriated by aestheticism in order to secure autonomy from both religion and science.

The third element of an analysis would move into the territory of *Homo Academicus*. The rise of English studies has been documented by D.J. Palmer: *The rise of English Studies* (1965) and by C. Baldick: *The Social Mission of English Criticism* (1983), but there has not been a systematic attempt to relate that particular transformation of the university curriculum to the changing function of the university in the period or to the changing social constitution of the student population. By attempting a historiography of the academic literary criticism of the work of Coleridge in parallel with a social history of the institutional contexts within which that criticism was generated, a Bourdieusian analysis would give detailed substance to the outlines suggested in T. Eagleton's: *Literary Theory: An Introduction* (1983).

This, roughly, would be the shape of an academic project which would use Bourdieu's concepts to de-consecrate Coleridge's work and liberate Coleridge so that he could be appreciated as an agent rather than an artifact. This would be an exercise in de-mythologizing. It would be almost in the tradition of Strauss's *Leben Jesu* or *Renan's La vie de Jésus*. It would be a quest for the historical Coleridge and involve an analysis, perhaps reductive and perhaps not, of the subsequent historical accretions. There is, however, as Bourdieu would himself want to argue, certainly one aspect of this Bourdieusian project which makes it unBourdieusian. It neglects Bourdieu's awareness that the institutional conditions of possibility for such a project have to be constructed against the institutions which depend for their existence on maintaining the consecrated status of the Coleridges of our culture. It will not surprise you to know that I have submitted this project as a research proposal three times unsuccessfully to the British Academy. Without an alternative locus such as that which Bourdieu has constructed in France around the research group in the Maison des Sciences de l'Homme and around the Actes de la Recherche en Sciences Sociales, the academic project could degenerate into the kind of academicism for academicism's sake of H.R. Jauss's reception theory.

This sketch of three forms of possible analysis of the work of Coleridge demonstrates sufficiently, I hope, that Bourdieu's conceptual framework can be applied productively to the work of a creative artist who lived and wrote outside the specifically French intellectual tradition within which Bourdieu's own thinking has developed. Even though Bourdieu may himself have applied his concepts self-fulfillingly to cultural producers with whom he had affinity, nevertheless, adopted academically or scientifically, they function cross-culturally to generate innovative explanations of different cultural phenomena. However, writing within his own culture, the effect of Bourdieu's project has necessarily been to consolidate his affinities and to legitimate his tastes and judgements. Students and researchers may in this way produce interesting findings within limited intellectual fields, but it may be the case that the more fundamental allegiance to Bourdieu's method should involve the articulation of affinities from within one's own culture rather than the application of concepts generated elsewhere.

Alternative projects on Coleridge might, therefore, follow Bourdieu differently in the sense that the responses to Coleridge might be unashamedly existential and be aspects of the personal intellectual development and social position-taking of individuals within their own cultures. One paradigmatic existential respondent to the work of Coleridge might be D.G. James. James was interested in the relation between private mythology and religious belief. In the Prologue to his *The Romantic Comedy* (1948), James isolated three issues raised by the Romantic movement which were of enduring interest. He wrote:

> These are, first, the need to employ mythology; second, certain beliefs about human knowledge and imagination; and third, a sense of the strange and unknown.[6]

James regarded the first of these as of most interest. He continued:

> But in those aspects of English Romanticism I have mentioned, and which are treated in this essay, it is the use of mythology which more than any other gives unity to what I have written. This, I think, is the crucial thing. ... We cannot come to proof and certainty; and therefore we cannot dispense with myth and story. Still, the narrative I have to tell does not end with story merely; or, if it ends with story, it is story with which there goes along, also, authority.[7]

The culmination of the account in *The Romantic Comedy* at which James hints in the Prologue – the story with authority, had already been anticipated in his *Scepticism and Poetry* (1937). In that work he was explicit about the dogmatic needs of contemporary England. He wrote:

What is of the greatest importance is to try to realize the place of dogma in religion and its necessity for a religion. To many people to-day, we may be sure, religious dogma is an inexplicable mystery which they feel it necessary to condemn wholesale. What makes dogma an impossible stumbling-block to many such is of course its assertion of the miraculous; but what alone can dispel, to any degree, its impossibility in this respect is the realization of the inevitability of miracle for religion, and the understanding that a great religion demands, as a condition of its vitality, a structure of belief in what is shot through with the miraculous. Unless we can realize that this is so, we shall either stand outside Christianity and condemn it, as Keats did, or we shall, if our attitude be religious, be one of the many modernist apologists for Christianity who, we may believe, do harm to their religion by seeking carefully to extract from it all element of miracle. Such teachers may, indeed they often do, reduce dogma to the status of a symbol, beautiful and expressive perhaps, but yet only a symbol; and they thereby weaken its vitality and value. The historical basis which Christianity claims is fundamental to its existence, and to deny it is to rob Christianity of its potency in the world.[8]

It is clear from this passage that James believed in the autonomy of religious dogma. The incarnation of Christ at a historical moment provided the explanation of experience in religious dogma with an authority that cannot be shared by other discourses which are the creations of different faculties of the human mind and hence differently divorced from reality. It was James's Kantian epistemological position which allowed him to emphasize the discreteness of several discourses subordinate to reality, and which allowed him to assume that science and poetry are different forms of limited cognition. Imagination is the 'prime agent', to use James's borrowing from Coleridge, of all human knowledge of the world, and science and poetry are two discourses which have their own strict rules. For James, the scientific imagination is necessarily mechanistic and he attacked Whitehead for attempting to change its nature. For James, science which attempted to use a non-mechanistic analogy either ceases or fails to be science. In the period leading up to 1801 Coleridge gradually accepted, or so James assumed, the distinction between a scientific and a poetic imagination. The purpose of *Scepticism and Poetry* was to place these two subordinate cognitions in the context of religious dogmatic truth, whilst the purpose of *The Romantic Comedy* was to show that both logically and historically an authoritative dogma was a necessary progression from scientific and poetic imagination. To put the paradox bluntly, James tried to justify dogmatic belief existentially. In the two works that I have mentioned,

James used Coleridge as the main instrument in his didactic purpose. James used Coleridge to demonstrate a transition from an allegiance to scientific imagination to an allegiance to poetic imagination, which was the main concern of the first book, and also to demonstrate a transition from an allegiance to poetic imagination to an acceptance of Christian dogma, which was the concern of the second book.

My point here is that it is possible to understand the historical conditions in which D.G. James developed a particular interpretation of the work of Coleridge – to understand the way in which his existentially engaged approach to the work of Coleridge had the effect of mobilising cultural support for the religious position which he wished to advance in the period from 1930 to 1960. I can hint at a comparably paradigmatic response to Coleridge in my own work from the 1960s. In a paper included in *Raymond Williams Now*[9] I recently recommended Bourdieu rather than Williams as a mentor for the kind of reflexive self-objectification that is socially necessary in a culturally pluralist society. I could propose a reflexive project on Coleridge which would be Bourdieusian without using any of Bourdieu's concepts. A response to Coleridge would be partly constitutive of and partly correlative to my own self-presentation in the same way as, I argue, *Le sens pratique*, is, for Bourdieu, a conscious assimilation of the objectivity of Algeria to his own self-presentation. A reflexive approach of this kind would elaborate, for instance, some of the following basic facts:

I studied English Literature as an undergraduate at Cambridge from 1963 to 1966. I had been attracted to the Cambridge English School because it had a tradition of seeking to analyse literary texts in their relations to their social contexts (in contrast with Oxford which traditionally had emphasized the linguistic or philological analysis of autonomous texts). I had been attracted to the work of the first generation of English romantic poets – Coleridge, Wordsworth, and Southey – whilst I was at school in Bristol. The attraction was partly that these poets had lived in Bristol in the 1790s, and, partly, that the first generation Romantic poets were philosophical poets. In the summer of 1965, I wrote a mini-thesis for submission for my undergraduate degree. It was on seven key social figures in Cornwall in the second half of the 18th Century. At that time, Cornwall was in the vanguard of the Industrial Revolution and I had been interested in exploring the relations between traditional cultures and technological change. In particular, Humphry Davy, the chemist who was to become the President of the Royal Society and mentor of Faraday, was a Cornishman who also wrote poetry. The time at which I was an undergraduate was the period of the upsurge of 'Cambridge Theology' which was most associated with John Robinson's *Honest to God*. What this really meant, however, was that there was a stimulating atmosphere of debate in the field of philosophical theology. I was particularly impressed by the lectures given by R.W. Hepburn as the Stanton Lectures in 1965 in which he examined the claims of religious discourse to have autonomous meaning. The 1960s was also the period of the 'Two Cultures Debate'. I attended seminars given by F.R. Leavis in which he often articulated his hostility to the conceptions of science and literature advanced by C.P. Snow. All of this combined to mean that when I graduated in 1966, I proposed to undertake post-graduate research on 'Literature and Science, 1770–1800'.

To offer this kind of analysis would explicitly be to offer the cultural artifact which is the canonical work of Coleridge and its constructed, reified 'context' as the facilitator for a process of socio-analytical encounter. As another aside, this is Bourdieusian in the same way as his analyses of Flaubert are elements of a confused position-taking in relation to Sartre – confused because, I think, Bourdieu remained sympathetic to Sartre's early view of the status of texts expressed in *What is Literature?* but hostile to the attempt made by Sartre to reconcile his existentialism with Marxism in the *Critique of Dialectical Reason* and, subsequently, to operationalize that reconciliation in literary biographies, such as that of Flaubert.

To try to conclude. I think this volume is appearing at a crucial moment in relation to the response to Bourdieu's work, certainly in the UK. We do not want to replicate the fate of Foucault. We do not want to generate a mini-industry about Bourdieu. In my view, the proper response to Bourdieu?s work is primarily political. We have to generate our own institutional structures to promote reflexive practice so that our interest in Bourdieu's work does not become a form of academicism. Pedagogically, we have to struggle to maintain the teaching and learning process as one of social encounter. Most of all, we must guard against the possibility that the concepts developed by Bourdieu become components of an arbitrary culture that is imposed unreflexively on others. Bourdieu's work can be used to produce new insights into our own cultural history and our own cultural present, but, above all, his work has to be imitated in that he provides an example of the way in which we can seek to articulate an engagement with our own culture which is an authentic expression of our position within it.

Notes

1 J.W. von Goethe, trans., R.J. Hollingdale, *Elective Affinities*, Penguin Books, Harmondsworth, 1971, 54.
2 P. Bourdieu, 'Thinking About Limits', *Theory, Culture and Society*, vol. 9, 1992, 41.
3 P. Bourdieu, trans. M. Adamson, *In Other Words*, Polity Press, Oxford, 1990, 3.
4 M.F.D. Young, ed., *Knowledge and Control. New Directions for the Sociology of Education*, Collier–Macmillan, London, 1971, 161.
5 Ibid. 162.
6 D.G. James, *The Romantic Comedy*, London, 1948, x.
7 ibid. xi.
8 ibid. 245–246.

9 D.M. Robbins, 'Ways of Knowing Cultures: Williams and Bourdieu', chapter 2 of J. Wallace, R. Jones and S. Nield, (eds), *Raymond Williams Now: Knowledge, Limits and the Future*, Macmillan, 1997, 40–55.

Bibliography

Baldick, C., (1983), *The Social Mission of English criticism, 1848–1932*, Oxford: Clarendon.

Bourdieu, P., (with Chamboredon, J.C and Passeron, J.C.), (1968), *Le métier de sociologue*, Paris: Mouton-Bordas.

Bourdieu, P., (1971), 'Intellectual field and creative project', in Young, M.F.D, (ed.), *Knowledge and Control. New directions for the Sociology of Education*, London: Collier-Macmillan.

Bourdieu, P., (1972), *Esquisse d'une théorie de la pratique, précédé de trois études d'ethnologie kabyle*, Geneva: Droz.

Bourdieu, P., (1973), 'The three forms of theoretical knowledge', *Social Science Information*, XII, 1, 53–80.

Bourdieu, P., (1975), 'L'ontologie politique de Martin Heidegger', *Actes de la recherche en sciences sociales*, 5–6, 109–156.

Bourdieu, P., (1980), *Le sens pratique*, Paris: Editions de Minuit.

Bourdieu, P., (1984), *Distinction. A social critique of the judgement of taste*, London: Routledge and Kegan Paul.

Bourdieu, P., (1988), *Homo academicus*, Oxford: Polity Press.

Bourdieu, P., (1990), *In Other Words. Essays towards a reflexive sociology*, Oxford: Polity Press.

Bourdieu, P., (1992), 'Thinking about limits', *Theory, Culture and Society*, 9, 37–49.

Eagleton, T., (1983), *Literary theory: an introduction*, Oxford: Blackwell.

Goethe, J.W. von., trans. Hollingdale, R.J., (1971), *Elective Affinities*, Harmondsworth: Penguin Books.

Green, J.H., (1865), *Spiritual Philosophy: founded on the teaching of S.T. Coleridge*, London: Cambridge.

Husserl, E., trans. Churchill, J.S. and Ameriks, K., (1973), *Experience and Judgement: investigations in a geneaology of logic*, London: Routledge and Kegan Paul.

James, D.G., (1937), *Scepticism and Poetry. An essay on the poetic imagination*, London: Allen and Unwin.

James, D.G., (1948), *The Romantic Comedy*, London: Oxford University Press.

Palmer, D.J., (1965), *The Rise of English Studies. An account of the study of English language and literature from its origins to the making of the Oxford English School*, London: Oxford University Press.

Robbins, D.M., (1997), 'Ways of Knowing Cultures: Williams and Bourdieu', in Wallace, J., Jones, R. and Nield, S., (eds), *Raymond Williams Now; Knowledge, Limits and the Future*, London: Macmillan.

Sartre, J.-P., (1967), *What is Literature?*, London: Methuen.

Sartre, J.-P., (1991), *Critique of dialectical reason*, London: Verso.

Szondi, P., (1974), *Poésie et poétique de l'idéalisme allemand*, Paris: Editions de Minuit.

Williams, R., (1961), *Culture and Society, 1780–1950*, Harmondsworth: Penguin Books.

Williams, R., (1971), *Orwell*, London: Collins.

The impact of market journalism:
Pierre Bourdieu on the media

Philippe Marlière

Introduction

As a French intellectual increasingly involved in the socio-political debates of his time, Pierre Bourdieu has made a number of attempts over the past fifteen years to make his thought accessible to a wide readership (Bourdieu, 1980 and 1992a). Among his most recent publications, *La Misère du Monde* (Bourdieu, 1993), a weighty synopsis devoted to the study of different forms of poverty and social suffering in France, has become one of France's social science best-sellers (Marlière, 1997a: 46–58). Several months ago, Bourdieu published another book entitled *Sur la Télévision* which falls largely into the same category. This slim volume immediately aroused controversy and provoked sharply divided reactions, either of support or outright hostility (Bourdieu, 1997a).[1] The book consists of the transcript of two lectures on the media which Bourdieu presented at the Collège de France. In view of the content of the book, it is ironic that the two lectures were filmed by the French channel, Paris Première, and televised in May 1996. Like *La Misère du Monde*, Bourdieu's new contribution was probably written with a view to stimulating political debate. The tone is at times polemical even though the author stresses that the book should not be taken as an attack on journalists, but as engaging in a debate with them in order to ensure that television – which according to Bourdieu 'could have been an extraordinary instrument of democracy' – does not become an 'instrument of symbolic oppression' [p. 8].

The great advantage of Bourdieu's thought is that it can be applied to any social object and is powerful enough to analyse forms of social practice (behind those that are obvious and taken for granted), which have hardly even been detected by previous research. This preliminary remark serves as a heuristic device with which to assess the success of his contribution to the media. Is Bourdieu's 'journalistic field' really an innovative idea which facilitates an understanding of how the media works? According to Bourdieu, the journalistic field is considerably influenced by commercial or economic constraints, but in turn imposes a structural constraint upon other fields [p. 62]. In particular he deals throughout his exposé with the interference between the journalistic field and other fields such as politics and academia. His in-depth critical analysis also leads to some clear-cut conclusions.

Media vision and market constraints

Bourdieu's verdict on the media is unyieldingly severe: for him, television not only endangers different spheres of cultural production (ie the arts, literature, science, philosophy, law), but also threatens political life and democracy in general [p. 5]. Bourdieu argues that television is not a free medium since it is constantly the object of acts of censorship from the political and economic fields. On the whole the management of television is determined by the channel owners, by the agencies which pay vast amounts of money to have their commercial clips screened or by the state which raises public money to fund it. Bourdieu says, for instance, that the ownership of NBC by General Electric makes it highly unlikely that this channel will ever make an investigative documentary asking people who live near a nuclear reactor what they think of it [p. 14]. A fairly obvious point perhaps, but Bourdieu's sociology of television goes on to become more stimulating as he delves into the very mechanisms of the symbolic violence enacted by television. He says that one of the functions of television is to draw people's attention to what he calls 'omnibus facts' (*faits divers*, p. 16), that is facts which are supposedly of 'common interest' and understandable by all. These 'catch-all-news' items have no particular political or social interest, do not annoy or shock anyone's beliefs and supersede important issues such as politics. Bourdieu appears to be right to stress that, given that television is the only source of information for most people, this creates a division between the few who read newspapers and who can therefore access all varieties of information and the majority who are deprived of it because they only watch television [p. 17]. Television does not encapsulate reality in the sense it tends to 'dramatize', transforming a minor event into a 'sensational' or 'spectacular' phenomenon [p. 18]. For instance, when television journalists report on the areas around big cities such as Paris or Lyons, the media tend to create an image of social problems for the public consumption which emphasizes the 'extraordinary', that is violent actions, fights between youngsters and the police, acts of vandalism, juvenile delinquency, the over-concentration of immigrant populations, etc. Media portrayal of these suburban areas 'stigmatizes' the people living there in all aspects of their everyday lives, thereby extending the 'bad reputation' of a place to its inhabitants. This explains the feeling of mistrust and aggressiveness, or sense of inferiority among the most politically active residents which manifests itself in reaction against journalist crews. This quite ordinary example demonstrates how the media produce 'reality effects' by creating a 'media vision' of reality which, in turn, tends to create the reality which the media claims to describe. This does not mean that journalists entirely fabricate stories or events, but it shows that some manifestations of social malaise can be distorted by the media when it does more than simply record them. In this case facts are constructed or re-constructed in favour of self-serving journalistic interests (Champagne, 1993: 61, 68 and 73–74).

In addition to his criticism of the general dullness of most newspapers and television programmes, Bourdieu denounces the increasing homogenization of newspapers and their 'de-politicization' [p. 23]. He maintains that the ratings-obsessed television industry is tending to replace more and more problematic and divisive programmes, such as politics and 'intellectual encounters', with universally appealing entertainment, such as sport or soap operas. He observes that even the media which appear to resist this trend the most (the BBC or Arte, for instance) still constantly make 'shameful compromises' (*compromis honteux*) for the sake of ratings [p. 58–60].

This is an important point with which many media analysts would probably agree, but when put in a historical perspective it is considerably less accurate. Indeed, contrary to Bourdieu's view, a study of the press and of television in the post-war period shows a gradual 'politicization' of the news. 'Political news' is in fact quite a recent invention in the Western press. If we take the example of Britain in the 1930s: while liberal/left-wing papers were beginning to cover political news concerning trade-unions, left-wing parties and campaign groups for the unemployed, the right-wing press treated all that was 'political' with haughty disdain. The outer pages of *The Times*, *The Daily Telegraph* and *The Daily Mail* were still devoted to advertising. In 1963, however, *The Daily Mail* introduced a 'Political News' column dealing essentially with parliamentary business to differentiate it from sports and general news (Benton, 1997: 141 and 144–145). In the same way the media approach to politics has become on the whole more civilized than it used to be in the pre-war period and political lampoonists who could write and report political news with a view to kill (or to destroy at least their political careers) are a species which has become gradually extinct. While extreme right-wing newspapers in 1930s France were able to publish abusive and antisemitic articles against the socialist prime minister Léon Blum, or launch in 1936 an orchestrated campaign of hatred and lies against the Interior minister Roger Salengro leading to his suicide (Ferenczi, 1995), today's French press is subject to strict controls.

Tackling the journalistic field?

Fully to understand the rules and rationale underlying media management, Bourdieu argues, one has to bear in mind that the media by and large form a journalistic field. By this, he means a 'microcosm which has its own rules, which is constituted autonomously and which cannot be understood from external factors' [p. 44]. In order to grasp the rules of the media, therefore, it is necessary to tackle and objectify a series of 'objective relations' between competing channels which are not perceived by the public (ie overall ratings of a channel, impact of commercial firms on its budget, the number of 'prestigious journalists' who work for a particular channel, etc.). To understand fully what a journalist writes or says, it is essential to know what his or her position in the journalistic field is, that is the very power and prestige the channel or newspaper he or she works for has in the field. That power can be of an economic nature but can also have a symbolic impact which, Bourdieu says, is more difficult to assess [pp. 45 and 47]. A particular sector of the media is in a dominant position in the field when it is capable of 'distorting the space around itself' and imposing its own views on the field. To be influential, such a media member has to combine considerable economic strength with high symbolic capital. Bourdieu argues that the newspaper *Le Monde* occupies this ideal position in the French press [p. 48].

Bourdieu's essay combines two types of argument. First, his observations on the way television deals with news (ie the search for 'sensational events', 'scoops', the homogenization of programmes, the importance given to sports and entertainment programmes, etc.) and the way in which speakers and guests are obliged to speak: concisely, precisely, technically. An obligation which reinforces the predominance and authority of those who speak the legitimate language over those who possess a lower level of linguistic capital, that is those who happen to be economically worse off (Bourdieu, 1982). Second, his stigmatization of 'the journalists' as an undifferentiated category, which is somewhat surprising because his condemnation of the media world appears to be too fierce and absolute to provide a realistic account of a plural and heterogeneous reality. Bourdieu's appraisal of the media warrants a degree of criticism for its lack of rigour in failing to give any precise definition of what journalism is. 'Journalism' for Bourdieu seems to refer to a unified category created by the illusion that it necessarily speaks and acts as one individual would. The lack of in-depth analysis of the different types of journalism and of the different categories of journalist (including those who dominate and those who are dominated) found in the press and on television, renders Bourdieu's account of 'journalism' somewhat confusing and annoying. It is confusing because it does not do justice to a complex situation and portrays the profession quite inaccurately as a homogeneous whole. This reinforces his point with the idea that the journalistic field – and television as a paradigmatic category – attributes a series of unified beliefs to its players, a view which allows Bourdieu to interpret and theorize the media world as a very unitary field. This is an annoying position which makes it difficult to follow Bourdieu's heavy-handed attack on journalists who are indiscriminately accused of 'anti-intellectualism' and 'conformism' [pp. 52–53]. It would be fairer to say that, in its heterogeneity, the journalistic field – like the academic field – has a variety of the brilliant and the dull, the hard-working and the ineffective, and the self-serving and the simplistic among its members. Furthermore, as has already been said, when looked at in historical perspective, media ethics and rigour have clearly improved and are not, as Bourdieu seems to say, in decline.

Bourdieu fails to acknowledge genuine forms of peer-assessment and peer-criticism which exist in the journalistic field. Most 'serious' European newspapers have developed a weekly supplement which is partly devoted to the introspective analysis of journalism as a profession. In some cases these ventures can lead to very uncompromising criticism of 'market-style journalism' which even use Bourdieuian narrative to express their views (Snow, 1997). Such rigorous self-analysis clearly shows that not all members of the journalistic field blindly follow the changing rules of the media marketplace. Many of them still continue to do their jobs as honestly, soundly and effectively as they possibly can.

Overlapping interests and fields at play

Bourdieu's analysis of the problematic overlap between the journalistic field and other fields and its consequences seems much more effective and innovative than his depiction of the media world. He considers the way in which the fields of politics and academia are jeopardized from within by 'heteronomous' agents (which Bourdieu calls 'failures', *des ratés*, p. 73). These agents offer little capital in terms of the specific values of the political or academic fields and therefore have an interest in undermining or bypassing the rules which govern them. These so-called 'dominated' agents search outside the field and within the journalistic field for quick and ephemeral forms of recognition and legitimacy which they failed to obtain, or do not have the patience to obtain in their own field [p. 73]. Bourdieu initially examined the overlapping effects of the journalistic field in relation to academia, but the political field can also be looked at in the same way, given the obvious and constant interferences between the two fields.

Political marketing and market journalism

In his rather harsh depiction of journalists' 'incompetence' and 'cynicism', Bourdieu takes very little notice of the negative role played by the political field itself in the subjection of television to the rules of the market (ie ratings, profit, commercialization and of programmes, etc.). This is all the more striking because France – the object of Bourdieu's case-study – is probably one of the few European countries in which the journalistic field is still not totally independent of political power. There were attempts by various socialist governments during François Mitterrand's first term (1981–1988) to grant the media more leeway than they had had under conservative rule by creating, for instance, a politically independent structure in charge of monitoring the running of French public and private channels in 1982 (currently called the Conseil Supérieur de l'Audiovisuel, CSA). The institution is now accepted by all political and media players. One of the reasons for such unanimity may be the fact that this controlling institution has very limited powers of coercion with which to sanction channels which infringe media regulations (Lang, 1997). Thus, despite the beginnings of democratization, the French media remain somewhat subordinated to political power. As a result many television journalists suffer from a 'deferential complex' *vis-à-vis* the French political class (Buob, 1997). The 'deferential complex' is to be seen at work whenever a major French statesman – above all the president of the Republic – appears on television for a so-called 'political programme' which, in most cases, turns out to be a mere 'communication programme'. When it was closely state-controlled, General De Gaulle's charismatic use of television was undisputed and seemed almost natural. Since the 1980s and the semi-independence gained by television from political power, the instrumentalization of television by politicians has become more subtle. Jacques Chirac, as president of the Republic, has shown remarkable skill at transforming political programmes into 'political shows': a political show falls into a new category of television programme where the boundary between 'politics' and 'entertainment' is very thin. It is now common knowledge that this type of 'political show' is strictly controlled by the French presidential staff (Halimi, 1997: 16–17). The programme is scheduled by presidential advisers, the theme is chosen by them, the interviewers undergo rigorous selection by presidential staff to prevent any embarrassing questions. They even dictate the studio set, seating arrangements and lighting. Their main objective is to control the form and the content of the political agenda and build up a sense of expectation among viewers a few days before the programme is scheduled in order to 'create an event'. The content is secondary and the 'political news' is not only scarce, but sometimes absent altogether. What matters in this context is the image or the look. François Mitterrand, in the middle of a political crisis in the mid-1980s, understood this very well. He decided to invite himself onto a series of 'political shows' with a supposedly 'cool' and 'fashionable' journalist as sparring-partner in order to show French viewers that he was a 'hip' president who could speak using the latest form of Parisian slang.

These examples shed light on one of the most worrying forms of political distortion in a democracy, namely the influence of 'political' or 'communication' advisers. These advisers have been playing an increasingly influential role in the decision making-process of most major Western political parties and governments. A detailed sociological study along these lines, revealing how in Britain the 1997 Labour party political manifesto was drafted, would be extremely enlightening. It would show the extent to which a limited number of 'campaign advisers' – none of whom were affiliated to the Labour party – were able to impose on the party as a whole the 'five key pledges' which were to form the fulcrum of the Labour campaign. These pledges were not determined by democratic debate at all levels of the party but through the widespread use of the 'focus group' technique conducted by these 'political advisers' (Marlière, 1997b). Thus, being neither political experts nor real journalists, the 'communication people' are not themselves driven by any strong ethical or political beliefs: they are on hand only to put across the right soundbite or the right image at the right moment. Their lack of political affiliation explains why, in a large majority of instances, they are able to switch political allegiance so easily (Cayrol, 1997: 48).

Another point which is tackled superficially by Bourdieu deserves to be looked at more closely. It concerns the role played by Western governments in the privatization of television channels. Over a period of fifteen years France has evolved from a complete state monopoly of the media to a hybrid situation, in which publicly and privately run channels are competing. Ironically, it was a socialist government which in the early 1980s launched the first ever private channels, Canal+ and Channel 5 (La Cinq). The former, a subscriber channel, has turned out to be the only successful and innovative venture. The latter was run by the press tycoon Robert Hersant and was influenced by the direct involvement of Silvio Berlusconi, director of Italy's Canale Cinque. As with Canale Cinque, the same light-weight variety shows and American soap-operas were broadcast 24 hours a day. The channel eventually went bankrupt after only five years. In 1986, the Conservative's return to office saw the privatization of the oldest and most prestigious channel, TF1, which was sold to a public building tycoon, Robert Bouygues. Far from ensuring a so-called 'pluralism' and 'diversity' on French television, these channel privatizations have led to a standardization of programme and a dramatic reduction in their quality. In addition, the sale of public channels to a handful of powerful businessmen has resulted in a media concentration which in most cases fails to maintain political pluralism (Bourges, 1997).

The negative effects of television channels subjected to the rules of market journalism as described by Bourdieu, are all to be found on French television. Unlike the BBC and Channel 4, ratings-obsessed French channels, both private and public have been destroying the 'pluralism' that their 'competing situation' was supposed to emulate. It follows that 'serious' or 'intellectual' programmes dealing with domestic or international politics as well as literary shows have disappeared from prime time showings, if not altogether. It is somewhat puzzling, therefore, that when Bourdieu attempts to analyse how the field of journalism works, the influence of political power is of so little consequence, despite his contention that the sociologist's first task is to tackle the 'objective power relations which structure the journalistic field' [p. 45]. It appears that in the overlap of the political and journalistic fields, politics still has the upper hand on certain occasions because political power is in a position to shape or structurally distort the journalistic field for better or for worse.

Academic imprimatur and media blessing

The main thrust of Bourdieu's argument is the idea that the media – and above all television – have been undermining the autonomy of the intellectual field. He believes that 'corrupting mechanisms' have become increasingly prominent in the academic milieu as television has come to occupy a central position in the field. Bourdieu argues that for the intellectual to be read and heard, it is more and more difficult to resist the growing pressure of market journalism. What is at stake, according to Bourdieu, is the preservation of autonomy in the intellectual field. By 'autonomous field', Bourdieu means a field in which the producers' 'clients' are their peers or direct competitors, that is those who 'could equally have made the discovery which they are presenting' [p. 71]. The trouble is, Bourdieu argues, that today television has the power to jeopardize this autonomy. He speaks of the 'Trojan horse syndrome' according to which the journalistic field favours the dominated agents on the intellectual field and helps them to receive a form of that they failed to obtain, or did not have the patience to seek in the academic arena [p. 69]. In other words, Bourdieu implies that in some cases 'complacent' intellectuals use television as a way of bypassing the traditional processes of intellectual legitimization within academia. He suggests that the academic seal of approval once awarded exclusively through the old mechanisms such as publication record and teaching performance has been superseded in some cases by television appearances. Bourdieu considers this new move into the media market a danger to the autonomy of science so vital for research. For him, the 'failures' have an obvious interest in crushing the autonomy of the intellectual field in favour of quick success in the journalistic field because there their lower level of scientific capital can still prove to be an asset. Indeed, 'dominated intellectuals' do not baffle journalists with technical jargon and are keen to broaden the disciplinary boundaries to include 'trans-disciplinary encounters' where anyone can assess and discuss anything [p. 69]. These 'over-adapted' intellectuals are appreciated by journalists because they can count on them to agree on and play by the rules of the journalistic field as presented by Bourdieu [p. 73]. Such 'media intellectuals' (Bourdieu takes the obvious examples of Bernard-Henri Lévy, Alain Minc or Jacques Attali) are public figures who have a say on practically any possible issue [p. 31]. They are what he calls 'fast-thinkers' who are asked to respond to complex (or irrelevant) questions in a few seconds. They are able to play the game because they merely reflect upon and regurgitate generally accepted ideas (in the sense of Flaubert's *idées reçues*, p. 30) – banal ideas, commonplaces, ideas which are so empty and obvious that they go without saying [pp. 30–31].

Inversely, a 'subversive thought' cannot access the media because it takes time to articulate it on television. And time is the last thing television can afford to grant its guest speakers [p. 31]. Bourdieu proposes a category of 'journalist-intellectual' who exploits affiliation to two fields in order to import into one skills which have been more or less well mastered in the other. This has two major effects: on the one hand, somewhere between academic esoterism and journalistic exoterism undefined forms of cultural production emerge; on the other hand, the individuals responsible occupy a position in the journalistic field which enables them to assess scientific production (including *social* scientific production) with apparent intellectual authority. Because of market constraints, they inevitably draw public attention to the 'easiest' and 'most commercial' products of a given discipline, to the extent that they even ignore the contribution of experts in the field. This, in turn, has another double consequence: it inclines cultural consumers to allodoxia[2] by establishing the excellence of minor productions and also directs the choice and policies of culture promoters (such as publishers) towards more marketable and less exigent products [pp. 89–90]. These intellectuals occupy overlapping and shifting positions depending on the field in which they evolve: they are dominated in the intellectual field, but dominant in the journalistic field. Bourdieu shows that even areas traditionally considered most protected from media ascendancy, such as the judiciary or scientific subjects *par excellence* like mathematics or physics, are also affected by the 'media fast-thinking' effect.

Bourdieu argues that the only way for the academic field to preserve its autonomy is to build a 'kind of ivory tower' within which field experts assess and criticise each other on equal terms, armed with the same scientific tools, the same techniques and the same methods [p. 71]. The re-establishment of autonomy within the scientific field is vital to Bourdieu because it enables specific laws to be laid down which in turn contribute to the progress of reason and knowledge and consequently reinforce the autonomy of the field (Bourdieu, 1997b: 140).

An Anglo-American readership will probably object that Bourdieu's rather apocalyptic depiction of the relationship between academia and television epitomizes a specifically Franco-French debate (Marlière, 1997c: 16). For it seems that even the most media-friendly intellectuals in America and Britain are only called upon to appear on television to deliver a clinical and highly specialized diagnosis of a matter which falls directly within their field of competence. By contrast some French intellectuals are not in the least reluctant to engage in debates beyond their immediate academic concerns. In this respect, Bourdieu's analysis merely puts forward situations of symbolic struggle between intellectuals in a particular national context.

Furthermore, Bourdieu seems at times to over-emphasize the impact of 'media blessing' and probably overdoes the capacity of 'intellectual-journalists' to do 'damage' as a result. His implicit fear that soundbites and media assessment of scientific work could jeopardize the autonomy of the intellectual field appears somewhat misplaced as well. The rules of the intellectual field are – at least in most academic disciplines – more strongly established and safe than Bourdieu suggests. French academia has not yet sunk to a level where television appearances are considered more prestigious and legitimizing than a lecture to the Collège de France.

Bourdieu's approach, however, does shed light indirectly on the fragility of knowledge in the social sciences despite its proclaimed 'epistemological break' with the immediacy of common sense. The uncertainty of disciplinary boundaries or the scarcity of symbolic rewards in a disciplinary field can perhaps explain the temptation of some scholars to abandon years of scientific autonomy painstakingly acquired in the anonymity of an academic institution, in the hope of greater symbolic and material rewards from the media. While Bourdieu offers a stimulating insight into the intricacies of the legitimization processes of scientific research, his diagnosis of the 'corrupting appeal' of television on intellectuals requires further precision. For what can be inferred from Bourdieu's position – despite all his denials! – is that any collaboration between the media and intellectuals is not only risky, but also quasi-impossible. In the opening pages of his essay, Bourdieu maintains that in some cases the intellectual has a duty to speak on television in order to share the fruits of his research with the uninitiated [pp. 12–13] – a claim which he seems to contradict in most other parts of his book. In addition, his rather uncompromising position could leave him isolated in comparison with other leading sociologists. For instance, Raymond Aron shared the strong belief that media exposure – and in his case in the written press – could provide sociologists with a fruitful way of bringing their work on society to society. The whole of his academic career was devoted to proving that journalism and academia can work together harmoniously. Bourdieu's experience has been less propitious to their harmonious combination, as I shall show.

Book reception and symbolic struggles

Until the publication of *Sur la Télévision*, Bourdieu's relative lack of interest – at least academic interest – in the media and television was rather surprising given the multidisciplinary nature of his sociology of cultural practices (Bourdieu, 1965, 1969, 1979, 1992b). Some readers of *Le Monde*, however, may remember that Bourdieu's contempt for television was already noticeable in an interview which he gave to the Parisian newspaper in the early 1990s (Bourdieu, 1992c), but he did not elaborate on this issue until *Sur la Télévision*, except a short article devoted to journalism and published in a special issue of his journal *Actes de la Recherche en Sciences Sociales* (Bourdieu, 1994: 3–9). Bourdieu's lack of research on this topic was all the more puzzling in view of the 'social centrality' of television world-wide. This short essay on television comes rather late in his work. By contrast, important segments of American or British social science have dealt quite extensively with the question of dominant ideology and its formation in capitalist societies by studying closely the role of the mass media and television (Garnham, 1993: 187–188).

One cannot give a fair account of *Sur la Télévision* without passing reference to the controversial reception of the book (Bougnoux, 1996: 182; Weill, 1997; Garcia, 1997). For instance, a typical negative response from one critic stressed that, behind the mask of scientific truth, Bourdieu's research on television was a mere pamphlet (Fabiani, 1997). Indeed, prior to the book publication, the French sociologist had been invited to appear on the weekly programme 'Arrêt sur image' on 23 January 1996. The show was devoted to television coverage of the lengthy strikes which had paralyzed most public services throughout France in December 1995. The programme was supposed to reflect on and assess the way television had presented the strikes to the public. The programme title, 'Can television speak about social movements?', seemed to indicate that the institution would engage in self-introspection and be open to external criticism. Following the show a bitter polemic raged in the pages of *Le Monde Diplomatique*. Bourdieu began by publishing a long article which revealed that he had been deceived by the programme editor (a journalist with *Le Monde* and media pundit). Most of the conditions the sociologist had set before agreeing to participate in the show (such as time allocated to speak, choice of other guests invited, of news extracts to be commented by him) had been blatantly ignored by the programme editor during the broadcast. In the article, an embittered Bourdieu concluded that this was proof that it was impossible to make a coherent and critical appraisal of television on television. The second part of the article outlined the main points of *Sur la Télévision* (Bourdieu, 1996). In the following newspaper issue, the journalist exercised his right to reply with biting irony. He adopted a Bourdieuian stance in order to objectify Bourdieu and pointed out that the sociologist's attempt to impose the conditions of a 'safe broadcast' for himself was an abuse of his superior cultural capital and prestige which enabled him to do and say whatever he wanted without criticism or interruption from journalists. The journalist concluded that Bourdieu had confused the broadcast with one of his lectures at the Collège de France (Schneidermann, 1996). *Sur la Télévision* appeared in French bookshops a few months later in the context of this row.

The criticism levelled at Bourdieu's sociology of the media by sociologists whose own work has been influenced largely by his theory reveals a widespread malaise. Even in the hostile field of French sociology, voices from within peripheral circles of the 'Bourdieu camp' have publicly distanced themselves from his repeated attempts to stigmatize 'journalists' as a monolithic category. They argue that such an argument represents a 'desperate and vain attempt' by a certain type of epistemology which confuses social sciences with natural sciences to draw artificial disciplinary boundaries in order to exclude any other type of discourse on the Social perceived as 'inferior' or even 'illegitimate', such as journalism. The critics point out that underlying Bourdieu's account of the media, behind the veil of scientific authority used to thwart journalists, is the dogmatic claim that the only truly informed observer of society is the sociologist (Fabiani, 1997).

Conclusion

So, does Bourdieu's contribution to the sociology of the media help tackle a new phenomenon or simply enhance the understanding of the specific rules already at play in this field? The answer cannot be straightforward. As ever, Bourdieu is a remarkably keen observer of social situations and is able to present a problem in a stimulating way. His study of the impact of the journalistic field on other fields such as politics and academia, and his articulation of what lies at stake in the growing loss of autonomy of the political and academic fields offers a valuable contribution to the subject.

Nevertheless, large parts of his work warrant some criticism for giving a sense of *déjà-vu* to any reader who is moderately aware of the way the media work. This dissatisfaction can be explained to some extent by the relative methodological weakness of his research. Quite surprisingly for Bourdieu, his sociology of the media does not appear to be based on in-depth empirical investigations. The absence of a systematic study of the political influence in the media privatization process or the over-simplification of positions in the journalistic field make the overall analysis somewhat under-developed. The fulcrum for his analysis is the situation in France and comparisons made with other countries (United States, Great Britain) are somewhat hasty. Given that some situations relevant to the French case do not apply to other national contexts, a genuine comparative study is needed. What is more unsettling for the reader is the difficulty of determining clearly the heuristic value of the research. Bourdieu claims to adopt a scientific approach, but the boundaries between a scientific discourse and a universally accessible polemical narrative on the media is not always clear. In fact, the essay constantly hesitates between the two genres. It would not be an exaggeration to say that, on numerous occasions, Bourdieu merely reiterates established points concerning the media. Despite the classic Bourdieuian conceptualization applied to some of the phenomena observed, it is sometimes difficult not to think that a number of his observations have long been taken for granted in the field of media studies or even in the media itself. For instance, his denunciation of the tyranny of ratings or the commercialization of journalism are now accepted as commonplaces.

This being the case, why write such a book? Bourdieu is adamant about this last point: he wants his research to make journalists explicitly aware of the 'perverse structural mechanisms' which instrumentalize them, so that they can react against them more effectively than they do at present [p. 63]. In the same way, intellectuals who appear on television are invited to negotiate with journalists in order to establish a sort of deontological code for both sides and to secure acceptable conditions for their collaboration with the media. In theory such proposals are readily acceptable. The trouble is that Bourdieu does not explain how the most critically aware journalists can free themselves in practice from overwhelming structural constraints imposed by the state and especially from the capitalist interests of their employers, that is channel owners and press tycoons.

Notes

1 I quote from the French version of the book throughout the chapter.
2 According to Bourdieu, *allodoxia* is an error of identification, a form of 'false recognition'. Because they are not really familiar with the most legitimate products and practices (which they have a very low probability of coming across in their own social milieu), the dominated and deprived agents' action *de facto* boils down to *imagining* what these products and practices are. As a consequence, there is a noticeable gap between the 'reality of things' and the actual representation which they make of it.

References

Benton, S., (1997), 'Political News', *Soundings*, 5: 137–148.
Bougnoux, B., (1996), 'Pierre Bourdieu, sociologue boudeur', *Esprit*, 222: 182–184.

Bourdieu, P., *et al.*, (1965), *Un art moyen. Essai sur les usages sociaux de la photographie.* Paris: Minuit.

Bourdieu, P. and Darbel, A., (1969), *L'amour de l'art. Les musées d'art européens et leur public.* Paris: Minuit.

Bourdieu P., (1979), *La distinction. Critique sociale du jugement.* Paris: Minuit.

Bourdieu, P., (1980), *Questions de Sociologie,* Paris: Minuit.

Bourdieu, P., (1982), *Ce que parler veut dire. L'économie des échanges linguistiques.* Paris: Fayard.

Bourdieu, P., (1992a), *Réponses.* Paris: Seuil ('Libre examen').

Bourdieu, P., (1992b), *Les règles de l'art.* Paris: Minuit.

Bourdieu, P., (1992c), 'Un entretien avec Pierre Bourdieu', *Le Monde,* 14 January.

Bourdieu, P., (1993), *La Misère du Monde.* Paris: Seuil ('Libre examen').

Bourdieu, P., (1994), 'L'emprise du journalisme', *Actes de la Recherche en Sciences Sociales,* 101–102: 3–9.

Bourdieu, P., (1996), 'Analyse d'un passage à l'antenne', *Le Monde Diplomatique,* April: 25.

Bourdieu, P., (1997a), *Sur la Télévision,* Paris: Liber-Raisons d'Agir.

Bourdieu, P., (1997b), *Méditations pascaliennes.* Paris: Seuil ('Liber').

Bourdieu, P., (1998), *On Television,* London: Pluto Press.

Buob, J., (1997), 'Le complexe de déférence', *Le Monde-Supplément Médias,* 16–17 March.

Bourges, H., (1997), 'Pour une régulation économique de l'audiovisuel', *Le Monde,* 26 August.

Cayrol, R., (1997), *Médias et démocratie: la dérive.* Paris: Presses de Science Po ('La Bibliothèque du Citoyen').

Champagne, P., (1993), 'La vision médiatique', in Bourdieu, P., *La misère du monde, op. cit.*: 61–79.

Fabiani, J.-L., (1997), 'Sociologie et télévision, arrêt sur le mage', *Le Monde,* 12 February.

Ferenczi, T., (1995), *Ils l'ont tué! L'affaire Salengro.* Paris: Plon.

Garcia, S., (1997), 'Pour Pierre Bourdieu', *Le Monde,* 1 March.

Garnham, N., (1993), 'Bourdieu, the Cultural Arbitrary, and Television', in Calhoun, C. *et al.,* (eds), *Bourdieu. Critical Cultural Perspectives,* Cambridge: Polity Press, 178–192.

Halimi, S., (1997), *Les nouveaux chiens de garde,* Paris: Liber-Raisons d'Agir.

Lang, J., (1997), 'Jack Lang souhaite une profonde réforme du CSA', *Le Monde,* 27 August.

Marlière, P., (1997a), 'Social Suffering "in their Own Words": Pierre Bourdieu's Sociology of Poverty', in Perry, S. and Cross, M. (eds), *Voices of France. Social, Political and Cultural Identity,* London: Pinter, 46–58.

Marlière, P., (1997b), 'Le "centrisme radical" de Tony Blair', *Le Monde,* 6 May.

Marlière, P., (1997c), 'Blessed and Cursed by the Box', *The Times Literary Supplement,* 17 October: 16.

Schneidermann D., (1996), 'Réponse à Pierre Bourdieu', *Le Monde Diplomatique,* May: 21.

Snow, J., (1997), 'Is TV News Telling the Whole Story?', *Media Guardian,* 27 January.

Weill, N., (1997), 'Pierre Bourdieu et le journalisme: exercice de défiance', *Le Monde,* 24 January.

Bourdieu and the art historians

Richard Hooker, Dominic Paterson and Paul Stirton

I have never had much taste for 'grand theory', and when I read works which might enter into that category, I cannot stop myself from feeling a certain irritation before a typically scholastic combination of false audacity and true carefulness. Bourdieu, 1996: 177.

The initial aim of this chapter was to review some of Bourdieu's comments on the history of art and to rebut, or at least answer, the charges that he levels against the discipline of art history. For several reasons, however, this would have been inadequate. On the one hand, it seemed restrictive to engage in narrow self-justification in a context which invites engagement with other methodologies and disciplines. On the other hand, Bourdieu's writings, from his 'postface' to Erwin Panofsky's *Gothic Architecture and Scholasticism* to his more recent book *The Rules of Art*, presents such a sustained attack on the discipline of art history that they demand a serious and more detailed response. The degree of partiality and misrepresentation in Bourdieu's reading of art history (at least, as it is understood in Britain and the USA) invites correction and some further elaboration to clarify the aims, methods and limitations of art history, both as a discipline and as a means of interpreting artifacts from the past.

Furthermore, there seemed only limited potential for a serious analysis of the issues if the discussion were taken into the area of sociology alone; that is likely to distort the arguments and cast the authors into the role of apologists. It was felt, therefore, that a more constructive approach would be to proceed with the unqualified responses of the art historian, without tailoring these views for a readership of sociologists. It is to be hoped, after all, that the chapter will elicit some responses across the disciplines.

There are three stages or loose groupings to this paper:

1. outlines the logical problems or inconsistencies that we feel exist in Bourdieu's critique of art history.
2. addresses the partiality and limited nature of Bourdieu's understanding, or at least his characterization, of art history as an academic discipline.
3. presents a critique of Bourdieu's reading of Panofsky, drawing attention to the misunderstandings that Bourdieu repeats regarding Panofsky's definition of iconology.

Part 1

By way of an opening, it seems appropriate to outline Bourdieu's critique of the discipline of art history, as it is developed in Chapters 8, 9, and 10 of *The Field of Cultural Production*.

Bourdieu's critique of art history re-invokes a well established criticism of the idea of the universal value of the particular aesthetic experience. It has long been argued by critics of this idea that it involves a projection of the unacknowledged provincialisms of its proponents. For example, it is argued that to claim that a painting of Renaissance Italy has universal value is to project values and assumptions embodied in the painting onto every possible potential viewer. As is clear from his 'postscript' to *Distinction*, it is the Kantian concept of aesthetic experience as universal and disinterested that Bourdieu contests and wishes to correct with a 'Vulgar' social critique of taste, conceived as a 'return of the repressed', a confrontation between 'pure' taste and the facile, disgusting, bodily tastes it defines itself against (Bourdieu, 1998: 485).

Extending the terms of this argument to art history, Bourdieu seeks to undermine the discipline by claiming that, as a deciphering process, it does not acknowledge the extent to which its procedures are framed by the narrow interests of the bourgeoisie; indeed it represses the fact. The discipline of art history thereby excludes those who are not privy to the conventions of bourgeois culture and education. Thus, according to Bourdieu, students of art history learn little or anything really new; rather, an education in art history serves to reinforce and affirm the natural appearance of specifically bourgeois values. He writes: 'Owing to the particular status of the work of art and the specific logic of training which it implies, art education ... like the teaching of a native tongue, ... necessarily presupposes, ... that individuals are endowed with previously acquired competence and with a whole capital of experience unequally distributed among the various classes (visits to museums or monuments, attending concerts, lectures, etc.)' (Bourdieu, 1993: 232). Broadening this argument to humanist education in general, Bourdieu says 'the school has only to give free play to the objective machinery of cultural diffusion ... for it to redouble and consecrate by its approval the socially conditioned inequalities of cultural competence, by treating them as natural inequalities or, in other words, as inequalities of gifts or natural talents' (Bourdieu, 1993: 233). It is an ideological construction of essence, or *being*, as the cover for social inequalities that Bourdieu targets. Art history is seen, due to its *structural homology*[1] with art production, as regarding art works as having an independent being, in a move that ultimately asserts the independence of the cultured individual.[2]

Presenting art history this way Bourdieu avails himself of the moral high ground; he is on the side of the culturally dispossessed, and will unveil bourgeois conceit. Art History vs. Sociology has become illusion vs. demystification.

Having understood the charge against the discipline of art history, we need to understand how, having posited this criticism, Bourdieu configures his own position in relation to art history. In a key passage he explains:

the history of the instruments for the perception of the work is the essential complement of the instruments for the production of the work, to the extent that every work is, so to speak, made twice, by the originator and by the beholder, or rather, by the society to which the beholder belongs. (Bourdieu, 1993: 224).

It is the idea that works of art are made twice, first in their production and second in their reception, that underwrites Bourdieu's field of cultural production as the object of sociological analysis. Bourdieu constructs his ambition as explaining culture as a symbiotic relationship between the production and reception of art. With art and art history characterised as a continuous *field*, there is no significant difference between them. Bourdieu can make his accusation that the discipline of art history never achieves a truly critical relationship to its objects because it never transcends its symbiotic relationship with them. With this Bourdieu supplements his claim that art history is a practice of bourgeois exclusion with the claim that it is epistemologically flawed. That is to say, art history is not just morally suspect, it is also systematically wrong. Art history never achieves a position of sufficient distance from its object, or its own practice, to gain the kind of insight Bourdieu claims he has of it.

In order to make this claim, Bourdieu privileges his own position inside the field of cultural production, asserting the reflexivity of his method and his ability to objectify his position (and thus take account of it in his analysis).

From the perspective of these art historians, this is an extremely problematic claim to make. In essence, Bourdieu is setting himself up as an intellectual predator with art history as his prey. Before responding directly to Bourdieu however, it is worth explaining our broad strategy.

If the responses to Bourdieu's charges which follow seem somewhat combative, then it needs to be appreciated that his argument implicitly and explicitly calls for the supercession of the discipline of art history by his own socio-genetic metanarrative. In other words, Bourdieu's argument is not simply an assault on the bourgeoisie, it is also an attack on traditions of scholarship, and ways of analysing cultural phenomena, which might be accurately termed part of a critical history of art.[3] Bourdieu makes some important criticisms of the discipline of art history as a mechanism of exclusion, but these criticisms come from someone who simultaneously exercises self-appointed and exclusive methodological superiority which is not only condescending in its attitude to art history, but often erroneous. It is with no little irony that we read Bourdieu attack 'those critics who rely "on a total" *oeuvre* which gives to its author the right to import into each domain the totality of the technical and symbolic capital acquired in others ... simultaneously defining rivals as partial intellectuals, or even truncated ones ... ' (Bourdieu, 1996: 210). As a consequence, the potential critical impact of his argument on art history is drastically reduced. This is unfortunate because his concerns often match those of art historians, and his conceptual battery provides useful ways of approaching issues (cultural appropriation, for example) central to much recent art historical discourse. In what follows we will offer a number of different explanations for why Bourdieu's critique of art history fails.

(a)

That we, as art historians, reject the notion of Bourdieu's superiority and resist his hostile take-over bid for art history could simply be put down to the inertia of bourgeois interests. As art historians we exist only to sustain the bourgeois machine which Bourdieu calls the field of cultural production. One of the milder criticisms Bourdieu makes of the discipline of art history is that it is hypocritical, proclaiming universal value while limiting its distribution because of our methods. How much more hypocritical are art-historians who, like us, have read Bourdieu, and yet continue to practise art history.

Part of our hope in the future of art history is straight-forwardly cynical and comes from reading Bourdieu. One gets the feeling that he sometimes becomes exhausted because there are so many wrongs to be righted and so many illusions to be shattered. Like a shoal of fish moving in unison to avoid a shark, the field of cultural production survives Bourdieu because he simply does not have the time or energy to completely explain the socio-genesis of every cultural phenomenon. As he says: 'The auto-constitution of a system of works united by a set of significant relationships is accomplished in and through the association of contingency and meaning which is unceasingly made, unmade and remade according to the principles which are all the more constant because they are completely unconscious' (Bourdieu, 1993: 229). That 'the delicious shudders of a bogus revolution' (Bourdieu, 1993: 255) generated by Bourdieu's argument will always be contained is because he sets up an ecology between his predatory socio-geneticism and his prey. On his own analysis, the supply of culture generated by the field of cultural production will always exceed the sociologist's demand for an object. It appears that Bourdieu's hostility to the field of cultural production is in direct proportion to his need for an object to criticise and earn his salary as a professional sociologist.

All the same, this is still not particularly reassuring for art history. As part of the field of cultural production, we rely on strength of numbers to avoid extinction, but we spend our lives looking over our shoulders, hoping that Bourdieu will not turn our way.

(b)

Art history can survive post-Bourdieu, but it survives ignominiously, at the bottom of the moral and disciplinary food chain. At the same time, this survival of art history poses another question for Bourdieu. If we accept the metaphor of Bourdieu as predator and art history as prey, then a very similar structure seems to pertain between Bourdieu and his object. Would it not be possible to follow Bourdieu's own strategy and argue that just as he claims works are made twice, so his argument just makes them a third time? The elision of art and art history by Bourdieu creates an object, namely the field of cultural production, to which Bourdieu orientates himself in the way he says art history orientates itself to art. When he says art history is completely unconscious of the way it remakes art, so it appears Bourdieu is completely unconscious of the way he remakes art history.

The problem with all meta-criticism, Bourdieu's included, is that it is vulnerable to its own strategies. As art historians we are as interested in the origins of Bourdieu's discipline as he is in ours. To make the kinds of claims he is making he must surely come from a disciplinary bloodstock untainted by the bourgeoisie! If it is wrong to separate art from art history, is it not wrong to separate the sociologist from society? Or, does Bourdieu exist outside society, a kind of meta-bourgeois, (that is an aristocrat), living in the highest parapet of the ivory tower, an ivory tower he shares with art history, and other university disciplines. A tower to which students in this country now have to pay to get into, whether doing art history or sociology.

To put it bluntly, most of the things Bourdieu says about art history, could just as well be said about his brand of sociology. A simple exercise when reading chapter 8 of *The Field of Cultural Production* is to substitute the words art history with the word sociology and see how very often Bourdieu reveals himself. In a sense this kind of criticism of Bourdieu will go nowhere, but he invites it when he accuses us of hypocrisy. If you are going to accuse someone of hypocrisy, then you need to be fairly sure you are not practising it yourself.

(c)

If one way to contest Bourdieu's claim for disciplinary superiority over art history is to point to our common hypocrisy, then another is to question the distinctness of Bourdieu's project from art history.[4] There are numerous examples of those who share his preoccupations, but who remain within his definition of the field of cultural production. Martha Rosler, an artist whose work has engaged with issues central to Bourdieu's questioning of the status of art and its exclusions (including in perhaps her best known work *The Bowery in Two Inadequate Descriptive Systems* (1974) the issue of representation within the tradition of documentary photography) articulates the validity (indeed the necessity) of this position perfectly. She describes the passage from 1960s counterculture, with its dream of the 'outside' to the point in the 1970s when 'people began saying, "There is no outside". Which I felt was misunderstanding what an outside means. If we are talking about specific social institutions, of course there is something outside the institution. No one is saying there is something outside the society as a whole' (Rosler, 1999: 77). Rosler is only one artist amongst many who have pursued varied artistic strategies informed by the understanding that critique needs to be specific, in art as elsewhere. For Bourdieu (1996: 169–70) such artistic practice is a 'concealment' of the truth about art, the 'unveiling' of which 'is the only unforgivable transgression'. Thus, despite giving perfectly good reasons why any critique can be located within the logic of the field of cultural production, Bourdieu presents his own 'truth' about art as irrecuperable. Bourdieu's claim to transcend the field of cultural production, thereby allowing him to reach his conclusions, does not (from the art historians point of view) seem to be borne out by the critical/ methodological debate within the field.

The problem can be summarized by an examination of Bourdieu's use of the word 'field'. This obviously implies an open space where, for Bourdieu, art and art history interact. In their interaction they also put up a fence to exclude those not appropriately educated into the conventions of bourgeois behaviour. The fence around the field is not however, just the work of those inside the field of cultural production. It is equally vital for Bourdieu's claim to 'field transcendence'. You cannot transcend something if you cannot contain it. The problem is that Bourdieu can only claim to stand outside the field of cultural production by relying on some fairly arbitrary distinctions between art history and sociology. Chief among these is the radical simplification of art history which, from inside the field, seems far more disparate and fragmented than Bourdieu allows. Ironically, his position-taking with regard to art history echoes that of his antagonist, Immanuel Kant. Kant's importance as a founding figure for art history lay not only in his conception of the 'purity' of aesthetic judgement, but also in the way in which he delineated its boundaries as a discipline. Art was key to Kant's project of securing philosophy within the boundaries of its competence as it defined a limit for philosophy, 'expressly by being outside, different, separate' (Cheetham, 1998: 11).

The principle of interdisciplinary exchange necessarily comes up against the rigid demarcation of competencies Kant established by means of his 'spatialization' of the field of art history. If Kant's spatial conception of art history can be seen as problematic, and excessively restrictive, can we perhaps look to Bourdieu's conception of the field of cultural production for a more suitable model? In his rhetorical moments Bourdieu clearly alludes to the 'field' he theorizes as an electrical field, with negative and positive poles, and dynamic movement between them; in practice the 'field' of cultural production is treated as a levelled piece of ground, on which to build his own theoretical edifice. Bourdieu is careful to outline to his readers the criticisms likely to be thrown at him, including the charge that he is 'levelling' culture, making the 'vulgar' equivalent to the truly artistic.[5] Art history can survive such procedures easily enough (they have, after all, been the basis of the strategies of the artistic avant-garde[6]); what Bourdieu in fact levels is not value but difference. His frequent use of two-dimensional diagrams to represent the field of culture confirms this. These appear to have been conceived as *maps* of the field. In his 1982 essay '*Representation, Appropriation, and Power*' Craig Owens mentions the map as a form of representation particularly privileged by its 'transparency': ' ... "transparency" designates a perfect equivalence between reality and representation; signifier and signified mirror one another, the one is merely a reduplication of the other. Yet such transparency can be achieved only through a strategy of concealment: for example, the legendary transparency of the picture plane prescribed in Alberti's *Della Pittura* was attained only by effacing the image's material support' (Owens, 1994: 98).

Owens wished to replace the art historical *theories* of representation with a *critique*. Thus he looked to Michel Foucault and Louis Marin, who had both written on the status of single-point perspective within a broader concept of Classical representation as defining the limits of the Classical episteme. Perspective ('literally, seeing through, *per-specere*, trans-parency' (Owens, 1994: 98)) is seen as defining the subject of representation through its bringing together of two contradictory axioms (corresponding to its dual status as 'window' and 'mirror') – one that attributes the representation to a specific human subject, one that establishes this subject as universal and abstract. 'In the Classical system of representation, then, the subject of representation is posited as absolutely *sovereign*. In other words, the person who represents the world is transformed, through the act of representation, from a subjective being enmeshed in space and time – by which he is, in a sense possessed – into a transcendent, objective Mind that appropriates reality for itself and, by appropriating it, dominates it' (Owens, 1994: 104). It appears, then, that the position Bourdieu is taking in his mapping of the cultural field is that of the sovereign. Yet the transparency which his maps suggest must, on this model, entail a concealment; specifically, a concealment of the suppressions of difference required to make all the products and practices of the cultural field appear comprehensible from a single point. In his 1964 seminar on *Anamorphosis* Jacques Lacan addressed the adequacy of the perspective construction to vision. He argued that 'this construction allows that which concerns vision to escape totally. For the geometral [transparent] space of vision ... is perfectly reconstructable, imaginable by a blind man. What is at issue in geometral perspective is simply the mapping of space, not sight' (Lacan, 1978: 86). To the art historian this confirms the feeling one has in reading Bourdieu – that his approach, despite its claim to give a total account of art, ultimately allows the substantive questions with which art history concerns itself to escape.

Bourdieu configures the field of cultural production as 'objectifiable' in order to confirm his own objectivity. Art, as a key site of difference, becomes crucial to the status of his own sociology. Without being able to analyse the field objectively, Bourdieu's own claims to reflexivity dissolve – his position taking becomes indistinguishable from that of the cultural aspirants he describes; in other words his approach to the cultural field can be seen as a *habitus*, a disposition towards a certain interpretation of empirical reality, that always finds its presuppositions confirmed.

Despite Bourdieu's claims to the contrary, within art history there are numerous precedents for his kind of argument. In the early 1980s John Tagg was coming to remarkably similar conclusions about the irredeemably bourgeois nature of art and art history, as has Gerhard Mermoz, both of whom emphasize the symbiotic relationship between art and art history. Bourdieu places particular emphasis on Hans Haacke, but Haacke did not arrive at his critique of the institutions of the art world from studying sociology. Rather, his work is part of a tradition of American art in the 1960s and 1970s which understood art objects as but one element within a complex field of interactions between history, society, institutions and criticism. Minimalism, Land Art, and Performance, are but the most obvious. That Bourdieu places such emphasis on Haacke is understandable (especially as in their *Free Exchange* the *structural homology* between their self-images is clear), but Haacke's specifically sociological concerns cannot be isolated from the wider disintegration of the art object taking place in America at the time. From this perspective, Bourdieu's insistence on a radical separation between the field of cultural production and his own sociology is not just an oversimplification; it is intensely misleading. What this adds up to, we suggest, is that Bourdieu's use of the term field has more to do with the methodological necessity for Bourdieu to appear separated from the field of cultural production than that which is actually the case. There are close precedents for Bourdieu's arguments which have come out of that field and there are attitudes towards understanding culture which are not very different from Bourdieu's. That Bourdieu is conditioned by his method to underplay these disciplinary overlaps and openings in the fence of the field of cultural production is because his socio-genetic method cannot co-exist with other methods, it must consume them if it is to survive. It often seems that Bourdieu's interest in art history is driven by an insatiable need to prove the superiority of his method and its claims, rather than by a real interest in trying to explain the function of society in configuring the field of cultural production.

Having emphasized the similarities between Bourdieu and art history, in terms of both their common hypocrisy and their overlapping concerns, we now turn to a basic difference between Bourdieu and art history, which is also the most important criticism of him.

(d)

There is a larger critique of Bourdieu's claims on precision or indeterminacy. Within the parameters of Bourdieu's attack on art history described so far, his strategy claims to reveal indeterminacies within the practice of the discipline. He then proceeds to reveal the socio-genetic origins of these indeterminacies, and so explain them, making them determinate. The reason why this is important is because, according to Bourdieu, it is at moments of indeterminacy, that bourgeois projections come into play, substituting claims for the universal value of art for the real socio-genetic origins of indeterminacy. Bourdieu (1993: 264) thus claims to restore necessity to cultural products, he writes: 'by removing them from indeterminacy (which stems from a false eternalization) in order to bring them back to the social conditions of their genesis, a truly generative definition. Far from leading to historicist relativism, the historicization of the forms of thought which we apply to the historical object, and which may be the product of that object, offers the only real chance of escaping history, if ever so small'.

What Bourdieu means by escaping history will be considered in due course. What is important here are three things: a) Bourdieu's hostility to indeterminacy; b) his equation of it with false eternalization; and c) his explanation of such indeterminacy as veiling suppressed socio-genetic factors. It is with this method that Bourdieu's argument manifests its claim to be more than field transcendent. That is, Bourdieu claims epistemological transcendence, bringing to bear a higher order of knowledge.

In both the pattern of his strategy, and his claims for it, Bourdieu shows remarkable parallels with Hegel. The most important similarity between Hegel and Bourdieu is their common hostility to indeterminacy. This hostility is matched by their common conviction that all indeterminacies are simply misunderstanding of a more profound, but obscured, clarity. The obvious difference between Hegel and Bourdieu is that Hegel holds that the principle of sufficient reason will remove indeterminacies. For Bourdieu, the principle of sufficient social genesis removes indeterminacies. Hegel's strategy, however, is markedly different from Bourdieu's.

Hegel understood that the principal of sufficient reason could not be simply claimed, it had to be demonstrated. To do this, his system sets out to demonstrate that everything can be sufficiently rationally described, and only when this has been done, can the truth of his hypothesis that reason is sufficient be guaranteed. Accordingly, at the beginning of his project Hegel simply calls the principle of sufficient reason the *Notion* and does not ask his reader to accept it until it has been demonstrated. Bourdieu is in a very similar situation because he is claiming the absolute validity of his method. Unfortunately, however, Bourdieu does not pursue indeterminacy with the same single-mindedness. Certainly, Bourdieu's critique of art history contains passages, reminiscent of Hegel, where he goes to great lengths to demonstrate the socio-genetic origins of a particular cultural form. On different occasions, however, his argument dissolves into vague promises that socio-genetic analysis will reveal the truth, such as at the end of Chapter 10 of *The Field of Cultural Production*. These, as yet unfulfilled, promises are the very indeterminacies Bourdieu seeks to bury.

With this argument we can revise the earlier characterization of Bourdieu as predator and art history as prey. Until Bourdieu can give a socio-genetic explanation for every cultural phenomenon, his claims for the superiority of his level of consciousness is not proven. Since he characterizes the field of cultural production as self perpetuating, this will never be achieved. Bourdieu, despite his claims to the contrary, is not in a position to deliver the certainty he promises. He is guilty of generating the illusion that he can make all indeterminacies determinate, and that the interests of bourgeoisie can ever be transcended.

This pessimistic prognosis is not the end of the story, however, because Bourdieu engages in an extremely problematic elision of bourgeois interests with art historical method. The site of this elision is his characterization of all indeterminacy as function of the bourgeoisie's false eternalization of art. In the second part of this paper we argue that the multiple indeterminacies of art history cannot be reduced to socio-genetic origins and conclude suggesting that art history offers an example of an alternative attitude towards indeterminacy from which Bourdieu could learn a great deal.

Part 2

In order to mount his attack on the discipline of art history, Bourdieu is forced into descriptions or characterizations of the discipline which are excessively narrow and monolithic. From the inside, art history seems far more disparate and fragmented than he would allow. Its arguments and controversies cannot be reduced to mere proprietorial squabbles amongst the custodians of the symbolic goods of the bourgeoisie; they arise from real differences of methodological and theoretical ambition.

Not the least of the causes of dissent and acrimony within art history since the early 1970s has been the influx of theory from without its borders – semiology, psychoanalysis, deconstruction etc. – and the engagement of prominent intellectuals from other areas in theoretical debates on art (Jacques Derrida and Frederic Jameson are but two of the most well-known examples). While this process has appeared at times to take the form of a *colonization* of the discipline, significant numbers of art historians have worked to acknowledge the pertinence of new theories and apply them to their practice. Craig Owens (1994: 88) for example, in '*Representation, Appropriation and Power*', straight-forwardly presented the antinomy between the critical thought of Michel Foucault, Louis Marin and Roland Barthes, and the humanist basis of art history, arguing that their poststructuralist critique 'could not possibly be absorbed by art history without a significant reduction in its polemical force, or without a total transformation of art history itself'. Owens concluded that a revision of art history was necessitated by the critique of representation as 'the founding act of power in our culture', and that the furthering of such a critique would inevitably be multidisciplinary (1994: 91). At least a section within art history has not been reticent in questioning its own philosophical, methodological, even sociological foundations. It is certainly not uncommon to see Bourdieu cited in art historical texts engaged in such questioning, but he is undoubtedly outnumbered by references to the names of Foucault, Derrida, Barthes, Lacan, Baudrillard *et al.* – a list that those suspicious of the value of interdisciplinarity may recognize with resignation as 'the usual suspects'. Bourdieu might complain that this is an instance of the intellectual field being reconfigured as a series of fashions – a consistent theme in *Free Exchange* – but we might note another difference between his critique of art history and the work of Foucault and Marin that Owens addresses. Whereas Bourdieu never introduces specific art works into his methodological apparatus in anything other than a perfunctory way (his persistent use of the work of Marcel Duchamp as an example of processes of transgression and recuperation, repeated in both *Distinction* and *The Rules of Art*, being a prime example of this), both Foucault and Marin present detailed, attentive analyses of art works to demonstrate the connection between representation and power. If Owens is explicit in his conviction that the humanist base of art history pushes it towards an uncritical 'antiquarianism', his own attentiveness with regard to both the specificities of cultural products and their conformity with social systems of representation brings to mind the art historian who most explicitly made art history a 'humanistic discipline', Erwin Panofsky.

It would appear that Bourdieu bases much of his view of art history on the work of Panofsky; undoubtedly a key area of the discipline but the view it provides is necessarily a partial one, which perhaps reflects his contacts or experience. Indeed, Bourdieu owes a debt to Panofsky for the development of certain of his key theoretical concepts, in particular *habitus*; a concept Bourdieu adapted from the conception of Scholasticism as a 'mental habit' Panofsky proposed in his *Gothic Architecture and Scholasticism*. It is instructive to look at the change in attitude towards Panofsky that occurs between two papers of 1966 – *Intellectual Field and Creative Project* and *Systems of Education and Systems of Thought* – where Bourdieu outlines the thesis of *Gothic Architecture and Scholasticism*, uncritically and at length, in support of his own arguments regarding the school as provider of a *cultural unconscious* or *habitus*, and the 1968 *Outline of a Sociological Theory of Art Perception* where Panofsky is accused of naturalizing what is in fact a visual faculty possessed only by 'the educated or competent beholders of our societies' (Bourdieu, 1993: 216). In 1966 Bourdieu sees the need for an analysis of what he calls *creative project*, the definition of which shows Panofsky's influence clearly: 'The creative project is the place of meeting and sometimes of conflict between the *intrinsic necessity of the work of art* which demands that it be continued, improved and completed, and *social pressures* which direct the work from outside' (Bourdieu, 1966a: 166–7).

In his 1968 paper Bourdieu makes no reference to the 'creative project' as an object of analysis, and it is clear that he envisages a sociology of art along the lines that he has subsequently developed it. Panofsky, he says, fails to address the conditions that make it possible to experience the work of art as *meaningful*. In doing he describes as natural what is in fact the *coded* character of all works, and the necessity of possessing the correct codes to comprehend them. Bourdieu applies the very lesson he had taken from Panofsky – that art works reflect the intellectual milieu in which they were made – to criticize him here for presenting the beholder's experience as immediate. The 'fresh eye' Panofsky is accused of describing is in fact 'an attribute of those who wear the spectacles of culture and who do not see that which enables them to see' (Bourdieu, 1993: 217). Bourdieu's *volte face* with regard to Panofsky becomes clearer when one considers that the other key project of Bourdieu's at this time was the empirically-based *The Love of Art*. We can, in retrospect, see an undercurrent in *Intellectual Field and Creative Project* that was to lead Bourdieu away from Panofsky, and from consideration of the work of art *qua* work of art; which remains at least nominally part of his project in 1966. Assessing the status of the academic he writes: 'Every intellectual brings into his relations with other intellectuals a claim to cultural consecration (or legitimacy) which depends ... on his relation to the university, which, in the last resort, disposes of the infallible signs of consecration' (Bourdieu, 1966a: 179). Thus a criticism of Panofsky as a 'consecrated' intellectual could potentially be made. *The Love of Art*, a study of European museums and their publics, addressed the question of consecration in detail. The implications of this research – that it is the art institution that legitimates art, and alienates the culturally uneducated – were only really integrated into Bourdieu's thought at expense of Panofsky's influence. As a result of taking the direction he does, away from investigating the 'creative project', and focusing on the 'objectivity' of the field, Bourdieu loses sight of two of Panofsky's greatest strengths – the opacity of his theoretical suppositions, and his commitment to the work of art *qua* work of art.

Bourdieu has made great use of religious metaphors in his writings on art. He opposes the sacrilization of culture, refers to the 'faithful' inheritors of academic traditions, and speaks of museums as temples, critique as heresy. It would not be stretching the truth to say that Bourdieu is temperamentally comparable to the geneticist Richard Dawkins, whose vigorous refutations of religious thought are based in the belief that complex effects result from simple procedures, and that explanations for diversity need not therefore be mysterious or beyond rational comprehension.[7] (This kind of connection is made by Bourdieu himself (1996: 188) when he describes the myth of the 'uncreated creator' as 'to the notion of habitus what the Book of Genesis is to the theory of evolution'). Thus Bourdieu can be seen in his early work to be making an uneasy compromise with Panofsky's humanistic outlook, which still harbours a view of art as irreducible to its context. Ultimately Bourdieu values sociological explanation (conceived as scientific, objective) over an address of the work of art *qua* work of art, because it enables him to 'demystify' through a simple cause and effect procedure: the art work is ultimately part of a power game amongst aspirants in the cultural field. This being the case it should not surprise us that in 1968, only two years on from his role as art historical back-up to Bourdieu's theorizing of the art/context relationship, we find that Panofsky has become the object of Bourdieu's criticism. The problem here is clearly that just because art is treated religiously in our society does not make sociology into a science because it seeks pragmatic explanations for art's value. Panofsky's questions still apply, because Bourdieu has not addressed them.

Ultimately, Bourdieu turns on Panofsky because he detects in his humanistic account of art a kind of residual religiosity, which it is his goal to remove from the understanding of art. The use of religious metaphors in Bourdieu's descriptions of the treatment of art in our culture, and in art history is by no means accidental. The Kantian aesthetic is read by Bourdieu purely as a manifestation of a bourgeois need to legitimate authority – the issue of the relationship between subject and object is not addressed in his critique. Despite Panofsky's importance for Bourdieu's own thought, ultimately the former's Kantian ambitions are anathema to him. In *The Historical Genesis of a Pure Aesthetic* Bourdieu (1993) attacks Arthur Danto (in relation to his famous encounter with Warhol's *Brillo Boxes*) for making sociological conclusions without acknowledging sociology's claim to circumscribe his own philosophical position. What Bourdieu has consistently presumed in his own work is that philosophy, or any other discourse, has no claim to circumscribe *his* position. As Alpers (1977: 119) says, 'For all of Panofsky's claims to employing an objective method (his three levels of meaning, for example), he accepted responsibility for his own thought and his commitment to certain values ...' It is precisely here that we can see Bourdieu as falling short of Panofsky.

Part 3

At the end of Chapter 8 of *The Field of Cultural Production* Bourdieu specifically targets Panofsky. The danger in this strategy is that, as we have seen, Panofsky was one of the most methodologically self-conscious and sophisticated art historians. Historians of the discipline and students of Panofsky's method have long recognized that a central aspect of Panofsky's project was an experience of alienation from the great works of the Renaissance. That is to say, Panofsky self-consciously understood his experience of great art to be flawed and incomplete. Bourdieu, it should be noted, does not allow for the idea that the art historian can experience real alienation from the work of art; there is always some kind of prior knowledge which frames such alienation within a reassuring context.

Notwithstanding Bourdieu's objection, Panofsky's hugely influential method of Iconology works within a framework which allows for an inadequate experience of a work of art to be progressively enhanced, but never become totally satisfactory. Panofsky defines three levels of interpretation in a work of art: Pre-Iconographic, Iconographic, and Iconological.

The first, the pre-iconographic, looks at the work of art on the basis of practical experience and interprets primary or natural subject matter. By Primary or natural subject matter, Panofsky means no more than identifying colour, shape, line etc. This might be important in a situation where a work of art has been repeatedly restored or repainted. In such circumstances it is difficult or impossible to distinguish between the original and its subsequent remaking.

The next level of reading is Iconographical analysis. Here secondary or conventional meaning can be derived with reference to literary sources. For a viewer from a non-Christian background this might involve identifying the literary sources for a nativity scene, or a crucifixion. For a catholic, this level of information might be so obvious as to fall into the pre-iconographic and she/ he might be more preoccupied with trying to identify an obscure saint.

Iconological interpretation, the third stage, then looks at intrinsic meaning or content. To reveal the meaning of works of art on this level we must familiarize ourselves with tendencies of the human mind as they are conditioned by cultural, social and intellectual conditions. The most famous example of this is Panofsky's paper *'Perspective as Symbolic Form'*, where he argues that the invention of perspective in the Renaissance was a pictorial expression of Renaissance ideas that space was measurable and infinite.

It should be noted that Panofsky understood these three steps as inseparable. That is, there is no hard and fast distinction between any of the three phases; they blur into one another. Moreover, one of the things which proved so influential about Panofsky's method was that it could be applied to an instance where an individual was relatively familiar with the conventions of a work, or completely unfamiliar.

Bourdieu misrepresents Panofsky in several ways, varying throughout his output. The most problematic is where he writes: 'According to Panofsky, the most naïve beholder first of all distinguishes the primary or natural subject matter or meaning which we can comprehend from our practical behaviour'. Bourdieu's sleight of hand is to misrepresent Panofsky as identifying the pre-iconographic mode of looking at works of art with the naïve beholder.[8] Panofsky does not anthropomorphize (or *anthropologize*) the category like this. In saying that he does, Bourdieu constructs Panofsky's three stages of analysis of the art work as discrete from each other, not as a continuum. He then organizes them in a social hierarchy with the art historians at the top. Bourdieu (1993: 221) says that 'Through sociological observation it is possible to reveal, effectively realized, forms of perception corresponding to the different levels which theoretical analysis frames by an abstract distinction'. With this the practice of art history becomes the practice of exclusion. As the art historian gains a more intimate relationship with the work of art, so she/he is becoming more and more remote from the naïve beholder. Now, we will not contest that through sociological observation these forms of perception can be seen to correspond to different social hierarchies. What we question is Bourdieu's claim that this completely displaces Panofsky's central presumption that history also plays a part in forming the levels of perception which take place.

Bourdieu, however, has established a dynamic which reappears throughout his critique of art history. This is because Bourdieu characterizes the art historians' experience of the work of art as a perfect, or potentially perfect. It is this perfection which contrasts with the alienation experienced by those outside the field of cultural production. On Panofsky's model of cultural criticism, by contrast, the art historian may well be bourgeois and educated, but she/he also experiences the barbarism of the imperfect experience Bourdieu cannot allow. He cannot allow this because, for the art historian to experience indeterminacy, means that she/he might share something of the barbarians' experience, and that art history is not completely unconscious of itself as a deciphering process. If Bourdieu was actually trying to understand Panofsky, rather than shore up his own method, he would find someone who, in his understanding of the inevitability of indeterminacy, contradicts Bourdieu in almost every assumption he makes.

If we do not accept Bourdieu's personification of Panofsky's method, then what are the consequences? First, as Panofsky often argued, the three discreet modes of analysis he describes are not definitively separable, rather they imply a progressive deepening of the relationship between work of art and viewer which takes place over time and does not presume anything about the viewer. Furthermore, the dynamic of this progression depends on a simultaneous experience of closeness and distance from the work. The experience of distance will certainly have a sociological component, but it is also historical. It is not just the social status of the viewer which configures the relative adequacy of their experience of the work of art. To take one simple, but obvious example, art historians and critics have long been troubled by the problem of how to describe colour. Max Kozloff describes this problem as a situational break-down inherent in the tension in any linkages among sensations, words, and memory. Now, this problem applies to the description of colour in any circumstance, whether or not we are dealing with a falsely eternalized work. It seems to us that it is simply implausible to suggest that this problem of how to describe colour using language can be explained as having socio-genetic origins. This is an indeterminacy which art history understands as an indeterminacy and does not attempt to resolve it. Art history, unlike Bourdieu it seems, works with indeterminacy and understands this as a function of its own terminal inadequacy in the attempt to derive satisfactory explanations for its objects.

What this is building up to, in conclusion, is to say that the mode of deportment Panofsky adopts towards the work of art is consciously paradoxical. This gives Panofsky's writing a humility and reflexivity which is absent from Bourdieu's. Ultimately this is the gulf between Bourdieu and Panofsky, between Bourdieu's sociology and art history, and it signifies a completely different attitude towards the object of analysis. Bourdieu is quite right to recognize that art history is at home with indeterminacy, but he overdetermines this indeterminacy as socio-genetic because his method will not allow him to do otherwise. The legitimate criticisms of art history are swamped by his preoccupation with maintaining his own strategic position and at the expense of sustained observation.

Bourdieu repeatedly uses the term *Charismatic Ideology* to describe that constituency which invokes the eternal value of art, an *illusio* that 'undoubtedly constitutes the principle obstacle to a rigorous science of the production of the value of cultural goods' (1996: 167). His critique of them would be more effective if his own charismatic faith in socio-geneticism was less intense. Here he can learn from art history and consider Max Kozloff (1967: 36) when he says that 'criticism seems most alive to itself when it is kept somewhat off guard by works of art – when a critic suspects that he must enlarge his frame of reference, or intensify his analytical tools, or even switch his methodological approach to make his experience intelligible in its own terms'.

Reading Bourdieu on art history, then, is like walking past a street preacher who is shouting of impending doom. It is difficult to ignore him, and he may even say something which pricks the conscience, but it is not enough to warrant anything like panic or thoughts of conversion. Other sights and sounds of the field of cultural production promise a more sustained interest and these art historians move on through its exciting and always unexpected indeterminacies.

Notes

1 The concept of structural homology is detailed in *The Rules of Art*, in the section on '*The Market for Symbolic Goods*', pp. 141–173.
2 Bourdieu develops this connection in *The Rules of Art*, where he describes both the belief in the autonomous art work, and in the autonomous creator, as instances of fetishism.
3 The term comes from Michael Podro's book *The Critical Historians of Art*, which presents a history of art historical thought which has attempted to address issues raised by Kant and Hegel in their conception of art. Given that it is one of this chapter's key arguments that Bourdieu's presentation of art history is overly monolithic it would hardly be fitting to speak in defence of 'art history' as a whole. Rather it is defended as a site where critical thought can, and does, emerge. Podro's criteria for criticality need not be seen as definitive – critical art history can be seen to continue past Panofsky; indeed we might say that some reckoning with the issues raised by Bourdieu's critique (though not necessarily on his terms) might be a contemporary criterion.
4 Thomas Crow (1996: 37) has pointed out that art historical accounts of modernism and theories of modernity and mass culture frequently begin with the same names – Adorno, Benjamin, Greenberg – but that 'Very seldom are these debates about both topics together. But at the beginning they always were: the theory of one was the theory of the other. And in that identity was the realization, occasionally manifest and always latent, that the two were in no fundamental way separable'. Thus a precedent is set for the mutually beneficial co-existence of art history and sociology. For an example of someone whose work has remained committed to the study of art works while examining the contexts in which they are made, presented and received, one could cite Douglas Crimp, whose critical approach is informed by the sentiments of the following quote from Walter Benjamin's *Theses on the Philosophy of History*: 'A historical materialist views [cultural treasures] with cautious detachment. For without exception the cultural treasures he surveys have an origin which he cannot contemplate without horror .... There is no document of civilization which is not at the same time a document of barbarism'. (Quoted in Crimp, 1997: 238).
5 See in particular the section in *The Rules of Art* on 'Questions of Method', as well as *Free Exchange*.
6 See Thomas Crow, 'Modernism and Mass Culture', in Crow, 1996.
7 Dawkins advances the key tenets of his position in *The Selfish Gene* (Oxford UP, 1976) and *The Blind Watchmaker* (Harlow: Longman, 1986).
8 This sleight of hand is taken further in the introduction to *Distinction* where Bourdieu (1998: 1–7) uses Panofsky's supposed characterization of naïve aesthetic experience as if it was an objective description.

References

Alpers, S., (1977), 'Is Art History?' in Kernal and Gaskell (eds.) (1993), *Explanation and Value in the Arts*, Cambridge: UP.

Bourdieu, P., (1998), *Distinction: A Social Critique of the Judgement of Taste*, London: Routledge.

Bourdieu, P., (1966a), 'Intellectual Field and Creative Project', in Young, M. (ed.) (1971), *Knowledge and Power*, London: Macmillan.

Bourdieu, P., (1966b), 'Systems of Education and Systems of Thought', in Young, M. (ed.) (1971), *Knowledge and Power*, London: Macmillan.

Bourdieu, P., (1996), *The Rules of Art: Genesis and Structure of the Literary Field*, Cambridge: Polity Press.

Bourdieu, P. and Haacke, H., (1995), *Free Exchange*, Cambridge: Polity Press.

Cheetham, M.A., (1998), 'Kant and the Bo(a)rders of Art History', in Cheetham, Holly, Moxey (eds), *The Subjects of Art History*, Cambridge: Cambridge University Press.

Crow, T., (1996), *Modern Art in the Common Culture*, Yale University Press.

Holly, M., (1985), *Panofsky and the Foundations of Art History*, London: Cornell University Press.

Kozloff, M., (1967), 'Problems of Criticism', in *Artforum*, Dec.

Lacan, J., (1978), *The Four Fundamental Concepts of Psychoanalysis*, trans. Alan Sheridan, New York: Norton.

Owens, C., (1994), *Beyond Recognition*, London: University of California Press.

Panofsky, E., (1997), *Perspective as Symbolic Form*, trans. Wood, C.S., New York: Zone.

Panofsky, E., (1960), *Gothic Architecture and Scholasticism*, New York: Meridian.

Panofsky, E., (1940), 'The History of Art as a Humanistic Discipline', in *Meaning in the Visual Arts*, New York: Doubleday and Anchor.

Panofsky, E., (1939), 'Iconography and Iconology: An Introduction to the Study of Renaissance Art', in *Meaning in the Visual Arts*, New York: Doubleday and Anchor.

Podro, M., (1991), *The Critical Historians of Art*, London: Yale U.P.

Rosler, M., (1999), interview with John Slyce, in *Dazed and Confused*, #54, May.

Notes on contributors

Simon Charlesworth was educated at Rotherham College of Arts and Technology, attended the universities of Warwick and Cambridge, and is the author of *A Phenomenology of Working Class Experience* (CUP 2000).

Roger Cook has graduate and post-graduate degrees in Fine Art from University College London (Slade School) and has been a Lecturer in the Department of Fine Art at the University of Reading for thirty years. As a result of the turn to critical and theoretical studies in the field of contemporary art, in 1992 he discovered the work of Pierre Bourdieu, which led him to undertake PhD research on contemporary art in the Department of the History of Art and Architecture. He has delivered papers at the two recent Bourdieu conferences at Southampton and Glasgow. His Southampton paper 'Towards a Sociosomatics of Art: Bourdieu's Reflexive Sociology, Contemporary Art and Education' appeared in Michael Grenfell and Michael Kelly (eds) *Pierre Bourdieu: Language, Culture and Education: Theory into Practice* (Peter Lang, 1999). He is a contributor and co-editor of a forthcoming collection of papers associated with the University of Reading MA in Body and Representation.

Bridget Fowler is a Senior Lecturer in Sociology at the University of Glasgow. She is the author of *The Alienated Reader* (Harvester Wheatsheaf, 1991), *Pierre Bourdieu and Culture Theory* (Sage, 1997) and various articles.

Richard Hooker is a lecturer in the History of Art at Glasgow University and is writing a book on Adorno's aesthetics.

Terry Lovell is a Professor in Sociology, and the Director of the Centre for the Study of Women and Gender at the University of Warwick, where she has lectured in sociology, women's studies and cultural studies since 1972. Her publications include *Pictures of Reality* (BFI Publications, 1980), *Consuming Fiction* (Verso, 1987) and a *Glossary of Feminist Theory* (with S. Andermahr and C. Wolkowitz). She is the editor of *British Feminist Thought* (Blackwell, 1990) and *Feminist Cultural* Studies (Edward Elgar, 1995). She has written extensively on feminist social theory and the sociology of culture.

Philippe Marlière is a lecturer in Political Sociology at University College, London. He was a Research Fellow at the French Centre National de la Recherche Scientifique (CNRS) and at the European University Institute,

Florence. He has published articles in the work of Pierre Bourdieu in English and is currently co-writing a book in French, with Yves Sintomer, on the sociology of Pierre Bourdieu (forthcoming, *La Decouverte*, 2001).

John Orr is Professor of Sociology at Edinburgh University where he teaches film and contemporary culture. His recent publications include *Cinema and Modernity* and *Contemporary Cinema*. His current publications include *The Art and Politics of Film* and a film reader, edited with Olga Taxidou, *Post-War Cinema and Modernity*, both published by Edinburgh University Press.

Dominic Paterson is a doctoral candidate in the History of Art at Glasgow University and is looking at the history of theories of the relation between art and power.

Louis Pinto is Directeur de recherche at the CNRS in Paris. He is concerned with the topics of culture, intellectuals and media (*L'intelligence en action: le Nouvel Observateur*, Paris, Métailié, 1984, *Les philosophes entre le lycée et l'avant-garde*, Paris, L'Harmattan, 1987, *Les Neveux de Zarathoustra. La réception de Nietzsche en France*, Paris, Seuil, 1995), as well as with others topics, including particularly consumerism and consumer society. His most recent book is devoted to Pierre Bourdieu's theoretical contributions to sociology and philosophy (*Pierre Bourdieu et la théorie du monde social*, Paris, Albin Michel, 1994).

Franck Poupeau is a doctoral student at the Centre de Sociologie Européenne, EHESS, Paris. He has published 'Le mouvement de contestation de la Seine-Saint-Denis. Elements pour une théorie du capital militant', *Regards sociologiques*, mars 2000.

Nick Prior is a lecturer in sociology at the University of Edinburgh. He is the author of several articles on the rise of national art galleries, including: 'Edinburgh, Romanticism and the National Gallery of Scotland', *Urban History*, 22: 2, August 1995; and 'The High Within and the Low Without', *Cultural Logic*, http://eserver.org/clogic/, 2: 2, Spring 2000. He is currently writing a book, titled *Museums and Modernity*, to be published by Berg in 2001.

Derek Robbins read English at Clare College, Cambridge and was supervised by Raymond Williams for his doctorate. He was a founding member of the School for Independent Study at the University of East London, where he is now a Reader and the Head of the Dept. of Social Politics, Languages and Linguistics. Since 1986 he has carried out research on and with Pierre Bourdieu. He has published *The Rise of Independent Study* (1988, Open University Press), *The Work of Pierre Bourdieu* (Open University Press, 1991) *Bourdieu and Culture* (2000. Sage), edited a four-volume collection of secondary articles on Bourdieu (2000, Sage), and written and translated numerous articles on his work.

Paul Stirton is a senior lecturer in the History of Art at Glasgow University and Visiting Professor at the Bard Graduate Center for Studies in the Decorative Arts in New York.

Loïc Wacquant is a Professor in the Department of Sociology, University of California at Berkeley and a researcher at the Centre de Sociologie

Européene in Paris. His research interests are in urban inequality and marginality; 'race' as a principle of social vision and division; carceral institutions in the government of misery; classical and contemporary social theory; culture and economy; violence and the body; extreme social systems. His publications include *An Invitation to Reflexive Sociology* (with Pierre Bourdieu), The University of Chicago Press, 1992, *Les Prisons de la misère*, Paris, Editions du Seuil, 1999, 'The Cunning of Imperialist Reason' (with Pierre Bourdieu). *Actes de la recherche en sciences sociales*, 121–122, March 1998 (in English in *Theory, Culture, and Society*, February 1999) and numerous other articles.

Index